EISENHOWER

& THE MASS MEDIA

CRAIG ALLEN

EISENHOWER

AND THE Mass Media

PEACE, PROSPERITY,

& PRIME-TIME TV

The University of North Carolina Press   Chapel Hill & London

© 1993

The University of
North Carolina
Press

All rights reserved

Manufactured in
the United States
of America

The paper in
this book meets
the guidelines
for permanence
and durability of
the Committee
on Production
Guidelines for
Book Longevity
of the Council
on Library
Resources.

Library of Congress Cataloging-in-Publication Data

Allen, Craig.

Eisenhower and the mass media : peace, prosperity, and
prime-time TV / by Craig Allen.

p.   cm.

Includes bibliographical references and index.

ISBN 0-8078-2080-6 (cloth : alk. paper). — ISBN 0-8078-4409-8
(pbk. : alk. paper)

1. Eisenhower, Dwight D. (Dwight David), 1890–1969.   2. Mass
media—Political aspects—United States—History—20th century.
3. Communication in politics—United States—History—20th
century.   4. United States—Politics and government—
1953–1961.   I. Title.

E836.A815   1993

973.921—dc20   92-35615

                                                                                    CIP

Permission to reproduce selected material can be found on p. 260.

97 96 95 94 93   5 4 3 2 1

For Galen, Ray, and Dorothy

CONTENTS

A section of photographs can be found following page 109.

ACKNOWLEDGMENTS

The most pleasing part of my odyssey through the Eisenhower realm is repaying the many people who accompanied me. At the top of the list are Patrick Washburn of the E. W. Scripps School of Journalism and Alonzo Hamby of the Department of History at Ohio University. Four other Ohio University lights—Charles Alexander, Ray Gusteson, Mel Helitzer, and Don Flournoy—are owed additional debts of gratitude.

My closest working associate was Dwight Standberg of the Eisenhower Library, who established many of the initial research parameters and made Abilene, Kansas, seem like a second hometown. Kathy Struss at the Eisenhower Library and Allan Goodrich, her counterpart at the Kennedy Library, helped immeasurably by allowing me to roam through their collections of film and videotape. The research was expedited by the generous financial assistance of the Eisenhower World Affairs Institute.

Enormous thanks go to Christi Stanforth, my copyeditor, and to Lewis Bateman, my acquisitions editor, both at the University of North Carolina Press. Working with Lew, Christi, Sandra Eisdorfer, and the others at Chapel Hill was a personal privilege.

Just as much of a privilege were my opportunities to contact and converse with many of the people I was writing about. They ranged from Richard Nixon, with whom I corresponded, to others whose media stories from the 1950s are told in this book for the first time. Several of the figures I interviewed graciously altered their plans and schedules in order to accommodate me, for which I am indeed grateful.

Others who helped with the project and earn heartfelt acknowledgment include Marian Buckley and Janet Soper of Arizona State University; Juan Pozo-Olano of Washington, D.C.; Carl and Judy Trevison and Don TeSelle of Hartford, Connecticut; Mark Mandel of Portland, Oregon; and Jim and Carol Ward of Chatham, New Jersey.

Finally, I would like to thank my wife, Galen Everly, and my parents, Ray and Dorothy Allen, to whom this book is dedicated. I was not sure whether, after seven years of hearing about Eisenhower, they would still "like Ike." They did, and the book would not have been completed without them on board.

EISENHOWER

& THE MASS MEDIA

INTRODUCTION

When Dwight Eisenhower was stricken by a heart attack on September 24, 1955, what began as a serious crisis wound up as a revealing episode in White House mass communication. The news traveled fast and left many unsure whether Eisenhower would survive, others fearing he might be too weak to continue effectively as president. Instantly endangered was an almost seamless public picture of Eisenhower, whose reputation for stability and trust had given not just scenery but also foundation to major presidential undertakings, including foreign policy initiatives, legislative pursuits, and programs for rebuilding the Republican party. This image of Eisenhower also contained an explanation for a national nirvana that existed, paradoxically, within the darkest moments of the Cold War. Millions around the world were uneasy. Yet few could have guessed that they, too, had been diagnosed as "patients." At precisely the hour that doctors were giving Eisenhower medical treatment, White House communications specialists were at work on a prescription for the general public. Like doctors, these communications experts knew what to do when the goal was making people feel better.

The heart attack had occurred in Denver on a Saturday; many top officials could not be reached. Chief of Staff Sherman Adams, like Eisenhower, had been vacationing. With no wince or pause, the first executive decisions after the heart attack came from these White House communications coordinators. That media advisers ran the government for a short time was not an odd state of affairs in the Eisenhower administration; these aides did more than write news releases. With an around-the-clock proximity to the president, Eisenhower's media staff was prominent in his leadership circle and one of the most energetic elements in his command. Eisenhower had come to rely greatly on these people. The heart attack would show why.

Murray Snyder, the assistant press secretary, had been the highest ranking official when Eisenhower entered Fitzsimons Hospital. Snyder telephoned his superior, Press Secretary Jim Hagerty, who, from Washington, notified as many government leaders as possible and had the first of several exchanges with Vice President Richard Nixon during which they improvised an emergency delegation of authority. Snyder kept the news a secret from the press for almost an hour, a move that bought time for Hagerty, who hastily arranged a military flight to Denver, determined to beat the throng of government officials and senior reporters to the scene. Seven hours later, Hagerty ordered a pilot to land in the middle of an early autumn monsoon that had pounded Colorado's front range and closed Denver's Stapleton Airport. When additional advisers, doctors, reporters, and family members finally arrived at the hospital, Hagerty was already on site and directing events.[1]

The first news out of Denver was extremely encouraging. Eisenhower responded favorably to treatment, and within twenty-four hours his vital signs had rapidly improved. Yet apace with the positive diagnosis were internal anxieties that began to shift from Eisenhower's condition to the public's long-term reaction. Doctors expected a slow recuperation; three months, in fact, would pass before Eisenhower resumed normal duties. While Eisenhower's health was the chief concern, advisers measured the political predicament posed by the president's long convalescence. Because a pillar of Eisenhower's leadership was his virile, redoubtable public presence, it was not enough that Eisenhower had survived. Just as important to the future was persuading the American people that the president was the same person in recovery as he had been prior to the illness.

This job required an image-building campaign that by the second day, while Eisenhower slept, had fully defined itself, with hidden ploys and procedural camouflage characteristic of this administration's efforts to impress the public. For example, a figure named Dr. Paul Dudley White was brought to Denver to serve as chief adviser to the presidential medical team. Eisenhower was already receiving expert attention, but his military doctors were unknown publicly. White, in contrast, was not only a prominent Boston physician but also one of the nation's most visible personalities from the world of medicine. The national media had often featured White as an authority on an assortment of recent medical advancements, a standard topic in the press during the 1950s. In addition, White was the author of a popular book that explained how modern heart attack victims routinely resumed normal lives. Without giving details, Hagerty placed a quick order for numerous copies of this book and told White to bring them to Denver. White complied and watched later as Hagerty circulated the free copies as "gifts" to the scores of gathering news reporters.[2]

In the following weeks Hagerty and White were quoted repeatedly in the press and became familiar faces on the nation's growing number of television screens.[3] They appeared mainly in news briefings. Early in the recovery there were as many as three briefings per day, each more assuring than the one before it. Drugged and confined to an oxygen tent, Eisenhower was too ill to offer personal direction except for expressing a desire for "candor." Much as he had several times in the past, Hagerty translated "candor" into a device for keeping the press firmly in line. Charts and drawings were regularly presented, and ongoing medical procedures were recited to reporters in squeamish detail. There was even news of Eisenhower's first bowel movement and others that followed. Some reporters were less than enchanted, and Eisenhower later sounded off when he learned of all that Hagerty had told the reporters. Yet the press had no choice but to go along, keep its questions focused on the improving president, and endure the clinically correct news briefings.[4]

The communications experts also carefully considered the channeling of news about governmental activities back in Washington. Nixon called meetings of both the National Security Council and the cabinet the week following the illness; the press office disclosed that members attended as if nothing was out of the ordinary. At the beginning of the second week, Eisenhower had improved sufficiently that doctors allowed him to meet with Adams. This news was reported, as were specifics of the temporary command arrangement, which had Adams remaining in Denver and Nixon handling routine duties from the White House. The president met briefly with Nixon on October 8 and saw Secretary of State John Foster Dulles on October 11; other cabinet members paraded to Denver in full media view at scheduled two- to three-day intervals.

In playing up Eisenhower's recovery, the administration played down everything else. While Hagerty kept the press corps focused on Eisenhower's injections, cardiograms, and bodily functions, little light was shed on Nixon's impromptu presidential role and questions that might have surrounded it. There were no White House news conferences with Nixon as a stand-in. Nor was the tapestry altered by looming issues about the future. With many looking ahead to the 1956 presidential campaign, now only a year away, Republican party chairman Leonard Hall insisted that Eisenhower would head the GOP ticket. Reporters did not believe him but were unable to get Hall or others in the administration to so much as breathe anything to the contrary.[5]

Instead, the flow of information was controlled from Denver, and reporters there received more than enough.[6] On September 27, Hagerty passed out an eleven-page news release that contained "get well" messages from eighty world figures, including Pope Pius XII and, notably, Soviet leaders Nikolai Bulganin and Nikita Khrushchev.[7] There were photo opportunities of a smiling Eisenhower in a wheelchair, enjoying fresh air on the hospital roof; interviews with family members who did not appear overly concerned; and reports that he was surrounded by mountains of telegrams and letters from well-wishers around the world. On October 6, the *New York Times* devoted part of its front page to a drawing of the president riding a horse, made and sent to Denver by his seven-year-old grandson, David.[8] There was also information on some of Eisenhower's bridge games.[9] On October 14, the cabinet produced a tape-recorded birthday greeting for the president that was released to the media.[10] Print and broadcast reporters had neither to seek medical experts for opinions on Eisenhower's health nor to dig for material to flesh out their stories. Information was given to them so frequently that little adverse speculation about either the president's condition or the government's status could be located in media outlets that reached the nation.[11]

The positive images flowed through November; the administration tuned masterfully to a concerned public as if it was nursing a sick member of the family back to health. With Americans following these events happily, few were inclined to dwell on the behind-the-scenes work that had provided so much good news. One group, the Democrats, had tried to do this: convinced that enough was enough, they began to complain about Eisenhower's manipulation of mass media, even coining a term for it—"hagertizing."[12] But these Democratic complaints were drowned in the presidential fanfare. When Eisenhower returned to Washington briefly on November 11, five thousand people greeted him at National Airport and hundreds more lined a motorcade route to the White House; both scenes were carried on national television under plans coordinated through the White House. Onlookers turned out again three days later when Eisenhower departed for his home in Gettysburg, Pennsylvania, for further recuperation. In late December, Eisenhower was cheered a third time when he came back to the capital as a fully recovered chief executive.

Christmas 1955 was a pleasant time in the White House, as it was in other homes across the United States. On TV and in the press, mingled with scenes of the holiday season, the public saw and heard a supportive government staff, a caring First Family, and a smiling president eager for a new year of peace, prosperity, and progress. Fate had determined a happy ending to the story; the administration's use of the mass media had made this happy ending known to all. Inside the White House, another "happy ending" came just months later. With a more positive medical prognosis, but also with much evidence that the public had been relieved of fears that he was too old and feeble to lead the country, Eisenhower pushed ahead with his plans for seeking a second term, as Hall had predicted. The final result was Eisenhower's greatest political achievement as president—his landslide reelection.

Eisenhower's heart attack is a well-known story in recent American history. Indeed, today readers can choose from a vast collection of nostalgic books about the 1950s and the Eisenhower era, many recounting in detail Eisenhower's triumph in fighting back from the heart attack, the first to befall a sitting president. Yet few of these works acknowledge that a key part of the "fight" was waged outside Eisenhower's hospital room, or that the heart attack and its aftermath became a "media event" by most definitions of the term. Importantly, this instance of turning a minus into a plus with persistent, coordinated, and considered application of the mass media was not an isolated case during the eight years Eisenhower served in the White House. Nor was it the only occasion when Eisenhower's media activities failed to register much of a blip on either contemporary or historical radar screens.

Along with dozens of other maneuvers, decisions, and innovations pertaining to Eisenhower's mass communication, the heart attack campaign offers yet another new perspective on the thirty-fourth president. Already known to readers as a rags-to-riches symbol, an astute military leader, and a capable chief executive, Eisenhower was also a master user of the U.S. mass media. Not only did Eisenhower preside over sweeping changes in the techniques and traditions of presidential communications, but there are also many indications that Eisenhower succeeded in repeated attempts to reinforce a positive image and promote a "personal" dialogue with millions of Americans. This evidence includes high on-the-job approval ratings and other displays of popular support, such as those following the heart attack, that have continued to fascinate historians.

Although few scholars have shown just how Eisenhower devoted himself to these tasks, the reasons why he did are recurring themes in his literature. Above all, Eisenhower was by nature a very public-spirited individual. A 1980s wave of "revisionist" studies, including those of Stephen Ambrose, Robert Ferrell, Fred Greenstein, and Robert Griffith, emphasized that Eisenhower had not led a cloistered existence during his long military career but instead had distinguished himself as a forceful internal communicator. Eisenhower's talents in mass communication were equally impressive when he moved onto the world stage in 1942 during World War II. Greenstein felt Eisenhower had an inborn tendency toward "building public support" that guided all of his affairs; it was inevitable that this habit would be a rudder when he sized up his problems and needs in the White House.[13]

Yet according to these historians, Eisenhower was driven by more than instinct; he also saw purpose in his mass communication endeavors. "One of his basic principles of leadership," wrote Ambrose, "was that a man cannot lead without communicating with the people"; news conferences, for example, helped Eisenhower "stay in control" and "set the national agenda."[14] Ferrell noted that Eisenhower had to use public relations "to secure his own position within the party, to make himself so attractive to voters that the GOP right-wingers would have to do what he asked."[15] Griffith discussed still broader motives. He maintained that Eisenhower conceived of the mass media as an instrument for rallying public acceptance of moderate principles. With a "non-political" political philosophy and with support that cut across all sectors in American society, Eisenhower considered himself uniquely qualified to rid politics of confrontation and divisiveness and thus to improve the nation's democratic experience. Eisenhower sought a mainstream leadership that espoused the organizational ethics of unity, harmony, and consensus, realizing he could not elicit a national spirit of cooperation by keeping quiet.[16]

Historians have tended to agree that Eisenhower's communication efforts were more reliable in reinforcing his personal attraction among Americans than in fulfilling political objectives. Even so, the individual steps taken by Eisenhower to apply this communication strategy are no less noteworthy. Eisenhower experimented with diverse mass media and was the first president to have much of his communications directed by New York–based media professionals. Eisenhower's disdain for public controversy led to an arms-length relationship with a sometimes-hostile journalistic community and to some historic strides in transforming press encounters into a White House soapbox. Eisenhower's communication efforts were intertwined with internal Republican party politics in the 1950s, an important yet all but overlooked area in his many biographies. An opportunity to extend Eisenhower's communication platform was seized in his 1956 reelection, when the Republicans raised record sums of money to crush opponents in a one-sided media campaign. After the success of 1956, Eisenhower found additional ways to use the media during a very tenuous period that followed the Soviet launch of Sputnik in 1957. Near the end of his presidency, because of ongoing technical advancements, Eisenhower mounted a series of worldwide crusades that were among the most elaborately orchestrated media events of his career.

Eisenhower's sense of the mass communication field, and much of his contribution to it, cannot be fully understood without immersion in the importance he placed on the "new medium" of television. Timed nearly to the day with the resumption of station licensing following the FCC "freeze," the Eisenhower years coincided with the greatest period of growth and expansion in TV history. The percentage of Americans who had TVs—around 30 percent when Eisenhower was first sworn in—stood at almost 70 percent when he was reelected in 1956 and around 90 percent when he passed the presidency to John F. Kennedy in 1961. Long before the FCC freeze ended, Eisenhower was a TV watcher of the first order. Rather than complain, as many did, about the banality of television, Eisenhower saw TV as a breakthrough in American enterprise. Eisenhower knew what he liked in a TV production, believed millions of other TV viewers shared his judgments, and was aware of the changes TV was creating in American society. Accordingly, Eisenhower wasted little time in establishing television as his dominant communications priority.

Although Kennedy has been regarded as the first "television president," most of the TV devices and practices that Kennedy and others would use in the White House had already been demonstrated by Eisenhower. Eisenhower attempted the first televised "fireside chats," introduced the first TV news conferences, conducted the first televised cabinet meetings, hired the first presidential TV consultant, and established the first White House TV studio. Eisenhower was also the first president to actively engage in televised "photo opportunities"; his 1956 reelection defined much of what is known today as the "television campaign."

While pioneering TV work was a controlling factor in Eisenhower's popular dialogue, its importance was overshadowed by the overall size and scale of his administration's mass media operations. Hagerty, the master strategist of the heart attack campaign, was Eisenhower's best-remembered media manager. Yet the press secretary was only one among dozens of people from numerous offices and agencies who worked behind the scenes to facilitate Eisenhower's public outreach, their names until now virtually unknown in the vast literature on presidential mass communications. The heads of the media-minded Republican National Committee were extremely influential, as were planners and specialists at Batten, Barton, Durstine and Osborn (BBDO) and Young and Rubicam, two giant advertising agencies that worked in official capacities within the White House scheme. Besides these and other official advisers, Eisenhower had assistance from a circle of personal friends that featured many of the founders and leaders of the nation's corporate mass media establishment. Included were publishers, Madison Avenue executives, and the heads of the TV networks. Like no president before him, Eisenhower had at his side the best and the brightest from the communications field.

Early in his presidency, Eisenhower told his advisers he wanted his public relations comparable to those of a "great industrial organization." They achieved this goal. However, although this statement suggests another brick in the revisionist argument that Eisenhower was an active and determined leader, his use of the media raises some new questions about his presidency. In this area, not all was sweetness and light, as many revisionists suggested. Ambrose, for example, wrote of Hagerty's position as "about as easy and rewarding a job for a public relations man as could be imagined."[17] The job might have been rewarding but most definitely was not easy. Hagerty and others were often driven to a frazzle in their attempts to both keep up with the expanding mass media and meet Eisenhower's enormous expectations. Ominously, these expectations included a domination of the nation's mass media system, preemptive use of the media in defusing critics, and, sometimes, media tactics aimed at knocking out political opponents. Although Eisenhower's communication work was fueled by much creative energy, it also ran on influence and enormous sums of money, at amounts greater than those collected by any past political figure.

In the context of the public looking glass, Eisenhower comes off a little more vain and assertive than in some of his past portrayals. He also emerges, perhaps, as more human, even humorous in some passages. Yet in the end, a media study counters the critical questions it generates by clarifying Eisenhower's status as a "politician," a distinction he spent a lifetime disclaiming. Some scholars have maintained that Eisenhower set up historical fogging devices so as not to draw attention to the political component of his legacy, a notion very much evident in his media affairs. In addition to drawing out the political side of Eisenhower, a media study may suggest that Eisenhower was wrong in believing that good politics has a bad odor. Eisenhower's communication with the public was honest; enduring media innovations sprang from his partisan applications. Given the technical advancements and new communicative opportunities available to public figures in the 1950s, serious doubts would gather around the worth of the revisionist interpretation, that Eisenhower was up-to-date and knew what he was doing, had he not been media active. That Eisenhower was in step with an iridescent period in media history helps confirm the positive view.

Although the 1950s have long been regarded as a vital era in the evolution of U.S. mass communication, they have remained a black hole in the important area of political media studies. What can be seen in the void are Americans moving rapidly into the information age, with a man in the White House possessing a rare combination of instincts, needs, and resources that made Pennsylvania Avenue a focal point of the changes.

FIVE-STAR
DEBUT IN WAR,
NEW STAGE IN
1953

Many of the details of good communication, if not the components of an effective public relations effort, were known to Eisenhower at a very young age. As a teenager in Abilene, Kansas, Eisenhower gained his opportunity to enter West Point after rallying the town's civic leaders into a letter-writing campaign on his behalf. When his athletic career at West Point was shortened by injury, he became a cheerleader for the Army football team. In World War I, Eisenhower yearned to be near the action. Yet the talents his superiors recognized were those not of a fighter but of a teacher, coach, and motivator. Because he had trained hundreds of troops for combat in the First World War but had never seen the battlefield himself, Eisenhower saw his Army career pointed toward oblivion. Nevertheless, as Stephen Ambrose observed, these early experiences had already put Eisenhower on the unique track that carried him to prominence in World War II.[1]

Because of World War II, Eisenhower was the twentieth century's link in a chain of figures that included George Washington, Andrew Jackson, William Harrison, Zachary Taylor, and Ulysses S. Grant: military leaders who attained the nation's highest office through the public zeal for wartime success. Yet as World War II unfolded, few were predicting that Eisenhower would sit atop the pyramid when the hostilities ended. While others advanced in line commands, Eisenhower's career was confined to staff positions, from which he reluctantly but actively accumulated years of knowledge in the intricacies of government, industrial mass production, cost-benefit ratios, weapons development, and worker-soldier morale. Eisenhower's talents for organizing, lobbying, leading discussion, motivating both civilian and military factions, and conceiving a "big picture" grew enormously. World War II still needed generals of the Grant variety, but its mobilized, bureaucratized, multinational dimensions required an Eisenhower even more. He had been a staff colonel when the Germans drove the Allies out of Europe at Dunkirk in 1940. He was the supreme Allied commander when Allied forces reclaimed the continent four years later.

World War II required something else that was new: a military leader who could inspire not only soldiers but also the domestic civilian population, on which depended the mobilization effort. Both Franklin Roosevelt and wartime Chief of Staff George Marshall had recognized this need, and they knew Eisenhower was especially qualified to fill it. Eisenhower's instincts as a communicator thus help explain his rapid rise in the military, something so meteoric that many continued to attribute it to a quirk of fate. Actually, Eisenhower's ascension to high military command had been quarterbacked, and no person had called more of the plays than his younger brother, Milton. If luck determined any part of Eisenhower's fortune, it arrived not in the 1940s but in 1929, when he began an extended tour of duty as a staff officer in Washington, D.C., eventually becoming assistant to Chief of Staff Douglas MacArthur. Milton Eisenhower had just moved to Washington also and had begun a meteoric rise of his own as an administrator and director of public information at the Depression-era Department of Agriculture. Although shaped by the driving presence of MacArthur, Eisenhower was influenced more strongly by his brother, one of the first wizards of agency public relations at the dawn of the "big government" era. For seven years, the two Eisenhowers shared each detail of their careers in a relationship that would remain as close as that between John and Robert Kennedy.

Dwight Eisenhower was justifiably intrigued by his brother's work, not just its large scale and forward look but its recurring evidence that things got done when public opinion flowed in the right direction. Milton supervised one of the largest press services in government and as early as 1930 had pioneered the use of national radio broadcasts for the issuing of public statements.[2] Most impelling to Dwight was Milton's Midas touch in cultivating the many newspaper reporters who, like the bureaucrats, converged on Washington during the New Deal. Milton did this on the job with candor and after hours with parties, cookouts, and get-togethers. Dwight regularly attended these affairs and, although only an Army major, grew to be well connected with many notable members of the national press, who knew him then as "Milton's brother."[3]

Milton Eisenhower also cultivated Roosevelt, and the mutual admiration between these two men enabled Milton to bring his brother's talents to the attention of those in the White House. Milton's closeness to Roosevelt started taking a historic turn shortly after Pearl Harbor, when FDR put Milton in charge of the study that led to the creation of the Office of War Information. Milton's blueprint for the OWI did everything but name his brother as Allied commander. It maintained that the government should not use war to usurp outlets of mass communication but, as in peacetime, should fill these outlets with public relations. The landmark recommendations of the study were the concepts of decentralization and diversion from the mass-produced propaganda tactics used in World War I by the Creel Committee. Accordingly, Milton proposed that much wartime information emanate from the battlefield, entrusted to leaders exposed to the processes of communication and sensitive to public reaction on the home front.[4] Roosevelt concurred with Milton, aware that the terms "radio chat," "news release," and "press management," while figures of speech to most generals and admirals, were concrete concepts to the elder Eisenhower. FDR was also aware that typical military figures associated victory strictly with firepower; few were inclined to conceive of "politics" as a bigger factor and express, as Eisenhower did, that "only public opinion does win wars."[5]

Eisenhower's handling of public communications as Allied commander was practically identical to the approach he advanced as president. Eisenhower realized that his most urgent responsibilities were not in the area of public information. Firmly believing in the fruits of a well-tended public dialogue, though, he delegated this duty not randomly, to a person whose name merely appeared on a seniority list, but to someone he had handpicked. Eisenhower sought a figure who was half publicist, half adviser, capable of winning public relations battles with flair and imagination, but above all loyal to the philosophies and decisions of the leadership.

The first Eisenhower "right arm" was Harry Butcher, a lieutenant commander in the Naval Reserve who drew some quizzical comment in military circles when Eisenhower plucked him out of the Navy in 1942 for service at Army headquarters. Yet Butcher's appointment, like Eisenhower's, was based on great logic. Butcher had been part of the Eisenhower milieu in Washington during the 1920s and 1930s; as an editor of a nationally circulated farm magazine important to the USDA, Butcher had been a focus of Milton's overtures to the press before professional courtesies turned into intimate friendships with Milton and Dwight. Butcher increasingly brought new media insights to the Eisenhowers as he too rose, initially at CBS News as its first bureau chief in Washington and later as a CBS vice president, a post he held at the outbreak of World War II. Butcher's principal duty at Allied headquarters was to serve as liaison between Eisenhower and the contingent of war correspondents. His goal was facilitating what proved an emblem of Eisenhower's wartime activity: the appearance, in Butcher's terms, of "complete frankness and trust" with the press.

Eisenhower seized an opportunity to win the press over in his first major public news conference. Held in London in July 1942, it was long remembered by those who attended. Butcher had arrived just days before, greeted by the war correspondents with a bill of particulars that targeted unfair reporting restrictions and several staff members who, they maintained, "looked with 'disdain' upon newspapermen and their work." The American reporters were particularly irate because their British counterparts were subject to much looser censorship policies. Informed by Butcher of this situation, Eisenhower began the news conference with some opening remarks, and before the correspondents had a chance to voice a single additional complaint, he had detailed a speeding up of censorship screenings and other procedures that put the Americans and British on more equal terms. "You blokes," he told the U.S. reporters, "are my first concern." CBS correspondent Ed Murrow, a former colleague of Butcher and a spearhead of the complaints, announced that "Ike made a grand impression."[6] This perception persisted throughout the war, largely because Butcher constantly ran this sort of interference. Butcher's presence during the war was a cornerstone of many future events because he was the model for what later emerged in Jim Hagerty, Eisenhower's White House press secretary.

Eisenhower's first experiences in controlling his own channels of communication also foreshadowed the future. During the war, Eisenhower was cognizant that people back home were for the first time encountering an American war on the radio and in talking motion pictures. He was not content to promote his sensitivity and instill a positive wartime outlook exclusively through press cultivation. Butcher's diaries from this period reveal elaborate preparations for numerous headquarters-designed media ventures, including Eisenhower's radio broadcast, expertly timed just hours after the Normandy invasion.[7] Although the primary target audiences of this broadcast and others were Europeans, efforts were taken to ensure that Eisenhower was also seen and heard in the United States. One of the most interesting Butcher schemes took shape as the Allies advanced toward Germany in late 1944: his plan was to use telephone lines and shortwave radio to beam across the Atlantic descriptions of the final battles, and Eisenhower's reactions, live from the scene.[8] While this idea was technically unfeasible, it represented the "think big" media planning that Eisenhower greatly fancied. Americans nonetheless had repeated opportunities to hear Eisenhower's voice on the radio in recorded form. In addition, Eisenhower appeared in at least a dozen newsreels produced in 1944 and 1945 by the U.S. Army Pictorial Service and even provided a voice-over for a half-hour Army film that described the U.S. crossing of the Rhine River two months before the European war ended.[9] These films were seen widely in movie theaters across the United States.

Long before the war was over, Eisenhower was a figure well known to most Americans. Yet it was not so much the words Eisenhower conveyed but rather his demeanor in communicating that did the most to establish his public acclaim. Eisenhower expedited the end of the conflict because he did not compete with the many U.S. and British field commanders for the personal fame and distinction that the war would carry as a prize. MacArthur, Eisenhower's supervisor through much of the prewar period, had been an influential reverse role model. "The flashy, publicity-seeking type of adventurer can grab the headlines and be a hero in the eyes of the public," Eisenhower wrote in his diary in December 1942, "but he simply can't deliver the goods in high command."[10] Secure in his command and thus willing to let other generals have the glory, Eisenhower communicated and behaved in unassuming ways. Pomp and circumstance were usually absent from the newsreels in which Eisenhower appeared, and he seldom appeared in military regalia. Most of the time, Eisenhower looked and talked more like an enlisted soldier than an officer. The result was a public sensation when he returned to the U.S. after VE Day. Eisenhower's magnanimity brought public honor to his achievements; as historian Alonzo Hamby wrote, "In contrast to the regal MacArthur, he built an image as a plain-living, plain-speaking democrat . . . [and] emerged over more brilliant generals as the great hero of World War II."[11]

Eisenhower's popular appeal continued while he served as head of the Joint Chiefs of Staff after the war. He wrote in his diary in March 1947, "By this time I thought that a soldier (unless he deliberately sought public notice) would be forgotten and left alone to do his job, whatever it might be."[12] In fact, Eisenhower did seek public notice after the war and did not disdain to polish his image. Both parties wanted him as a presidential candidate in 1948, a prospect President Harry Truman discussed with Eisenhower as early as 1945.[13] In 1946, Eisenhower abruptly terminated his twenty-year association with Butcher and began preparations on a wartime memoir when he failed to block Butcher's publication of the official headquarters diaries; in these diaries, Butcher had recorded several occasions when Eisenhower impugned the British.[14] Largely to expunge this blight from his reputation, Eisenhower accepted numerous postwar speaking engagements, particularly between 1948 and 1950. During this time he was president of Columbia University, where one of his specialties, in his words, was "public relations." Academic figures at Columbia wondered about the school's leadership as Eisenhower traveled extensively around the country, speaking to every conceivable group and organization. In St. Louis on Labor Day 1949, Eisenhower drew much attention in the news media when he digressed from soldier talk and complained about the excesses of liberalism and an "ever-expanding federal government"; his lesson on what he called a moderate "middle way" was a pretext and springboard for his entry into the next presidential campaign.[15]

While Eisenhower remained in the public eye after the war, in private he was learning still more about the inner workings of the American mass media. His residence in New York made him a magnet for eminent figures in the communications field who deeply admired him as a military leader and, now, as a public figure. Eisenhower formed close associations with William Paley of CBS; David Sarnoff of NBC; Henry Luce of Time, Inc.; and Bruce Barton and Ben Duffy of BBDO, the world's second-largest advertising agency. Sigurd Larmon of Young and Rubicam, the third-largest agency, assumed a special status. Larmon became one of Eisenhower's closest personal friends, joining a group that referred to itself as "the gang." Eisenhower had as much respect for these media figures as they had for him. Just as Eisenhower was awed by the production capacity and human ingenuity in the defense plants and industrial facilities he had visited, he was similarly captivated by the enormity and potential of the nation's mass media establishment. Eisenhower appreciated not just the corporate orientation of the mass media but also its professional end. He never cared too much about the technical and engineering breakthroughs that were changing the media. He did, however, relate to the techniques of verbal and visual communication and was drawn to media specialists who could employ them for great public effect.

Through the late 1940s, the public heard from Eisenhower in print, on the radio, in newsreels and, now, on television. Eisenhower's World War II memoir, the best-selling book *Crusade in Europe* (1948), spun off into a TV series the following year; many episodes featured on-camera and narrated segments that he had recorded. During this period David Levy of Young and Rubicam, on temporary duty as a Navy lieutenant assigned to the radio division of the Treasury Department, became Eisenhower's first regular media consultant. In preparing a series of broadcast appeals that urged public support for the Marshall Plan, Levy recalled in Eisenhower not only natural on-air abilities but also a striking level of openness to direction and criticism. "I debated with him over content," Levy explained, but as for his delivery, "Eisenhower did what we told him to do." Vanity was one reason Eisenhower accepted this professional advice, according to Levy. Of greater concern, though, were details "beyond his control" that might reduce the impact of what he had to say.[16]

When Eisenhower took a leave from Columbia to serve in Paris as commander of NATO (the North Atlantic Treaty Organization), many of the print and broadcast associates he left behind in New York became leaders of the Citizens for Eisenhower movement that heralded his entry into politics in 1952. Because so many Citizens figures had communications backgrounds, the media steered much of the planning when Eisenhower returned to the United States to run for president, then led a campaign that later received scholarly attention for its innovations, particularly in TV. Kurt and Gladys Lang have shown how Eisenhower's supporters helped overcome front-runner Robert Taft by clamoring for TV coverage of a credentials hearing at the 1952 GOP convention; Taft wound up on the wrong side of a debate about "fair play" while Eisenhower snared the nomination.[17] John Hollitz and Stephen Wood described the ease with which Eisenhower accepted the advice of advertising specialist Rosser Reeves, who had the candidate appear in the first political TV commercials.[18] Steve Barkin revealed that Eisenhower was receptive to a secret "TV Plans Board," composed of more New York television professionals, who urged him to stress informality in his campaign broadcasts.[19] It was also the year the GOP bought air time in order to test Richard Nixon on TV after revelation of a secret GOP slush fund; Nixon's "Checkers" speech saved his spot on the ticket.[20]

The 1952 campaign had many media reference points for scholars, but not for Eisenhower himself, because he defeated opponent Adlai Stevenson by waging the most intensive whistlestop campaign up to that time. Nationally broadcast TV appeals were only side attractions in the fall of 1952, because by then control of Eisenhower's campaign had passed from the Citizens to the party machine, which insisted that a traveling strategy must be first priority. Thus Eisenhower wound up as an instrument of GOP political advisers who sent him into every nook and cranny of the country. A key outcome of 1952, after the exhaustion of almost 53,000 miles of nonstop traveling, was Eisenhower's determination never again to be placed in such a situation. Another outcome followed indirectly from the efforts of his advisers to emphasize specific issues, including alleged economic setbacks, corruption, and mishandling of the Korean War by Truman and the Democrats. The issues were clear, but in almost every outing Eisenhower's personal attraction seemed to overpower them. "All I remember is the crowd yelling, 'I Like Ike,'" recalled Edward Folliard, who covered the campaign for the *Washington Post*. Later, Folliard asked a spectator, an older-looking fellow, to explain this reaction. "Well I don't know," the man said. "I'd like to have old Ike cook me a steak."[21]

This phenomenon was not forgotten by the candidate and his advisers when they moved into the White House in 1953.

Despite many years of contact with the mass media, as president Eisenhower was never limited by his communication efforts. Fred Greenstein maintained that public communication was a distinct Eisenhower leadership strategy but only one of several. To become and remain a popular president, Eisenhower's fundamental tasks were forming a responsive government, advancing a viable legislative program and, above all, keeping the nation out of war. No amount of communication work or imagery could associate him with peace, prosperity, and progress if there were no substance to such claims. Yet Eisenhower was fit to deliver. His staff-oriented military background had given him a vast understanding of workings in the capital, and there was, arguably, nobody anywhere more knowledgeable about foreign policy. He also had energy. Before his inauguration in January 1953, he had personally defined the duties of the entire White House staff, had delineated procedures for the cabinet, and was working to "establish several lines of communication between the Executive and Legislative branches."[22] Eisenhower's internal organization and communications during his first weeks and months as president were the building blocks for what he believed was an admirable first-year administrative record. Public communication began as a relatively low priority; more than a month passed before his first presidential news conference.[23] Yet Eisenhower's outreach enlarged as a focal point of White House concern as advisers faced several developments not anticipated in the early planning.

Foremost among these developments was Eisenhower's troubled relationship with Congress. This relationship made for interesting reading in the press because conflicts existed almost entirely within the Republican party. Although the Republicans controlled both the House and the Senate, the center of power in Congress was the GOP's conservative wing, which the moderate Eisenhower had clipped badly at the 1952 convention. Eisenhower, hoping to ply his wartime skill as a behind-the-scenes unifier and harmonizer, sought to surmount the conservative ideology by first dividing then conquering its individual proponents. Seeing through this tactic, many proponents proceeded to make the conservative cause a shrill public issue. Just three weeks into his presidency, Eisenhower was writing of "Republican senators" who were "having a hard time getting through their heads that they now belong to a team that includes rather than opposes the White House."[24] Republicans fought Eisenhower over presidential appointments and demanded that he reduce taxes, defense spending, and public works appropriations. "We have had a number of misunderstandings, . . . [some] my own fault," wrote Eisenhower in April. "More frequently, I think, they result from the readiness of political legislators to fly into print at every possible opportunity." [25]

Two widely publicized controversies involving GOP senators had, by spring, emerged as roadblocks to the consensus style of leadership, and the image of it, that Eisenhower wanted to implement. One was a proposed constitutional amendment by Ohio's John Bricker that would have limited the president's authority in making international agreements. Eisenhower, always cordial to the senator in public, privately blasted Bricker and his "fortress America" idea, writing of Bricker's amendment as "his one hope of achieving at least a faint immortality in American history." [26] The more jarring controversy was the anticommunism crusade of Wisconsin's Joseph McCarthy, which gained momentum in 1953 when McCarthy became the chair of the Senate Permanent Investigations Subcommittee. McCarthy's actions "irritate, frustrate, and infuriate," Eisenhower confided in April. "I really believe that nothing will be so effective in combating his particular kind of troublemaking as to ignore him"—a course of action that stirred the controversy even more. [27]

While Eisenhower was sensing that loud-talking conservatives were controlling the public's impression of government, he was also starting to discover another factor: Washington-based news reporters who were apparently eager to highlight the infighting and divisions in government. The size of the press corps, around 200 members, was not conducive to the informal relations he had enjoyed with reporters in the military. Moreover, in his military career Eisenhower had been executing the policies of Roosevelt and Truman, and as Ambrose explained, reporters "did not ask him about, much less criticize, his plans and intentions." [28] Reporters now did this often. More than a mere nuisance, the press formed a breech in the president's consensus-building aspirations, which rested in part on his assumption that journalists would offer their wholehearted support, as they had during the war.

Ironically, Eisenhower's consensus philosophy itself became a repository of much press criticism. The Bricker amendment was an obvious affront to Eisenhower; in the view of the press, he was letting the matter fester by trying to compromise with Bricker. In a series of columns in the *New York Times* in April 1953, Arthur Krock reported that "the President's leadership thus far has not been firm" and that Eisenhower was off to a "slow start." [29] Bricker's Senate colleague from Ohio was majority leader Robert Taft, the person Eisenhower had cut down to win the 1952 nomination. Eisenhower's overtures to Taft gave reporters additional reasons to wonder about the president's firmness. "He is a little ill at ease," wrote the *Times*'s James Reston in his syndicated column that May. "[T]he President's way has always been to try to meet everybody's point of view as much as he can. He is not yet prepared to break out of this familiar cycle."[30] In another column, Reston complained that Eisenhower's courting of Taft and other conservatives was like "trying to lead a covey of mechanics through the wilderness. . . . [He] has been concentrating on the uniting of his party rather than leading the country."[31]

The same theme pervaded press interpretations of the McCarthy investigations. When McCarthy's probe of the Voice of America in early 1953 led to scores of firings, columnists Bruce Catton, Richard Rovere, and Walter Lippmann publicly deplored Eisenhower's inaction.[32] Similar complaints were sounded throughout the year.

Eisenhower accepted no blame for the McCarthy affair. He saw McCarthy and his other frustrations with Congress as aberrations, nagging though they were. Eisenhower continued to have faith in his ability to narrow differences among political opponents; to that end, he was acting in close company with most legislators, interest groups, and opinion leaders from all walks of life—including, to some extent, the news media. Eisenhower felt he was making headway in such pursuits as expanding foreign trade, encouraging free enterprise, balancing labor-management relations, and reducing government expense. The Korean War was over by summer.

Even so, as Eisenhower neared the end of his first year, he perceived a shortcoming in his administration's operation: the promotion of its achievements. Eisenhower discovered that good government, unlike a decisive military or political campaign, did not sell itself. This realization would bring about diverse steps in presidential communications, all of them in some way rooted in Eisenhower's instinctive scorn for what he sometimes referred to as "hiding one's light behind a bushel." He was helped to this conclusion by further problems and by the reactions of advisers who felt that more active communication by Eisenhower himself was part of the solution.

Sentiment had reigned among these advisers that Eisenhower, burrowed too deeply in his private dealings with Congress, was not taking advantage of his formidable public esteem evidenced in the 1952 campaign. These advisers shared this sentiment for a very good reason:

many of them had been senior members of the Citizens for Eisenhower movement in 1952. Not only had they seen Eisenhower demonstrate the power of his public appeal, both in person and in the media, on many occasions in 1952, but they had also created many of those opportunities. These were the same advisers who had pushed diversified media in 1952; now in the White House, they saw no reason for Eisenhower to follow in the footsteps of Truman, who had confined his day-to-day communications mainly to issue-intensive news conferences and public statements. As in the campaign, they wanted Eisenhower to appear on television and in newsreels as much as possible. They also believed that through the visual media Eisenhower could personalize speeches, remarks, and accounts of even the blandest aspects of his programs, thus establishing a direct channel to the public that would not be tainted by opponents and skeptics. Some were emphatic in predicting that this course of action would produce useful political leverage.

Just prior to the inauguration, Maxwell Rabb, the president's Oval Office–cabinet liaison and an adviser on minority affairs, had outlined the central proposition. Rabb proposed a monthly series of White House telecasts in which Eisenhower would talk in simple, personal terms about the goals of the administration. This move, explained Rabb, "enables the President to present his message over the head of Congress directly to the people in a way that cannot be criticized, and would help prepare public opinion."[33] Gabriel Hauge, Eisenhower's economics adviser, expanded on this go-to-the-people notion in May and June. "Television," stated Hauge, "is a medium that provides sight, sound, motion, immediate action, and creates great intimacy." Hauge, feeling that the administration was not using television to its full potential, conceived an array of presidential program formats that, if billed properly as innovations, would attract large audiences. One of Hauge's formats was a televised cabinet meeting.[34] Rabb, Hauge, and others submitted TV ideas to White House Chief of Staff Sherman Adams, who filed them away for further consideration.

Later that fall, because of a sequence of events stemming from a new wrinkle in the McCarthy affair, this White House "broadcast file" was retrieved, and it stayed open through the rest of the year. In early November the Justice Department confirmed the resurrection of an investigation into the affairs of Harry Dexter White, an assistant secretary of the treasury early in the Truman administration, now deceased, who had been accused of subversive activities. Truman reacted

with a vengeance, using numerous public statements and a national
TV broadcast to clarify White's past role and savage Eisenhower for
his alleged embrace of McCarthyism. Eisenhower believed he had
solid reasons for the White probe and tried to discuss them at his news
conferences, his only readily available means of communication at the
time. But these news conferences only made matters worse. Reporters
listened to Eisenhower's explanations, then persisted in asking him
to respond to Truman's personal attacks, with questions Eisenhower
was equally persistent in refusing to address. On two occasions, events
escalated into an uncontrollable barrage of questions. Eisenhower had
never seen such displays of hostility among reporters. These two news
conferences left lasting impressions.

On October 30, as heat from the White matter was building, U.N.
ambassador Henry Cabot Lodge, Jr., added his voice to those who
felt an immediate need for better communication in the White House.
This latest plea was not funneled through Adams but instead went
directly to Eisenhower, who at the time considered Lodge his closest
political confidant. For months, in response to Eisenhower's brood-
ings about Congress, Lodge had maintained that the White House was
moving too slowly with TV: Eisenhower had been seen on TV only as
often as President Truman, about once every three or four months.
Lodge summarized an October Gallup poll indicating that one-half
of American homes now had television. In Lodge's estimation, this
was "another confirmation" of the importance of more television appearances and "the value of your becoming the 'T.V.' President." Not
only would this be "a very convenient medium for you and one which
would save your energy and strength," it would also be "particularly
effective."[35] It was possible that Lodge wanted this television outlet in
the hope that Eisenhower would use it to denounce McCarthy. Numerous other advisers were encouraging just that. One of the most
adamant was C. D. Jackson, a *Time* magazine editor loaned to the
administration by Henry Luce.[36]

Although Eisenhower resisted all attempts to divert the administration from its policy of ignoring McCarthy, he rather boldly exercised
his agreement with Lodge that White House communications now
needed to be stepped up. A week after he received the Lodge letter,
Eisenhower touched on many of its themes in a confidential memorandum sent to each cabinet member. Eisenhower demanded a "more
widespread and aggressive campaign to publicize [the] gains and activities" of the executive branch. "While key and top echelon figures

in the fields of journalism, publication, and public relations are pro-administration, . . . [the] lower echelons have not been too successfully wooed." Eisenhower's case in point was the "over worked red herring of McCarthyism," which threatened "inestimable damage" to the administration.[37] On November 23, Eisenhower circulated another version of this memo to White House staff members. "We have a task that is not unlike the advertising and sales activity of a great industrial organization," he said. Eisenhower characterized the administration as a "good product to sell"; now, he insisted, "it is necessary to have an effective and persuasive way of informing the public of the excellence of the product."[38]

Press Secretary Jim Hagerty figured prominently in many subsequent moves aimed at directing the selling effort. Up to this point mostly a background figure, Hagerty now found Eisenhower more attentive to input from the press office. Within weeks, Hagerty and Eisenhower were working on an overhaul of existing procedures for the news conferences.

Nevertheless, as the White controversy peaked in November, the selling tactic discussed most often in the White House was the one Rabb had proposed months before: a continuous series of Eisenhower reports to the nation on live television. Stanley Rumbough, the president's staff-cabinet liaison, discussed Eisenhower's November 5 memo with a number of people who had received it; Rumbough reported to Adams that enthusiasm for the informal Eisenhower telecasts "was the unanimous opinion of almost everyone."[39] Lodge had mocked up a script of such a telecast, no less, and sent it to the White House on November 12. "[W]hat I'm trying to do," explained Lodge, is to "establish the General as our first television president."[40] The following week, Adams had Charles Willis, his assistant, bounce the TV idea off a number of GOP figures, including moderates in the House and Senate who had been giving Eisenhower consistent support. With no hesitation, Willis reported that "the President can eliminate many of his troubles with Congress by going to the people periodically with a report."[41]

Thus a decision was made to arrange airtime on all of the TV networks for an Eisenhower telecast in late December. The program would be carried simultaneously on the radio networks. It was to be a different type of White House broadcast, not an urgent presidential address. The White furor lingered but in a dissipated form; internal security would not be the topic of the program. Nor would it really be a sketch of Eisenhower's 1954 legislative plans. Unofficially, those at the networks and in the White House understood the "news" in this broadcast to be the broadcast itself, a new living-room experience for the American public: a person-to-person style program hosted by the nation's chief executive. The date selected for the event was December 24—Christmas Eve, an indication of what was to come.

It was one thing to order a presidential telecast that imparted information yet left viewers with a warm feeling. It was something else to have such a telecast achieve the desired effect, especially with the public growing more accustomed to high-quality programming. The visual component of television had created complications that had never existed in radio: since audiences could now enjoy natural performers by sight as well as sound, they began to expect a level of visual appeal in all types of programming. However, Eisenhower was no Jackie Gleason.

When advisers talked about putting Eisenhower on television, they began from a common reference point, perhaps the most indelible image from the 1952 campaign. After Eisenhower had decided in June 1952 to run for president, he traveled from Paris to his boyhood home of Abilene, where AT&T and CBS, at great expense to the Citizens group, arranged live coverage of the formal announcement. It was history's first demonstration of bad political television. Spectators were unsheltered from a rainstorm that hit at airtime; viewers saw Eisenhower stumble through an ill-prepared speech with water dripping from his glasses. It was so glaringly bad that historian Herbert Parmet has argued that a news conference the next day in Abilene saved Eisenhower's political career.[42]

The upcoming December program was not Eisenhower's first appearance on live TV as president. He had conducted three nationwide TV addresses earlier in 1953; that summer, Eisenhower had gone on TV to introduce his new Department of Health, Education, and Welfare and its first secretary, Oveta Culp Hobby, the second woman ever named to a cabinet post. Yet his White House broadcasts seemed to lack spark and imagination; they looked unprofessional compared to the programs that preceded and followed them on the network schedules.

The lesson of the 1952 Abilene broadcast, and of more recent ones, was the same: someone was needed to supervise the production of the telecasts, work directly with Eisenhower, and anticipate every imaginable technical glitch. Eisenhower had had this supervision during the autumn phase of the 1952 campaign and his telecasts in that period had been considered effective.

Yet the process involved in drawing out Eisenhower's personality on TV was not the only reason a supervisor was required. Before a switch could be thrown on any presidential television broadcast, a thicket of technical and logistical details had to be worked out surrounding the bulky and unwieldy television cameras of the day and the supply of cables, lights, amplifiers, and control panels that were also hauled to the scene. Simply installing this equipment in the White House was comparable to moving a small family into a new home. Once the equipment was in place, a squad of technicians was needed to operate it. These logistical hurdles more than any other factor accounted for the relatively small number of White House television broadcasts through 1953.

No one on the White House staff had the time, inclination, or knowledge to confront these matters and make the Eisenhower broadcast a memorable viewing experience. Outside help was needed; it came from Hollywood celebrity Robert Montgomery, who volunteered to produce the Christmas telecast and wound up beginning a formal association with Eisenhower that would continue until he left office in 1961.

Montgomery had much in common with the future president Ronald Reagan—so much that if Reagan's life represented a typical White House track, a Montgomery presidency would not have been far-fetched. Both were extremely effective on TV and both were actors with political motivations and talents. Nevertheless, much unlike Reagan's, Montgomery's life had been one of several unfulfilled career ambitions.

Born in 1904, Montgomery was raised in a secure New York family before he ventured from home and began to earn money cleaning locomotives and tending deck on an oil tanker. Several stage plays that he wrote from these experiences carried him to Broadway, and in 1928 he began eighteen years as a contract actor for Metro-Goldwyn-Mayer and RKO. Among his forty movie credits was *Night Must Fall* (1937), for which he received an Oscar nomination. Most of Montgomery's work was not Academy Award caliber.[43]

Like Reagan, Montgomery grew restless with the movie routine. After service as a Navy lieutenant in World War II, Montgomery wanted to be a film director, but his experimental *Lady in the Lake*

(1946), in which cameras served as the eyes for detective Philip Marlowe, bewildered many critics and moviegoers.[44] The same year he began a fourth term as president of the Screen Actors Guild, which he helped organize in 1933, only to see his leadership undermined by a studio workers' strike that did not have his approval. Soon after this, Reagan became head of the union.[45] In 1949 Montgomery tried again to mix his show business and political interests as a weekly radio commentator. Montgomery's commentaries were weak, notable more, in the words of the *New York Times*, "for charm than profundity"; he quit after one year.[46] Yet the actor's next move, into television, carried him to the peak of his public acclaim. This came during his tenure as host of an hour-long dramatic anthology series on NBC called "Robert Montgomery Presents." The show premiered in 1950 and had respectable ratings for the next five years.

Montgomery had become known to the GOP hierarchy when he offered to make several public appearances for Eisenhower in the 1952 campaign. Many popular actors and actresses had done likewise, yet none of the other entertainers had contributed as many hours as Montgomery. This service had pleased Eisenhower's campaign managers, especially Lodge and to some extent the less publicly minded Adams. Although Montgomery was one of the most popular and widely known figures in the country, he had neither an overworked ego nor a desire to catch a free ride on the Eisenhower bandwagon. During the campaign, for example, he had provided suggestions for improving Eisenhower's appearances. Advisers took note of Montgomery's authoritative perspective from his lifetime of actual on-camera experience.

Montgomery made a powerful impression when he arrived at the White House in December. He reviewed the sample script that Lodge had written and listened to several White House figures as they tried to articulate what they hoped to see. Finally, Montgomery told them that what they wanted was a television version of Franklin Roosevelt's "fireside chat." Montgomery not only knew how to give them a fireside chat; he could boast firsthand experience, having worked briefly for FDR as a radio adviser during World War II.[47] Eyes opened as Montgomery explained how cosmetics, studio direction, and proper lighting could make the Eisenhower chat particularly appealing. He also had ideas on future appearances and improvements for primitive TV facilities at the White House, the Executive Office Building, and the Capitol, where Eisenhower's State of the Union address would be delivered in a few weeks.[48]

That Christmas Eve, Eisenhower went on television in a modified "fireside chat" set up on the south lawn of the White House. While there was no "fireside," there were plenty of candles and softly illuminated Christmas decorations to warm the nighttime scene. In this setting, the president urged Americans to join him in counting holiday blessings: troops who had fought the Korean War were home this Christmas, postwar inflation was now curbed, and economic stability was bringing jobs to millions of people. Each of these subjects was part of Eisenhower's first-year political agenda; he spoke more formally of the same topics a few weeks later in the State of the Union message. That Christmas, though, average Americans may not have sensed that Eisenhower was talking politics, especially at the end of the telecast, when he and his family lit the national Christmas tree.[49]

The staff was pleased, but no more pleased than Montgomery, who, on the first day of 1954, got two things that few in his profession would have expected: a permanent position as special consultant to the president and an office at the White House. He also received a promise of more media work in the future.

2

THE BUSINESS
OF PERSUASION,
1954

The Christmas Eve telecast had been a big success, but even Robert Montgomery, the new TV consultant, had found it an ordeal. A second Eisenhower fireside chat two weeks later on January 4, prior to the president's daytime State of the Union address on January 7, was no less strenuous. In preparation for that broadcast, Eisenhower had to stop working in the Oval Office and leave while technicians outfitted it with cameras, lights, and sound equipment. Thus the administration decided to delay further fireside chats until Montgomery had streamlined technical arrangements. One of Montgomery's next projects was establishing a fixed presidential TV studio in the White House.

Even so, there was no lessening of interest in the new medium as relations with Congress remained strained in 1954. John Bricker and Joseph McCarthy, still setting the pace in the news media, were joined by new congressional challengers unhappy with the president's budget proposal for the 1955 fiscal year, the first budget submitted by his administration. Conservative Republicans considered the budget too extravagant, while the Democrats considered it too stingy. Democrats on Capitol Hill fought Eisenhower's plans to cut farm price supports, limit federal aid to housing and health care, and privatize the nuclear power industry. With an election ahead in November, 1954 shaped up as a major test of Eisenhower's consensus-building leadership, a time to accelerate selling of the "good product" he discussed at the end of 1953. Associates continued to view Eisenhower as the chief salesperson.

During the winter and spring of 1954, with live television on hold, the administration kept Eisenhower in the public eye by staging numerous minor events in the White House aimed at generating news media publicity, particularly that with a visual orientation. Camera crews from the television networks joined those from the newsreel companies in filming these affairs. One such event, a gala White House reception for Turkish president Celal Bayar on January 29, was among the few that had some semblance of serious news value. In contrast, on January 19, Eisenhower filmed a message honoring the upcoming birthday of Abraham Lincoln. A contingent of teenagers representing various parts of the country, all members of the Young Republicans, visited with Eisenhower on February 5. On March 15, he pressed a button at the White House that activated a hydroelectric generator at Ft. Randall Dam in South Dakota, 1,500 miles away. On April 8, news cameras assembled so that Eisenhower could unveil a new eight-cent stamp.

These White House "photo opportunities," as they would later be called, were not new. They could be traced to the newsreels of Woodrow Wilson and the still photos of the bearded Abraham Lincoln from the previous century, if not in paintings and renderings of presidents in even earlier eras. What was different in 1954, though, was a marked increase in these events and their integration into the president's regular schedule. Thirteen photo events had been held in 1953; that number would almost triple to thirty-four by the end of 1954, and photo events continued on close to a one-per-week schedule in the years that followed.[1] Television explained this expansion. Each network had nightly newscasts carried in prime time that were attracting ever-larger viewing audiences as more people purchased TV receivers. Filling these newscasts, even though they were only fifteen minutes in length, was not easy. Producers had an eye for high-profile visual material; while they sought news value, they also concentrated on finding events that could be conveniently recorded.[2] Press Secretary Jim Hagerty, initially with Montgomery's help, ensured that these events had as much convenience as possible. The press office was assisted by several publicity-oriented White House staffers, including the speechwriting team and others, such as Special Assistant Charles Willis, Deputy Abbott Washburn, and Appointment Secretary

Thomas Stephens, who proposed subject matter and formats, often with the creative flair needed to entice the news producers.

Eisenhower's thirty-four media events in 1954 did not include others that were held in various executive branch departments; Hagerty found he had to function as a traffic cop, spacing out the events in order to achieve "fuller coverage."[3] Also missing from the list of media events were around ten additional photo opportunities, even more visually appealing than those from the White House, that Eisenhower conducted on the road later in the year during the 1954 fall campaign. In August an Eisenhower appearance was broadcast live from Denver, and a week later he was filmed at the Iowa State Fair. In September Eisenhower appeared on TV breaking ground at a nuclear plant in Pennsylvania, dedicating a dam in Oregon, and visiting smoke jumpers in Montana.[4] Montgomery accompanied Eisenhower on many of these trips; Hagerty was on board for all of them.[5]

While Eisenhower continued to get snippets of exposure on the evening news broadcasts, Montgomery had been expediting work on Eisenhower's live TV appearances, in the process writing more of his own job description as the first presidential TV consultant. Logistical problems continued to bottleneck progress. Still, Montgomery saw himself as a producer-director, not a technician, thus his personal interest was what appeared in front of the cameras. Before long, Montgomery had broadened his domain to include Eisenhower himself; the role of the TV consultant as a personal stage manager was defined accordingly.

Montgomery answered officially to Sherman Adams and worked closely with Hagerty, but his status in the White House was drawn around a growing comradeship with the president, who opened himself to the actor for many reasons. It was true that Eisenhower was not one to rally around show business figures. After acquainting himself with numerous entertainers after the war when he joined their company of national celebrities, he privately considered the majority frivolous and overpaid.[6] Montgomery emerged as an exception. Although he did not possess the corporate, organizational vision that attracted Eisenhower to other people, the actor's drive, businesslike manner, and mainstream political ideas appealed to the president. Montgomery had been honored for distinguished service in World War II and remained in the Naval Reserve; when he attained the rank of reserve captain in 1956, Eisenhower personally acknowledged the promotion.[7] It was no handicap that Montgomery played war-hero roles in the movies, including *They Were Expendable* (1945), in which he starred with John Wayne, one of the president's favorite screen figures. Montgomery also helped his position by charming Mamie Eisenhower, whose happiness was often sacrificed by events in her husband's career; sensitive to this problem, the president seized every opportunity to please her.[8]

That the First Family had an affinity for movies and television was of no small consequence in the president's relationship with the actor. Eisenhower often watched TV as a form of relaxation and had a sense of the programs, personalities, and visual techniques that held a viewer's attention. Eisenhower and his wife enjoyed the popular "Fred Waring Show" on CBS because of its mixture of music and variety.[9] Eisenhower was also a fan of Arthur Godfrey, appreciating both Godfrey's down-home style and his longevity on the air.[10] Nothing in the media brought Eisenhower more delight than a good Western drama. "I know they don't have any substance to them and don't require any thought to appreciate," Eisenhower told Nikita Khrushchev when the Soviet leader visited the U.S. in 1959, "but they always have a lot of fancy tricks."[11]

Thus Eisenhower could savvy Montgomery's strategy, which was to better establish the president on the air as "plain folks," while preserving the leadership aura that had been associated with him since World War II. Eisenhower, not a natural orator, was at his best in informal settings; even though he was not a dashing figure on camera and could not speak with a resonant voice, his physical appearance was appropriate for the fatherly-but-presidential image Montgomery wanted to project. Montgomery was intrigued by at least one physical trait: Eisenhower's warm, animated smile, which could instantly lighten grim moods and situations.[12]

Projecting this image of the president required much work. Montgomery revealed some of his strategy in a short essay collection he called *Open Letter from a Television Viewer*; written shortly before Eisenhower died in 1969, it contained Montgomery's only published account of his TV work in the White House. "What I did attempt to do," Montgomery recalled, "was . . . to educate him about the uses of television, a medium unfamiliar to him except as a casual viewer." Advisers and friends, including Winston Churchill, had told Eisenhower he must avoid impromptu remarks and confine his movements and gestures on TV because they were considered distracting. Montgomery had insisted that these "horror stories" were "nonsense." Eisenhower "accepted my advice without reservation. As far as television was concerned, no authority was to supersede mine."[13]

Eisenhower's third fireside chat under Montgomery, on March 15, was dissatisfying, in part because the timing was bad. The same day, Communist forces in Vietnam began their climactic siege of the French installation at Dien Bien Phu. Three days before, an Army report was made public which accused McCarthy of misdeeds in his investigation of subversion in the military and set the stage for the Army-McCarthy hearings. Yet Eisenhower's topic that night had been taxes and his refusal to support Democratic tax cuts beyond those he had previously specified. Eisenhower was happy with the broadcast. He felt that through it he had swayed opinion leaders in Congress, both Democrats and Republicans, who went on to approve the president's tax program.[14] But Montgomery sensed that the telecast had not reached average Americans. In the process of dashing hopes for lower taxes, Eisenhower had looked stern and detached, and had failed to maintain the character prescribed in a fireside appearance. A viewer's letter sent to Eisenhower the following day, and in turn given to Montgomery, confirmed the actor's suspicions: it spoke of visual distractions, including odd camera angles and the president's unappealing wardrobe.[15]

Montgomery had another opportunity on April 5, when the president used a national TV broadcast to calm fears about U.S. and Soviet H-bomb testing. In this telecast, political expectations were more urgent. Reporters had been badgering the White House and the Pentagon for information on America's H-bomb and on reports that nuclear tests in the South Pacific were so devastating that radioactive fallout was harming people as far away as Japan. Meanwhile, Eisenhower was privately engaged in the case of atomic scientist Robert Oppenheimer, an opponent of the H-bomb, whose security clearance had been secretly removed; Stephen Ambrose has shown that during this period Eisenhower worked nonstop to keep McCarthy out of the potentially explosive Oppenheimer investigation.[16] Eisenhower's goal was to get the H-bomb off the front pages; what proved to be an almost flawless TV broadcast, one in the "Checkers" tradition, helped him succeed.

In the March 15 telecast, Eisenhower had spoken from behind a platform with his eyes glued to a teleprompter, a complicated device that facilitated eye contact by projecting words in front of a camera lens. Because Eisenhower had not yet mastered the teleprompter, for the April 5 telecast Montgomery told him to ad-lib the entire speech and use not words but the force of his personality to wring the emotion out of the H-bomb issue. To enhance the effect, Montgomery directed Eisenhower to leave his chair, walk slowly toward the cameras, and sit casually on the front of his desk. He gave the president complete freedom with his natural gestures, including his trademark impulse of folding and unfolding his arms. *Life* referred to the result as Eisenhower's "most professional TV performance to date." [17] Eisenhower knew instantly that the show had been a hit. "That's what I've been telling you boys for a long time," he said. "Just let me get up and talk to the people. I can get through to them that way. I don't feel I do when I have to read a speech or use that damn teleprompter. It's not me and I feel uncomfortable." [18]

Interestingly, Montgomery worked in almost total anonymity. Journalists, for example, did not follow Montgomery's attempt to create a fixed presidential TV studio, nor what became of it. Had reporters pursued this story, they could have revealed much about White House communication priorities. Such a studio was designed using a vacant kitchen in the basement that easily accommodated the TV equipment and the many technicians needed to operate it. Although Eisenhower would use this studio many times through 1960 to record filmed messages and conduct some of the photo events, Montgomery decided that future live broadcasts would revert back to the Oval Office, where there was far less space and inordinate confusion. He made this decision because the ceiling in the kitchen studio was so low that the giant TV lights could not be positioned in a way that did not highlight Eisenhower's bald head. The Oval Office was the only available location where the lights could be elevated.[19]

Also seldom mentioned, but very visible, were cosmetic changes. The actor revamped Eisenhower's wardrobe, replacing light gray suits with darker ones and eliminating the president's array of white and striped shirts in favor of those of solid light blue; these were more flattering on camera. Montgomery also vetoed Eisenhower's black-rimmed glasses and ordered a less distinct shell-rim design, although Eisenhower usually complied with the actor's request that he not wear glasses at all. Montgomery also taught Eisenhower how to apply facial makeup. Decisions about makeup, shirt color, lighting angles, and camera positions were made after studio tests with stand-ins resembling Eisenhower in height, appearance, and skin texture.[20]

The actual broadcasts were the biggest challenge, as Montgomery found that instilling in Eisenhower a sense of timing, poise, and animation at levels the actor was used to seeing at NBC was a slow process. One problem in 1954 was that telecasts were still many weeks apart. Eisenhower remained unsure about the teleprompter, and, like a piano teacher, Montgomery insisted that he practice. Eisenhower had also been rattled by frenzied behind-the-scenes technical activity. Until the president grew accustomed to this activity, Montgomery draped a solid black curtain in front of the technicians and video paraphernalia; all Eisenhower could see were camera lenses protruding from holes cut in the cloth.[21]

Still other measures were sometimes needed to help the president. Ray Scherer, an NBC White House correspondent who became a friend of Montgomery's through their common association with the network, recalled humor and practical jokes. One example came on a stressful day when Eisenhower was not paying proper attention to floor directions prior to a telecast. Montgomery went out on the south lawn of the White House, where Eisenhower spent time each day with his nine iron, and returned with a badly damaged golf ball. He thrust the ball into the president's face a minute before airtime, demanding to know what had happened to it. Eisenhower burst into laughter and then continued through the broadcast with ease.[22]

None of this, in Montgomery's estimation, represented an attempt to remake Eisenhower or leave viewers with a spurious sense of what the president was really like. "What an impertinence it would have been," Montgomery wrote, "for me to have tried to influence a President with Mr. Eisenhower's broad background of experience."[23] Accordingly, Montgomery accepted as off-limits the substance of Eisenhower's speeches and remarks, allowing him good relations with Emmet Hughes, Bryce Harlow, and Kevin McCann, Eisenhower's main speech writers. Always encouraging Eisenhower to be natural, Montgomery had no interest in altering Eisenhower's often convoluted and ungrammatical syntax; this may be one reason why it got so much attention from critics. Montgomery spoke up, though, when he felt that others were putting words in Eisenhower's mouth that sealed him away from average viewers at home. Once in early 1954, according to Hagerty's personal papers, Montgomery helped in "handling"

Henry Cabot Lodge, who "tried to get in the way [by] insisting on changing simple words into $2 ones."[24]

Montgomery served on the White House staff through a curious arrangement. His position was voluntary and he was never paid for his work. There was a practical reason for this. With his movie royalties and NBC compensation, he was already earning more than anyone else in the executive branch and thus did not need the taxpayers' money. What Montgomery got in lieu of a paycheck were his White House office, invitations to White House social events, frequent rides on presidential aircraft, and numerous thank-yous and platitudes from Eisenhower. Montgomery did not hide his "Special Consultant to the President" title in biographical materials churned out by his agents.

Another unusual angle was Montgomery's work schedule. After hosting "Robert Montgomery Presents" from NBC's New York studios on Monday nights, he would usually fly to Washington on Tuesdays, spend a day or two, and return to New York later in the week.[25] This routine, though, was very irregular and depended, week by week, on the TV activities that had been scheduled. Many White House staff members, apparently including Hagerty, sometimes complained that an entertainer had choice office space near Eisenhower but was often not there.[26]

Montgomery's presence in the administration revealed some insights about Eisenhower that other advisers may not have grasped at the time. Most of those who headed the White House staff had been former military associates, academicians, lawyers, and others closely connected to northeastern GOP politics. Eisenhower regarded the assembling of this staff, and the fact that it stayed intact through most of his eight years, as one of his achievements. Even so, Eisenhower wanted to bring to the executive branch a perspective that was different from that held by most of those he had appointed. Basically, Eisenhower wanted to hear from more people whose careers had been shaped by America's competitive free enterprise system. Eisenhower obtained this perspective in some of the people he named to the cabinet: Secretary of Defense Charles Wilson had been the president of General Motors, Secretary of the Treasury George Humphrey the president of the Hanna Company in Ohio, Secretary of Commerce Sinclair Weeks a Boston business figure, and Agriculture Secretary Ezra Taft Benson an agent for the farm cooperative system in Utah.

Yet Eisenhower found it difficult to attract the best from the nation's private sector, even when he used a characteristic tactic of selling government service as a call to duty. Eisenhower sensed that in the wake of the New Deal, the nation's capital was an alien, perhaps even a hostile place to those from the business field. This situation irritated Eisenhower because he had intense respect for the knowledge of the "self-made" person who had endured the test of the free enterprise experience. "The result," Eisenhower wrote in his diary, "is that sooner or later we will be unable to get anybody to take jobs in Washington except business failures, college professors, and New Deal lawyers. All of these would jump at the chance to get a job that a successful businessman has to sacrifice very much to take."[27]

Communication was one area in which Eisenhower accepted guidance only from those groomed in the private sector. His experiences in public relations prior to becoming president had suggested to him that mass communication was not a domain for lawyers and bureaucrats, but instead demanded hands-on practitioners, professionals, and people who knew, as he did, that the nation's marketplace of information was a business. Eisenhower was willing to bend a great deal to enlist these types of figures.

Montgomery was a good example. Eisenhower kept Montgomery happy and allowed him an awkward arrangement not just because the actor cost him nothing or because they became close friends but because Montgomery represented clear success in private enterprise. While many could not get past a perception of Montgomery as a Hollywood leading man, there was no denying that the actor had climbed to a high pinnacle of a fiercely competitive field. With Eisenhower using the same mass media channels as others in this field, it was a mark of distinction to have somebody like Montgomery in the White House.

Eisenhower's interest in the corporate model of mass communication extended beyond his recruiting efforts. He maintained the close personal contacts with leading mass media entrepreneurs that he had developed after the war. Many of them were key figures in the publishing field, including publisher Henry Luce of Time, Inc.; Helen Rogers Reid, owner of the *New York Herald Tribune*; William Robinson, publisher of the *Herald Tribune*; Arthur Sulzberger, publisher of the *New York Times*; and Douglas Black, president of Doubleday. Hagerty, the press secretary, was a product of this print environment. Eisenhower also cultivated Madison Avenue, winning the loyalty of the American Association of Advertising Agencies (AAAA) and its

Advertising Council, which created and distributed a large quantity of material in the form of public service announcements for use by print and broadcast outlets. Historian Robert Griffith explained how Eisenhower, who viewed the Ad Council as "one of our great agencies for the preservation of freedom," influenced the content of these announcements. An Ad Council campaign promoting "Confidence in a Growing America," for example, was an Eisenhower device aimed at softening another political problem in 1954, a nagging recession.[28]

In addition to its output, the logic of the business world attracted Eisenhower and played a role in shaping his public dialogue. Corporate America did not begin from a starting line, but instead worked backward from an anticipated bottom line. It was somewhat the same in the Eisenhower administration. Results, obviously not measured in sales and dividends, were nonetheless charted in many different ways. Votes were a politician's ultimate bottom line. Yet consensus building needed more up-to-the-minute parameters; Eisenhower obtained some of his benchmarks through a variety of public opinion research that was funneled into the White House.

It cannot be said that Eisenhower was a captive of this research, nor that it was always used to set White House goals. The only time in his private diaries that Eisenhower acknowledged even reading the results of opinion research was in the period before he decided to enter politics, when pollsters showed him a probable presidential candidate.[29]

It is known from many White House materials, though, that Eisenhower was extremely attentive to public opinion research and got this information regularly. Some of the research reports that reached Eisenhower in his first two years as president appeared in the records of Gabriel Hauge, the White House economics adviser; these reports included a twelve-month breakdown of trends in Eisenhower's approval ratings up to March 1954.[30] Hagerty was especially active in gathering and synthesizing published public opinion research.[31] There was also ongoing guidance from the Republican National Committee; in addition to the input it received from state and local GOP committees across the country, the RNC obtained formal research from the Batten, Barton, Durstine, and Osborn advertising agency (BBDO).[32] By 1954, the Eisenhower White House had more sources of research information, and generated more research itself, than any previous administration.

One reason for this interest in research was George Gallup, the founder of the Gallup Poll, who was closely tied to the administration throughout its eight years. Gallup had been a protégé of Sig Larmon, a member of Eisenhower's "gang" and head of the Young and Rubicam advertising agency. Gallup's career break had come in the early 1930s, when Larmon lured him from a professorship at Northwestern University with a lucrative job offer at Young and Rubicam in New York. For three years Gallup headed research at the agency before leaving in 1936 to begin his public polling business. Larmon had loaned Gallup the money he needed to get started.[33] Gallup never stopped thanking Larmon for this gesture. Not only had the Depression made money tight; in the aftermath of the *Literary Digest* uproar, in which surveys by that publication mistakenly predicted Alf Landon's victory in the 1936 election, a polling business was deemed a highly risky venture. In 1952, Gallup's research suggested public distress with communism, the Korean War, and alleged corruption in the Truman administration; each became a theme in Eisenhower's first campaign.[34] After 1953, Gallup was sometimes brought to the White House to explain in more detail the simpler sets of numbers that appeared in his nationally syndicated newspaper column.[35]

The 1952 campaign had also marked the beginning of a research program that provided White House advisers with their most frequent source of information, known as "tracking." Tracking was a procedure advanced by BBDO as a way to test and market products and maximize sales for the agency's clients. BBDO had been hired by the Republican National Committee to coordinate advertising for Eisenhower in 1952; after the campaign, the RNC signed a four-year retainer contract with BBDO which made the agency a White House operation. Every Sunday night, agency representatives at BBDO's twelve branch offices contacted 50 to 100 people by telephone to determine public concerns and interests.[36] Results were tabulated and circulated in the White House on Monday afternoons.

The tracking went on throughout Eisenhower's presidency. Although it was unscientific, the object was to determine fluctuations in public attitudes in time for Eisenhower to take corrective action. One example influenced policy during the 1954 recession, which had begun in the spring and lagged through the summer, pushing unemployment close to 6 percent. When Defense Secretary Wilson returned to Detroit in 1954 and told an audience that the unemployed reminded him of kennel dogs who "sit on [their] fanny and yell," BBDO research immediately detected mounting public indignation.

Public relations needs were particularly acute because this recession was the first during a GOP administration since the Great Depression had struck Herbert Hoover in the 1930s; also, an election was ahead. The day after BBDO circulated its findings, and after a lot of debate, Eisenhower agreed to break policy and publicize a half-completed labor survey indicating a decline in unemployment, thus smudging the controversy as the economy rebounded.[37]

Eisenhower, who became accustomed to receiving this research, sometimes took action when he felt he was not getting enough. On February 2, 1954, he wrote a letter to the head of the BBDO office in Minneapolis that explained the need for better information from the Minnesota "listening post" on public reaction to farm policies.[38] The week before, Eisenhower had personally requested and received from Roy Howard, the president of the Scripps-Howard newspaper chain, a research database on a variety of issues that Howard's company was compiling from surveys undertaken by its publishing outlets across the country.[39]

The results of this research were remarkably coherent throughout 1954. After two wars in a ten-year time span and a variety of economic ups and downs, the people were ready for stability and contentment. The dominant public concerns were war and peace, articulated in apprehensions about the military power of the Soviet Union and nervousness about nuclear arms. Yet the people were baffled by such things as test-ban treaties and megatonnage; they seemed simply to want a president who could calm their fears. They were especially vigilant about personal matters such as employment, taxes, the cost of living, and the economy. Domestic communism was still an issue, but less so as the year wore on. Southerners were concerned about desegregation in the wake of the *Brown v. Board of Education* ruling that May. Farmers were irate about sagging agriculture prices and sputtering support programs. Even though the nation's problems were amplified in the news media, research suggested they distressed only pockets of the population. Gallup's research later in 1956 showed that 74 percent of the public felt no group had been treated unfairly by the administration.[40]

Contentment was also illustrated in Eisenhower's public approval ratings, the subject of Hauge's report in March 1954. There had been a quivering downward slide through the end of 1953; after the president scored a "75" in August 1953, respondents who approved Eisenhower's handling of his job had diminished to 60 percent the following November. By mid-1954, Eisenhower's approval rating was back above 70 percent. One of his goals now, and through the rest of his presidency, was keeping the rating at that very high level.

Eisenhower was interested in research, but never consumed by it; on the other hand, he did have a passion for the processes that might be used to achieve good numbers. As he looked to his own needs, he did not see persuasion as a micromanaged, "dollar-a-holler" proposition the way other politicians, including his predecessor Harry Truman, had seemed to. Eisenhower intended his November 23, 1953, memo, in which he told advisers their job was "not unlike the advertising and sales task of a great industrial organization," to be taken literally.[41] The words "selling" and "promotion" appeared in Eisenhower's written materials innumerable times, particularly in late 1953 and even more frequently in 1954.

Much of Eisenhower's promotional effort was internal. The White House staff was generally responsive to public relations, but Eisenhower often had to sell the idea of selling to cabinet members, many of whom had never been taught to think in such terms. On February 12, 1954, Eisenhower indicated to William Robinson of the *New York Herald Tribune* that Secretary of State John Foster Dulles had an image problem—that Dulles let himself be portrayed in the news media as too crusty and obtuse. Eisenhower was convinced Dulles could be "a truly great Secretary of State" if "the publicity media of the country [would] take up this theme and promote it."[42] Even more of an image problem followed Agriculture Secretary Benson, a villain to most farmers because of Eisenhower's insistence on leveling commodity price supports. Later, in 1955, Eisenhower told Benson that he needed to start concerning himself more with "plain education and a lot of salesmanship, dressing up—persuasiveness is the word." Eisenhower explained, "What we want to do is get phrases to show we are working like dogs; we are building the dam and getting things done."[43]

Eisenhower preached public relations in private because he did not have the time to build the dam by himself. In fact, an attempt to delegate this entire responsibility led to one of the major internal pursuits in the Eisenhower White House in 1954: the creation of an executive branch public relations operation of large scale, one that would borrow from Madison Avenue principles. Its mission would be to refine the goals of the administration into a few easy-to-grasp concepts and promote those concepts through a coordinated use of the media. Eisenhower did not know exactly what he wanted, but he sketched his ideas in the November 23, 1953, memorandum and others in 1954. He gave the proposed public relations operation the working title of "board of strategy."

The same factors that had brought Montgomery to the White House, his skill and experience in the professional mass media, guided the president's thoughts on this new White House unit. He wanted a "director of communications," a position that many large businesses had created by the 1950s. Eisenhower refused to put this operation into the hands of a bureaucrat or allow any current administration member to develop it; he was determined that the board be headed by a truly distinguished figure from the professional mass media field. Because of the difficulty he had already encountered in drawing prominent people from the private sector, this was from the beginning a monumental task.

Nevertheless, Eisenhower felt that this operation could be organized much like a unit he had developed in his international communications work. This was his Psychological Strategy Board (PSB), a descendant of the psychological warfare unit created by Truman in 1951, which used channels of foreign propaganda to destabilize the Communist world and exploit events that reflected unfavorably on the Soviet Union and China. One of its successes, as Blanche Wiesen Cook detailed in *The Declassified Eisenhower* (1981), came immediately after the death of Josef Stalin in March 1953, when a well-timed early version of Eisenhower's "atoms for peace" proposal "literally blanketed the world" via broadcast and printed materials distributed by the U.S. Information Service, the CIA, the State Department, Radio Free Europe, and the Voice of America.[44] Eisenhower's PSB had begun operations on February 16, 1953, under C. D. Jackson, a veteran of the government's "psy-war" activity in World War II but better known as an editor-executive at Time, Inc. With Luce's help Eisenhower had lured Jackson away from New York into a year of government service. He considered Jackson a prize catch, even though it was inevitable that Jackson would return, as he did in April 1954, to his high-paying job at Time.[45] Jackson remained an unofficial adviser for the remainder of Eisenhower's presidency.

Eisenhower thought it possible to recruit a similar private industry veteran to become manager of the domestic board of strategy. Accordingly, Eisenhower's job description had two primary dimensions. First, the ideal candidate needed a philosophical closeness to the administration in order to be trusted with strategy and security. Second, the person had to be an expert on the domestic mass media. In late 1953 and most of 1954, word went out through the White House underground for possibilities; at various times the names of CBS chairman William Paley, CBS president Frank Stanton, BBDO president Ben Duffy, New York political publicist Earl Newsom, and the *Herald Tribune*'s Robinson were discussed as possible appointees.[46]

The person Eisenhower most wanted, though, was the sixty-two-year-old Larmon. Larmon was more than just a captain of the advertising industry; there was nobody with a media background who was closer to Eisenhower personally. After succeeding Raymond Rubicam as president of Young and Rubicam in 1944, Larmon had been active in public service; following some joint projects in New York during the president's tenure at Columbia, and many golf and bridge games, Larmon and his wife moved permanently into Eisenhower's innermost circle. Larmon had been a principal organizer of Citizens for Eisenhower, the volunteer organization that helped Eisenhower get elected in 1952. Like Montgomery and Jackson, Larmon represented the self-made business person who had risen to the highest corporate echelon and who would have to sacrifice money and personal influence to accept a post in Washington. Therefore Eisenhower, formally in January 1954 and informally several times that winter, appealed to Larmon to join his administration.[47]

In a sense, Larmon was offered a job he helped to conceive, since, like many former Citizens figures now in the White House, he had encouraged Eisenhower to put a big business spin on his public relations. Larmon had been instrumental in helping Eisenhower obtain the support of the AAAA's Advertising Council.[48] Eisenhower had also eyed Larmon as a possible successor to Jackson as head of the PSB. In either case Eisenhower promised Larmon the same flexibility and authority Jackson had, with a similar arrangement: an office at the White House and a one-year "tour of duty."[49]

Although Larmon eventually joined the government as a member of the part-time U.S. Advisory Commission later in 1954, he declined Eisenhower's requests to join the White House staff, citing his responsibilities at Young and Rubicam. Eisenhower accepted each rejection graciously. Other people were considered for the position through the spring of 1954, but the recruiting effort lapsed by summer, and the board of strategy never materialized.[50]

Eisenhower had wanted too much from the corporate common-wealth, but recruiting difficulty did not entirely explain the unfulfilled plans for a senior-level domestic media board. During the period Eisenhower was attempting to locate a director of communications, Hagerty was making a remarkable rise inside the White House. This had been an unexpected development; in fact, Eisenhower had wanted Larmon, or whoever was chosen as communications director, to function as Hagerty's supervisor. Hagerty had been a newspaper reporter and, for eight years, the press secretary to New York governor Thomas Dewey. Unlike many of his White House coworkers, Hagerty's role in Citizens for Eisenhower had been minor; Hagerty was indirectly linked with the group in 1952 only through Dewey, who more or less willed Hagerty to Eisenhower that year. In Eisenhower's 1953 correspondence sizing up his selling and public relations needs, Hagerty's name was rarely mentioned; Hagerty did not even receive a copy of the November 23 memo that first outlined the board of strategy.

Indeed, in the beginning Eisenhower regarded Hagerty as something like a second lieutenant in charge of his first platoon. At age forty-two, Hagerty was the president's junior by twenty years; a decade later, after they had left the White House, Eisenhower was still referring to Hagerty as "my boy." As Eisenhower was assembling his staff after the 1952 election, the only personal direction he gave Hagerty was a lecture that took place as the two sat in a golf cart. "You'll know everything I'm doing," Hagerty recalled him saying, "and I'll keep you fully informed. If you get any questions, don't shoot off your mouth before you have the answers. If you have anything you don't know . . . , come to me and I'll tell you." [51]

Hagerty went to Eisenhower often, especially during the Harry Dexter White furor in late 1953, when White House press relations had produced sparks for the first time. Eisenhower kept his promise, left his Oval Office door open, and soon detected in the press secretary many unique and useful administrative talents. Hagerty had been hardened by some turbulent times as Dewey's press secretary, notably Dewey's humiliating 1948 loss to Harry Truman; as a stabilizing force in Albany, Hagerty helped Dewey regroup and achieve reelection in 1950. Eisenhower found Hagerty intelligent, hardworking, inventive, personable, and extremely diplomatic. Hagerty had become a spearhead of the administration's internal communications, illustrated in the energetic assistance he lent Wilton Persons, the Oval

Office–Capitol Hill liaison, whose job—dealing with Congress—was one of the most important and perhaps most frustrating White House assignments. In the spring Hagerty and Persons helped persuade Senators Karl Mundt and Everett Dirksen to structure the rules of the Army-McCarthy hearings in a way that put McCarthy on the defensive.[52] Eisenhower became impressed with Hagerty's wide-ranging knowledge of almost every facet of the administration and his reputation as a denizen of the executive branch who did not limit himself to the formal job requirements of a press secretary. The reputation that preceded Hagerty was followed by real substance. His personal diaries would describe numerous encounters where he informed Eisenhower of important happenings of which the president had no prior knowledge.

What the president saw in his midst was another Harry Butcher, the Navy officer who had managed Eisenhower's press relations and public image during the war but who had disgraced Eisenhower, and turned a tidy profit, with his unexpurgated war diaries. Because Hagerty had the same qualifications as Butcher but was a product of the next generation, somewhat awestruck by his duties and not a self-professed peer of the president, Eisenhower was ready again to confide in such a person and wager that the Butcher experience would not be repeated. Eisenhower's wager paid off. Hagerty evolved into the public-private pulse of the entire administration and died in 1981 without having profited from any book, memoir, or published personal account of the details.

In the summer of 1954, Eisenhower was still concerned about needed refinements in his public relations and, as he told Lodge, "things the administration is doing [that are] not getting out."[53] By then, it was clear that Hagerty was going to take on this assignment. On August 4, Eisenhower related again to Robinson his "growing need for sound and continuous counsel and some operational help in the field of public relations." In this letter, Eisenhower praised Hagerty and his assistant Murray Snyder and pondered an expansion of the White House press office, which "would free Jim—who daily proves himself of real calibre—to think about all these important matters and do the necessary planning."[54]

Hagerty did this planning and also became one of the most visible personalities during the remaining Eisenhower years. As a committed chain smoker, a less-than-expert dresser, and a New Yorker with a heavy accent, Hagerty lacked Eisenhower's communicative style. Yet Americans saw much of him in the years that followed.

Media planning assumed an increased measure of political meaning toward late 1954, even though the two senators who had inspired much of Eisenhower's early interest in White House public relations, Bricker and McCarthy, had been removed as deterrents to the president's consensus-building efforts. In late February, Eisenhower mustered enough votes to keep the Bricker amendment from the needed two-thirds majority in the Senate. The end for McCarthy had been public reaction to the televised Army-McCarthy hearings, which had begun in April. When the hearings adjourned in June, Eisenhower personally commended Joseph Welch, the attorney for the Army. Welch responded by saying that he felt he had succeeded in keeping McCarthy "in front of the television sets for quite a while, long enough to permit the public to see how disgracefully he acted."[55]

Yet there was no glow in the White House as the year wound down. Although Eisenhower had brought about, in his words, "the virtual ending of the fights which set Republican against Republican," the results of the fall election suggested there was still considerable ground to cover toward persuading the rest of the American public of this success.[56] The GOP lost seventeen seats in the House and two in the Senate, enough to put both sides of Congress back in Democratic hands. Against the advice of Lodge, who had anticipated these results and did not want 1954 to become a vote of confidence in Eisenhower, the president had campaigned intensely, both personally and in the media, for several GOP candidates.[57]

The 1954 setbacks caused Eisenhower to analyze his public relations once again. He blamed the defeats on the two years of escapades by noisy, headline-seeking conservatives; "[t]hese," he wrote to his close friend Swede Hazlett, "have come to mean 'Republicanism' to far too many people."[58] With a Democratic Congress about to convene, Eisenhower could see that he would have to play an even more active public role to give the GOP the moderate, forward-looking image he wanted it to have. Many factors were working in his favor, including the improved television appearances under Montgomery, his synthesis of research by public opinion specialists, and a comprehensive public relations effort coming together under Hagerty.

Nevertheless, an important communications need outlined at the beginning of 1954 had not been realized by year's end. Because of several complications, Eisenhower still lacked a means of channeling his information, visions, and philosophies directly to the American public on a timely, consistent, and reliable basis. By early 1955, this need would be fulfilled.

CIRCUMVENTING

THE PRESS,

1953–1955

The most significant single media advancement in the Eisenhower era came on January 19, 1955, when the first televised presidential news conference was held. Eisenhower got some impressive public relations mileage out of this event because his administration had taken steps to recognize the young field of television journalism. With TV reporters now able to cover the news conferences with cameras and microphones, the television industry applauded Eisenhower for liberating these events from traditions that had made them a bastion of print journalism. The National Academy of Television Arts and Sciences gave Eisenhower an Emmy award for his contribution to TV news. Eisenhower was later credited in much the same way by some scholars, including James Pollard, who felt that the administration's news conferences put TV "on a more equal footing" with newspapers.[1]

Although the TV news conference was a breakthrough in electronic journalism, it represented the culmination of an idea that had, by then, been discussed among Eisenhower's advisers for more than two years. The objective, as Press Secretary Jim Hagerty would write in his diary, was to "go directly to the people" with news and information from the White House. It was the same concept Maxwell Rabb had outlined in January 1953 in recommending the fireside chat: that of enabling the president to "present his message over the head of Congress" and other opponents "in a way that cannot be criticized." From the perspective of the White House, the TV news conference was the fireside chat in a different form.

The TV news conference did not appear magically in 1955. Its story began with Eisenhower's distress about Joseph McCarthy in late 1953, moved ahead despite some setbacks with the TV networks over airtime availabilities, was influenced by technological constraints, and finally climaxed, after the first news conference was televised, with some political footwork by the White House. Besides a turning point in the evolution of presidential mass communication, the TV news conference was a window on Eisenhower's less-than-satisfying relationship with the American news media.

A metamorphosis in Eisenhower's attitude toward the press was one of the by-products of his rendezvous with politics and elective office. He had been a darling of the press during his military career; with wartime press adviser Harry Butcher by his side, Eisenhower had cultivated reporters who, in turn, basked in the attention he gave. Even so, while valuing Eisenhower as a general, many of the same reporters had seen him as an unlikely occupant of the nation's highest office. The president had had the endorsement of 80 percent of the nation's newspaper publishers in 1952. Yet two-thirds of the reporters who traveled with Eisenhower in the campaign intended to vote for Adlai Stevenson. Another complicating factor had been a steady erosion of Eisenhower's interest in the working press, which coincided with his introduction to the corporate media world after the war. Many of the reporters who had known Eisenhower as "one of the guys" in 1944 and 1945 were covering him again in 1953.[2] He was not the same person; some reporters were put off by what they called the "new 'businessman's government.'" "[T]he Trumanites would keep you up until 2 A.M. talking about what they were doing," one correspondent spouted to *Time*. "The Ikeman sees you for fifteen minutes in his office."[3] Eisenhower did not often begin a news conference with a warm greeting. Instead, he confronted reporters with one fist impatiently jammed on his hip, starting the conference with the squib, "Do you have any questions you want to ask me?," which signaled to reporters a "let's get it over with" attitude. Eisenhower had not wanted this distance but was unable to narrow it himself; the more obliging Hagerty was indispensable in keeping press relations in a workable state.

Although Eisenhower had an instinct for warming to the press, his presidency removed the impulse. Above all, he did not have the time to court reporters as he had in the military. In addition, the watchdog, adversarial function of the news media bothered Eisenhower, revealing what he viewed as a dark side to the press, including reportorial tendencies that he personally rejected. Perhaps in an old-fashioned way, or perhaps not, Eisenhower had always defined the task of a journalist as energetic research and a straight, objective, ordered presentation of facts. He repeatedly complained about the colorization of news by "columnists." He was not referring to syndicated writers and editorialists; rather, he was talking about general news reporters who were allowed to begin stories with their bylines. Bylined accounts permeated every page and section of a typical newspaper. Eisenhower deplored this practice, believing the greatest good came when reporters behaved as soldiers, faceless worker bees, and distributors of information that allowed society to make its own judgments. Signed news stories not only cleared the way for interpretation; to Eisenhower, they were a symbol of journalistic vanity that inspired reporters to regard themselves as influential national figures, when, in fact, they were outside observers with limitations. Even the best could not be 100 percent informed.[4] "I haven't read [Walter] Lippmann since I left Columbia [University]," Eisenhower related in 1967. "When I saw him writing about Germany, with no knowledge of it at all, I quit reading him."[5] Eisenhower's sentiment was confirmed in 1968, when he read his first Lippmann piece in more than twenty years. In it Lippmann hypothesized that Eisenhower's support of the Vietnam War forestalled a GOP opportunity that year to support a negotiated peace. Just as he had two decades before, Eisenhower complained of Lippmann's "fuzzy thinking" and journalistic "habit of setting up a straw man that he can enthusiastically destroy."[6]

Eisenhower needed evidence for such conclusions, and the McCarthy affair in 1953–54 proved to be an epiphany. If McCarthy brought ill repute to the democratic process, so, too, did the general performance of the news media, at least in the view of many historians, including Robert Griffith, who observed in 1987 that "McCarthy never screamed, but the headlines did. . . . Most reporters had neither the time nor the research facilities to evaluate properly the senator's many charges, and the wire service tradition of printing the most arresting facts at the head of a story distorted even the most intelligent presentations."[7] While historians would give the McCarthy era press stern reviews years later, Eisenhower was performing the same analysis at the time the actual events were unfolding. Almost every criticism of McCarthy in Eisenhower's personal diaries contained a reference to the senator's need to make headlines and the media's willingness, without fail, to give him this opportunity. Eisenhower expressed his vitriolic assessment particularly well in July 1953, after his close friend Swede Hazlett urged the White House to crack down on McCarthy. Eisenhower flatly refused, calling the affair a "newspaper trial." "When you have a situation like this," Eisenhower declared, "you have an ideal one for the newspapers, the television and the radio, to exploit, to exaggerate and to perpetuate."[8]

Eisenhower had a simple explanation for the honor some journalists seemed to bestow on people like McCarthy: reporters needed confrontation. Fighting and confrontation made a news story more interesting; the more interesting the story, the greater the likelihood it would end up on page 1, thus increasing the acclaim of the person whose byline it followed. Eisenhower had fathomed just this in the media's attempt to discredit his consensus efforts with the GOP conservatives and in their perception of his leadership in 1953 as "milquetoast." While consensus politics did not make news, personality contests clearly did. The main themes in the news media in 1953, as the president saw them, had been Eisenhower versus Robert Taft, Eisenhower versus John Bricker, Eisenhower versus Harry Truman, and Eisenhower versus Joseph McCarthy.

The president's diminishing confidence in the press reached a low point in the firestorm over his decision in late 1953 to reopen the Harry Dexter White investigation. There was a natural level of intrigue in this case because White, an accused Communist spy, had been a high official in the Truman administration. Yet Eisenhower could not understand why the media seemed infatuated by this story and excluded dozens of others that reflected more positively on the workings of government. A picture of White, who had been dead for four years, made the cover of *Time* on November 23. This coverage, in part, had prompted an Eisenhower memo regarding the "slanting" of news by reporters and the "inestimable damage" it could bring.[9]

Eisenhower claimed he was not an avid reader of the newspapers. Yet Assistant Press Secretary Murray Snyder, among others, maintained that he was, and that he had daily access to the *New York Herald Tribune, New York Times, Washington Post, Washington Star*, and other newspapers.[10] Even so, Eisenhower's opinion of the press was not shaped so much by what he read as by his direct dealings with reporters, notably in their lines of questioning at the news conferences. In the midst of the White controversy, it seemed to Eisenhower that stories eventually written from these news conferences were guided more by the reporters' questions than by his answers.

The news conference on November 11, 1953, was memorable: it was the first time reporters had breached the unofficial courtesy at these affairs and, as a group, confronted the president with questions he refused to answer. The reporters wanted Eisenhower's response to personal attacks by Truman that the White investigation was a White House front for McCarthyism. Eisenhower cut the conference off after just twenty minutes and walked out. James Reston of the *New York Times* called it "the stormiest White House news conference of recent years"; Robert Donovan of the *Herald Tribune* reported that "at times the President appeared to be restraining his temper with conscious effort." [11]

Neither in late 1953 nor at any subsequent point in his presidency did Eisenhower consider the news media an enemy of his administration. That many of Eisenhower's closest friends were publishers and broadcast executives made this impossible. Yet it was because of these friendships that Eisenhower's press expectations created an extra measure of frustration. While Eisenhower had respect for Henry Luce, William Paley, Helen Rogers Reid, and other media owners who daily braved the risks of free enterprise, he could not fully comprehend why these people would surrender so much influence to their minion reporters, who operated in a safe haven, did not seem to possess any extraordinary talent, and had obtained their jobs through happenstance. Eisenhower knew, of course, that any attempt by these publishers to actively intervene in the labors of their own employees would result in charges that they were trespassing on "freedom of the press." This realization, however, scarcely mitigated Eisenhower's reasoning that reporters were interlopers who clogged the communication channels. Eisenhower believed, further, that changes among reporting personnel would not improve the situation, because the reporters were, in his view, as interchangeable as drill bits.

The best course of action was not fighting with reporters, treating them as opponents, or exerting pressure through their employers, but rather defusing them and disconnecting their capacity for unilaterally interpreting presidential activities. This concept was the foundation of a press strategy that would ignore individual reporters and use what was truly important, their outlets of communication, to the administration's best advantage. Considering that the public cared infinitely more about Eisenhower than any individual news media personality, this strategy made a lot of sense.

However, it was a strategy that had a number of initial booby traps. The stepping up of White House photo events in 1954 helped. Eisenhower also consented to more interviews with reporters and was instructive about having others in the administration appear on nationally televised press panel shows, including "Meet the Press" on NBC and "Face the Nation" on CBS.[12] Yet it was clear, particularly to Hagerty, that any attempt to use the news media as a conduit for White House information would inevitably rest on the news conferences. The news conferences were the only occasions when Eisenhower regularly met with reporters in person; they were also the only occasions when the press corps—all 200 members—gathered together as a group.

The news conference was problematic because it was an invention of the press corps, not the White House, and steeped in journalistic tradition. Except for Franklin Roosevelt's decision to dispense with reporters' written queries by soliciting questions spontaneously, the news conference had changed little since Woodrow Wilson instituted it in 1913. There had been talk from time to time of broadcasting the news conferences; any president beginning with Warren Harding could have done this. As late as 1953, though, this idea was incompatible with the protocol of these events. News conferences had been private gatherings that had given reporters opportunities to interact with presidents informally. Wilson's procedure of having reporters gather around him in the Oval Office continued until the presidency of Harry Truman, who had to use an auditorium to accommodate the expanding numbers of the press corps. The theoretical aim of the conferences, moreover, had been to provide background information: reporters did not have recording devices, and direct quotations were allowed only with permission. Although the press office indicated the day after the inauguration that future news conferences might be broadcast, even Hagerty, to a degree, saw this as a wild prediction.[13]

Preserving this press corps protocol had faded into a low priority in the White House by November 1953. Determined to kick McCarthy off the front pages, Eisenhower was told by Hagerty and others that the news conference would be the most expedient vehicle. Eisenhower was also presented with the proposition that full use of the news conference could be achieved only if he was willing to change many existing procedures, take protocol away from the press, place this control more firmly in White House hands, and risk potential outcry. Any inhibitions Eisenhower may have had about taking these steps were removed after the rowdy performance by the press corps at the November 11 news conference and another much like it on November 18.

One of the first moves in what would soon be a transformation of the presidential news conference came at Eisenhower's next meeting with the press, on December 2. By then McCarthy had intervened in the White turmoil with a declaration that domestic communism would be a major issue in the 1954 elections. This time, rather than appearing at the news conference as a passive "answer man," Eisenhower came armed with a prepared statement implying that McCarthy was wrong and that by election time communism would not be a serious menace. This statement was not long, and it did not satisfy all of Eisenhower's advisers. C. D. Jackson had recommended this addition to the news conference procedure in the hope that Eisenhower would use it to blast McCarthy. Instead, after Jackson drafted a statement to that effect, Eisenhower "slammed it back" at him "and said he would not refer to McCarthy personally—'I will not get in the gutter with that guy.'"[14] Nevertheless, the reporters listened intently, and Eisenhower got his message across to the public.

Eisenhower had not been the first president to use a news conference for issuing a prepared statement. However, by doing this on December 2 he set the stage for a major revision in the news conference at his next meeting with the press, on December 16. Again he read a statement—not about McCarthy but instead about Eisenhower's hopes for success in the three-day summit with GOP legislative leaders that was scheduled to begin the following morning. Wanting leverage over conservatives who were already attacking his program for the 1954 session, Eisenhower again got his message across; subsequent questions by the reporters also gave him a chance to elaborate on some other initiatives, including his "atoms for peace" proposal, unveiled the week before at the U.N.[15]

After the news conference broke up, Eisenhower reviewed what he had said, then made a decision that caught many reporters by complete surprise when it was announced that afternoon. Hagerty told the press corps that the president had "agreed" to lift the news conference no-quotation rule and put the entire affair on the journalistic record. This announcement was followed by another: a tape recording of the December 16 news conference would be released to the radio networks. Hagerty also indicated that all future Eisenhower news conferences would likewise be put on the record.

With this move, Eisenhower had taken a sizable stride toward achieving a routine means of placing his exact words before the public and having them stand alone against potential journalistic distortion and interpretation. And, as it turned out, there was no ruckus about it. The reporters were delighted. There was one catch: they still had to work from official transcripts edited by Hagerty. Nevertheless, a *New York Times* editorial proclaimed that the news conference "has under President Eisenhower become a completely public, on-the-record institution," similar to the British question-and-answer period in Parliament. Columnist Arthur Krock maintained that a "wooden curtain" no longer separated the presidency from the press and public.[16] In this celebratory atmosphere there was almost no objection to a feature of the new protocol that Hagerty had assumed would draw some complaint: the broadcasting of the news conferences on radio.

The first set of Eisenhower news conference innovations was rounded out by a superb display of public relations maneuvering. By giving no advanced indication that changes were in the offing, Hagerty not only reduced second-guessing within the press corps; he also affirmed that the White House was now in complete control, even persuading reporters to believe they were participants in a historic event. Eisenhower added his own touch by referring to his easing of quotation restrictions as a "Christmas present" to the press corps.[17]

His diaries from this period, however, make it apparent that Eisenhower had little desire to hand gifts and bouquets to the press. A month later, he marked his first anniversary as president with some pungent private reflections about the U.S. journalistic community. "The members of this group are far from being as important as they themselves consider," he wrote. "[T]hey deal in negative criticism rather than in any attempt toward constructive helpfulness. They love to deal in personalities; in their minds, personalities make stories." Citing an "extraordinary amount of distortion and gross error," Eisenhower emphasized that for twelve years he had been at "spots in the world that have been considered newsworthy" and had witnessed firsthand "the actual incidents reported. . . . Rarely," he stressed, "is such writing accurate." Eisenhower felt that the professional motivation of a typical journalist was "a certain thrill out of seeing his name in black type."[18]

The decision to formalize Eisenhower's press appearances with transcripts and audiotape recordings had cleared a path toward the TV news conferences, but they were not yet a fait accompli. Technical restrictions related to lights, cameras, and cables, not unlike those that impeded the fireside chat series, were a factor. More important, though, was an uneasiness in the White House about enlarging the audience for the news conference and making it a true public event. Radio coverage was one thing; but print reporters, while appreciating Eisenhower's open quotation policy and accepting the radio recordings, were much more likely to make an issue out of the obtrusive presence of television and the stage management that it would require. Eisenhower himself doubted whether the spontaneous news conferences should have a living-room following, fearing that before millions of viewers he might inadvertently divulge security information or embarrass a subordinate.[19] He did, however, see some pluses. With his spoken words now in print, he "soon learned that ungrammatical sentences in the transcript caused many to believe that I was incapable of using good English."[20] The audio recordings released to radio mitigated this dilemma, but not to the extent that TV could.

Even so, advisers hesitated on the TV news conferences mainly because they could not guarantee Eisenhower total control of what would be seen. On paper, it was a brilliant tactic for reaching the public, but it was one that could just as easily backfire if millions of Americans from coast to coast saw more hostile displays from the reporters, such as those in November 1953.

The early part of 1954 gave the White House ample reason to persist in these fears but also to consider additional steps. This period was a time of growth, perhaps of consciousness raising, for Hagerty; during his eight years as press secretary to Thomas Dewey and his first year under Eisenhower, the press secretary had still considered himself a reporter at heart. He was close to his father, James A. Hagerty, who by June would retire from a distinguished career with the *New York Times*. Yet the battle over the Bricker amendment—now at the "wisecrack stage," in Eisenhower's opinion—dominated headlines in the first two months of 1954, prior to its defeat. Then a buildup began in the press for the Army-McCarthy hearings. Like the president, Hagerty was insulted by the representation of these affairs in the news media and the insinuation that the executive branch was sitting down on the job.[21] On March 3, James Reston of the *Times* wrote that Eisenhower was "turning the other cheek" on McCarthy.[22] "To hell with slanted reporters," Hagerty confided to his diary the next day. "We'll go directly to the people who can hear exactly what [the] President said without reading warped and slanted stories."[23]

Eisenhower's fireside TV chats, receiving the increased scrutiny of Robert Montgomery, continued to be the president's main point of personal public outreach. Meanwhile, Hagerty was promoting a number of tactics designed to short-circuit adverse images of Eisenhower; these were drawn from his intimate knowledge of the individual and collective tendencies and foibles in the press corps. Hagerty had long been attentive to such avenues. Knowing, for example, that reporters often inflated the value of their own stories, in 1952 he had ordered pictures taken of a Stevenson rally in a location where Eisenhower had appeared earlier and had drawn twice as many spectators; when reporters wrote that the crowds were the same size, Hagerty circulated his photos and obtained more accurate coverage.[24] Hagerty also knew that reporters thrived on the "scoop" and liked to be part of history in the making. Thus, in March 1954 he proposed that Eisenhower put aside his White House preoccupations for a time and make a visit to Europe that would culminate in a return to Normandy on the tenth anniversary of D-Day; this idea of a foreign publicity tour, while not approved in 1954, would be resurrected during a similar period of press difficulty in 1959.[25] Nevertheless, one Hagerty scheme did achieve results beginning in August 1954, when he persuaded Eisenhower to leak sanitized transcripts of cabinet meetings to Donovan of the *New York Herald Tribune*. These transcripts put the reporter on course toward a very upbeat construction of the administration in his book *Eisenhower: The Inside Story* (1956), which stayed on best-seller lists for months when it was published.[26]

Nothing served Hagerty better than his sense of the vanity that existed in the press corps. Although Hagerty knew that reporters were not the egomaniacs Eisenhower made them out to be, he was aware of the high level of fraternal self-esteem among them. Because of his own background as a reporter, he easily slid in and out of this fraternity. When he called reporters on the telephone, he dispensed with White House formality and simply announced himself in newsroom style as "Hagerty." This approach flattered reporters, as did Hagerty's procedure for handling factual errors and journalistic lapses. Eisenhower often complained loudly when these occurred, but when a reprimand was in order, the president abided by Hagerty's insistence on calling the reporter directly rather than creating unpleasantness by contacting an editor and threatening the reporter's job security.[27] This practice alone gained for Hagerty almost unanimous respect among the reporters; many of them remembered it years after Eisenhower left office.[28]

The respect was mutual. Manipulating reporters was simply part of Hagerty's job, not personal warfare. Indeed, in order to help steer Eisenhower's communications and still remain a friend of the press, Hagerty relinquished most of his private life during his eight years in the White House. Almost religiously, Hagerty and his assistants briefed reporters every morning and afternoon; many briefings were held on weekends. Hagerty would later disclose that he received an average of six telephone calls each night between 11 P.M. and 7 A.M. Before Eisenhower embarked on trips or vacations, Hagerty often slept in his office while coordinating advance arrangements, then worked eighteen hours or more on the road each day to accommodate the needs of the reporters who covered them.[29] Still, while forthcoming to reporters, Hagerty acted in Eisenhower's best interests, not theirs. "I had friction," he recalled, but "I didn't pay much attention to it. I used to let each side sound off. Then we'd go ahead and do what we wanted to do and what the President wanted to do."[30]

Hagerty's determination finally led to the decision to put the Eisenhower news conferences on television, although the impetus was not a new flurry of press sensitivities but trouble from an unexpected quarter: the network offices in New York. By June 1954, after improvements in Oval Office TV procedures and in Eisenhower's on-camera delivery, the White House was ready to put the spurs to its schedule of fireside chats. Accordingly, Hagerty was personally dispatched by Eisenhower to the headquarters of ABC, CBS, and NBC to commence arrangements for the airtime needed for these and other broadcasts. The timing was important because Eisenhower wanted the telecasts on the schedule for the 1954 fall election campaign. Hagerty had made similar arrangements with the networks in the past, usually with red-carpet treatment. This time, however, Hagerty discovered a resistance on the network executives' part to committing to these long-term airtime requests.

The hangup had been the FCC's "equal time" rule, a sudden new intruder in the administration's media planning. The networks surrendered to Eisenhower some summer airtime that had previously been discussed, but sent Hagerty back to Washington with a warning that these shows and others must be "as non-partisan as possible" in order to avert certain requests for airtime by Democrats under the equal time rule. For the same reason, the regular Eisenhower "talk" was in serious doubt; reluctantly, Hagerty told Eisenhower that the administration must now "play it by ear." [31]

Networks executives had new reasons to be firm about equal time. It was not just that 1954 was an election year, and the first in which a majority of Americans had had television. Basically, the networks were confused about equal time—and they measured the uncertainty at about $2,500 in lost advertising revenues for every minute of airtime they might be forced to yield. In an affair that March that had little to do directly with the election, Stevenson, the Democrat who lost to Eisenhower in 1952 but now held no office, denounced on TV the administration's partnership with McCarthy. When the networks allowed a response from Vice President Richard Nixon, it appeared they would be forced to give the Democrats another opportunity and then kiss away more airtime and revenue to McCarthy, who flamboyantly persisted in such requests.[32]

It was for this reason that the networks liked the idea of a TV news conference. Because it was a news event, they could give exposure to their friend Eisenhower and have legal footing for denying others equal time. Also, the news conferences would be cheaper in the long run, at least compared to the fireside chats that had run during prime time. CBS and NBC planned to air kinescopes or films of the news conferences in time periods that did not interfere with their profitable commercial shows. Although the TV news conference was later seen as a benefit to broadcast journalism, network executives did not tend to link these plans to the needs of their news divisions; for a while, they discussed with Hagerty the possibility of sponsoring the programs.[33] They also saw value in the conferences' novelty. During the June meetings, William Paley and Frank Stanton of CBS had urged the White House to pursue "something dramatic" on TV.[34] Hagerty moved ahead with televised news conferences and, according to a 1967 interview, worked out many of the details by himself that fall.[35]

The TV news conferences were not ready in time to help with

the 1954 elections. Despite Eisenhower's numerous traveling appearances, he was unable to keep the Democrats from winning both the Senate and the House. Televised news conferences likewise played no role in the demise of McCarthy, who was condemned by the Senate that December. The reason the news conferences were not ready in 1954 would convince a number of critics later that the true motive behind a year of White House surgery on these events was that of circumventing reporters and submerging their voices with direct communication from the president.

In putting the news conferences on TV, Eisenhower faced a decision. The most expedient course would have been to carry them on live television. In October, Montgomery demonstrated how live cameras could cover a large indoor event when he fulfilled earlier plans and staged the first TV cabinet meeting.[36] Lessons for this project had come from the Army-McCarthy hearings that spring, also carried live. Live coverage entailed logistical hardships, but none were insurmountable; the major requirement would have been transferring the news conferences from the Indian Treaty Room at the old State Department building into a larger auditorium, a move accomplished by John Kennedy just weeks after he became president in 1961.[37] The alternative to inviting live cameras was recording the news conferences for delayed playback. This option was not viable at the time, because motion picture film was the only recording format, then requiring more artificial lighting than any available facility could accommodate. Nevertheless, because Hagerty was in contact with a team of engineers at the Kodak laboratories who were about to unveil a new light-sensitive film, the White House sat back while the technology was perfected.

The new film was worth waiting for; in fact, live TV was never seriously considered. The news conferences could remain in the Indian Treaty Room, across the street from the White House. Location was an advantage; but a much larger advantage was the possibility for control. Film was a safety net for the "surprise" factor that loomed in every news conference. If a reporter asked a question that put Eisenhower on the defensive, or if the press corps ganged up on him, these scenes could be edited out of the final broadcast, with the viewing public no more the wiser. Furthermore, such edits could be justified under the same protocol that allowed the White House aegis over the quotation transcripts. Also, through film Eisenhower could reach large audiences at night from news conferences he could still hold during the day.

The Kodak engineers came to Washington in October and conducted several trials, including the filming of a mock news conference subsequently screened by Eisenhower, who was, as Hagerty recalled, extremely pleased.[38] Nevertheless, almost three months and seven additional news conferences elapsed before this new technology was applied, so that Hagerty could run more tests on the film and complete a "survey" for Eisenhower and the staff on the overall question of moving ahead. Hagerty reported that there would be few distractions from the TV paraphernalia and that the news conferences could continue in normal fashion. One procedure that remained normal, but took on new importance amid concerns that reporters might upstage Eisenhower, was the pre–news conference briefing, which had been instituted in 1953. These briefings now took on the appearance of a TV rehearsal as advisers prepped Eisenhower, sometimes by asking him anticipated news conference questions as if they were readying him for a debate. The rehearsals usually ran between thirty and forty-five minutes.[39]

The press office told Eisenhower it was fully prepared for adverse reaction from print reporters. Complaints would come in one big burst because Hagerty had again kept preparations a secret; only network executives, their technicians, and others who needed to know were informed.[40] Although Hagerty got the advice of TV journalists in orchestrating the televised news conferences, they and their print colleagues had only sixteen hours of advance notice before the first was finally held.[41]

This debut took place at Eisenhower's fifty-eighth presidential news conference, on January 19, 1955, an ideal day for turning a meeting with the press into a straight-to-the-people political production. First questions pertained to a Communist Chinese attack on a small, Nationalist-held island; Eisenhower's brief responses affirming support of the Nationalists were certain to make headlines. Yet this day also marked the exact midpoint of Eisenhower's first term: not headline material, but nonetheless interesting to reporters, whose questions gave Eisenhower a chance to extemporize. When asked to speculate on "the next two—or maybe even next six years," Eisenhower could not resist creating a guessing game about his reelection plans for 1956. "It looks like a loaded question," he chaffed. The laughter of the reporters was seen and heard in an estimated eight million U.S.

homes that night, along with a five-minute Eisenhower monologue on the successes of his administration.[42]

As it turned out, the TV news conference itself joined China as big news, at least in the *New York Times*, where pictures and accounts of it were spread across four columns at the top of the front page, accompanied by two additional stories inside. It "went off quietly and well," said one story. Columnist Jack Gould termed it "democracy at work" and a "significant victory for TV as a journalistic medium."[43]

Still, as Hagerty anticipated, the opposition was vigorous. Critics wasted little time in preying on the main feature of the new protocol: the use of film and Eisenhower's control of it. The news conference had rested on a cooperative venture between the White House and the networks, which agreed to rotate coverage of the news conferences in a pool arrangement and submit each film to the White House for screening and editing. Many journalists felt that this screening was censorship and were convinced there had been no breakthrough in public affairs coverage, but rather a carefully conceived political maneuver. For this move to represent progress for journalism, many argued, the people who actually did the filming needed to have editorial control. A later *New York Times* editorial branded the affair "a show," and the *Times*'s Arthur Krock suggested in a lengthy analysis that it "will fortify [Eisenhower's] national and political leadership."[44] *New York Post* editor James Wechsler attempted a crusade against "censorship imposed by the White House," which he said was "supinely accepted" by the networks.[45]

The White House viewed this "censorship" debate in a completely different manner. The policy for screening the films was identical to that established in December 1953 when Eisenhower, to the acclaim of the print reporters, had lifted the news conference no-quotation rule. Under that policy, reporters had freedom to quote the president so long as they used official transcripts edited by Hagerty. The White House claimed to see no difference between editing transcripts and editing films—even though the transcripts went to around two hundred reporters, while the films went out to millions of home viewers.

The press office was in a good position to squelch the controversy. Further complaints came from the wire service correspondents who unofficially spoke for the press corps; the Associated Press reported in March that up to seven minutes had been cut from the first few news conference films.[46] Hagerty dealt with the criticism by refusing to elaborate on the cuts, while also reminding the wire services that TV stations were a growing part of their clientele.[47] Officially, the White House Correspondents Association accepted Hagerty's claim that the TV news conferences were inevitable, perhaps because the association was headed by Donovan of the *Herald Tribune*, a newspaper usually loyal to Eisenhower.[48]

The White House was more immediately concerned about political opposition, and the TV news conference became a fixture, for all intents and purposes, when none was offered. The *New York Times* reported that the Democratic National Committee, though bothered indeed by the propaganda potential of the news conference, had already conceded that its hands were tied. The Democrats could not for the moment request equal time, because 1955 was not an election year. Even when 1956 arrived, the DNC envisioned a thicket of difficulties in separating the partisan components of the news conferences from those that journalists would regard as newsworthy and germane to the presidency.[49] Hagerty summed up the event in his diary as a "very potent way of getting the President's personality and viewpoints across[,] . . . almost the same thing as the start of Roosevelt's fireside chats on radio." Hagerty stressed that "the Democratic National Committee was considerably concerned about it. The Democrats, however, can do nothing at all about it."[50]

Within very little time the novelty of the TV news conferences diminished. The only two networks to regularly carry complete versions of the films in prime time were the weak ABC network and the Dumont network; the latter folded in mid-1955. The CBS and NBC networks usually only aired the complete films when content was extremely newsworthy. Long excerpts from the films, though, became regular features of the evening news broadcasts on all networks.

Although few of Eisenhower's future TV news conferences drew as much attention, or as many viewers, as the first, the White House was entirely satisfied. When adviser Gabriel Hauge complained in June 1955 that the news conferences were taking a beating in the ratings, Hagerty assured him the events were serving their desired purpose of preserving a regular channel of communication.[51] Eisenhower subsequently held an average of twenty-two news conferences per year. All of them were filmed, and virtually all of the films were seen, in whole or in part, on all of the TV networks. Millions of visual and verbal impressions were made, with almost no additional fine-tuning from the White House after January 1955.

Hagerty was proven correct in his assessment that the Democrats could do nothing about the new type of fireside chat. This outcome was welcome news to the leaders and strategists of what was then a beleaguered and outnumbered Republican party. The political experts Eisenhower had assembled to run the GOP were no less media-oriented than those in the White House; they had been following very closely Eisenhower's blossoming television communications, as well as the public interest he continued to generate.[52] Some enormous possibilities seemed to be in the offing for a political party that needed, in the mid-1950s, to get moving in a hurry.

CHANNELING

MODERN

REPUBLICANISM,

1954–1955

Internal activity in the Republican party was robust during Eisenhower's first years as president. Eisenhower had agreed to run for president as a Republican because he wanted to block the party's isolationist figures, notably 1952 candidate Robert Taft, and because he felt a duty to rebalance the two-party system, which he believed was endangered by two decades of Democratic control. At the time Eisenhower did not really identify with either party, writing that the "extremists . . . of reaction" on the Republican side "and of so-called liberalism" on the Democratic side "should be abjured like the plague." Eisenhower's "profound conviction" was in his middle-of-the-road approach. Yet when he became persuaded by Republican moderates that his internationalist outlook and middle-of-the-road ideals could find a home in the GOP, Eisenhower's commitment to the Republican party was total.[1] In the beginning he saw himself as a savior of the GOP and sought to do for the Republicans what Franklin Roosevelt had done for the Democrats in the 1930s.

This goal was never accomplished, largely because Eisenhower's strategy for strengthening the Republican party amounted to another public relations campaign, one that did not work. Unlike Roosevelt, Eisenhower did not entertain visions of building a coalition from complex ideological, demographic, and geographic interests. Believing that Americans were more alike than they were different, the binding factors Eisenhower conceived were patriotism, personal prosperity, security, and hope for an ever-brighter future. It was logical to Eisenhower that these simple themes be assembled in package form and promoted to the public through mass communication. The phrase Eisenhower coined to trumpet this effort, "Modern Republicanism," not only carried political meaning. It was short, simple, and easily transmitted by the media.

The first sign of serious difficulty had been the 1954 elections, when, just two years after the Eisenhower sweep in 1952, the House and Senate fell back into Democratic hands. The adjournment of the Republican Congress in 1954 became, in retrospect, a historic event; as of 1993, nineteen sessions later, the Republican party was still unable to wield majorities in both houses. The moderate Eisenhower blamed the conservative wing for the party's 1954 losses, likening the outcome to the progressive-conservative split in the William Howard Taft–Theodore Roosevelt rivalry in 1912. There was "no amalgamation of thought," Eisenhower bitterly complained.[2]

Whatever the reasons for the 1954 defeats, the tactics of the Republican party in the mid-1950s, and the problems it then faced, were not unlike those that have prevailed through the rest of the century. Besides failing to win back Congress in subsequent attempts, the GOP was able neither to recruit large numbers of new members nor to inspire grassroots organizational activities in all regions of the country. The Republicans during this decade made their most concerted attempt to deal with these matters in the 1956 campaign, the last to feature the popular Eisenhower as head of the national ticket. The Republicans' success that year was in starting a thirty-year trend that allowed the party to win the White House several times while struggling elsewhere.

With its weaknesses in the 1950s, it was inevitable that the GOP centralize its activities and use the expanding mass media to carry its themes directly to the public. Still, in terms of its nuts and bolts, Modern Republicanism represented an attempt to jump-start a weak and unattractive Republican party. Eventually, the phrase "Modern Republicanism" was overwhelmed in the public's mind by another: "I Like Ike." Well liked, Eisenhower was nonetheless frustrated by his failure to make the GOP a true party of the people.

Contemporary evidence suggested that the Republican party was listless and catatonic in the 1950s, unappealing to millions of Americans who knew the party for its vehement conservative calls for isolationism and its attacks on Roosevelt's New Deal policies. The Survey Research Center at the University of Michigan reported in 1952 that only 30 percent of American voters called themselves Republicans, compared to more than 50 percent who considered themselves Democrats; that year, Eisenhower was elected president only because millions of Democrats crossed party lines to vote for the popular war hero.[3]

Weaknesses in the party affected Eisenhower directly through his troubled dealings with the conservative Republican Congress in 1953 and 1954. While the news media was questioning Eisenhower's overtures to the conservatives, even Eisenhower's closest political advisers were puzzled by his preoccupation with shoring up the GOP, believing that the president could better execute programs through a nonpartisan coalition of moderates, a tactic he was ultimately forced to use. Yet Eisenhower criticized Henry Cabot Lodge for telling him in 1954 that party matters were irrelevant when the public, without regard to party identification, had unswerving trust in the president. "I earnestly wanted a Republican Congress," insisted Eisenhower.[4] Because his most consistent support in Congress actually did come from Republicans, Eisenhower did not believe the party was in disarray as the news media suggested; he sensed that the trouble was above all an image problem. Eisenhower's solution was a program "so dynamic, so forward-looking, and so adapted to the needs of the United States" that a loyal party member "would have a distinct advantage."[5]

The news media and some advisers may have been confused by Eisenhower's party-building aspirations, but his goals were understood clearly at the headquarters of the Republican National Committee. For the three previous decades nothing had better reflected the regressive state of the party than the conflict-ridden, high-turnover operation at RNC headquarters. Because of this weakness, and because he had opponents in the GOP, Eisenhower kept the national committee on a short leash. People there knew that Modern Republicanism was as much a management directive as it was a political slogan. The order was to "modernize" and shape up.

Restructuring party headquarters had been an early Eisenhower priority. A fierce internal struggle following Thomas Dewey's 1948 defeat had given the party chair to ultraconservative Guy Gabrielson, a Taft zealot who had little interest in expanding the GOP's popular base. Bertha Adkins, the assistant chair at the time, recalled that she was "not sure what Gabrielson wanted me to do."[6] In 1952 Arthur Summerfield headed the party long enough to get Eisenhower elected, then joined the cabinet as postmaster general. C. Wesley Roberts then served four months as chair in 1953 before Eisenhower fired him for his role in a 1951 lobbying incident. Eisenhower got results, however, under Leonard Hall, a more gregarious and visionary figure than any of his immediate predecessors.

Hall, a lawyer who hailed from Long Island and was fifty-three years old at the time of his appointment in 1953, had a rotund frame, big smile, and baritone voice, and was widely known around the capital. He was a welcome guest at parties and informal affairs because of his sense of humor—and the political musical parodies that he composed and sang. He seemed to get along with everybody, including Eisenhower's critics in the news media.[7] Hall had tremendous affection for the president, but his loyalty was not to Eisenhower personally but to his Republican label, one reason the two never became especially close. Yet in many ways he was an ideal choice for Eisenhower. Hall supported moderate politics, shared Eisenhower's concept of a changing America, and sought a young, up-and-coming Republican party. Moreover, he was a proven pitchman. Hall demonstrated his salesmanship in his very first test, when he tactfully persuaded Taft and the rest of the conservative wing that he, a moderate easterner, could do a good job as chair.[8]

In the 1950s a national party chair was still considered an extremely powerful post. The overall duty of the chair was to combine the party's diverse, state-by-state interests into some sort of national political alloy just prior to a campaign. In many ways, the national parties existed only on paper outside of these four-year intervals, although the political influence accorded the chair had often been second only to that of the president. The party chair had to be one part cheerleader and two parts name- and number-cruncher. Hall savored both pursuits.

Yet Hall realized that the heyday of the national party leader was waning—the reason prompting the "go to the people" communications that Eisenhower was perfecting in the White House. Communication tactics designed to circumvent the press also tended to circumvent the national party organization. Hall was thus caught in a time warp, a gap between an old style of organizational politics and an emerging system based on mass persuasion and personality projection. The newer priorities did not automatically convert Hall, for he had had a long history as a cog in political machinery. As he was growing up in Oyster Bay, New York, his family depended on political patronage: his father was the coach driver and later White House librarian for their neighbor, Theodore Roosevelt. The younger Hall represented Nassau County in the House from 1939 to 1953; his most notable achievement was building the National Republican Congressional Committee, which for eleven years allowed him to dole campaign funds to his Capitol Hill colleagues.[9]

A backroom political tradition may have run in Hall's blood but it did not complicate his thinking. In fact, Hall had worked up a GOP political ledger identical to Eisenhower's. The party's liabilities were its Hoover-era image, its spotty grassroots structure, and its two-to-one membership inferiority to the Democrats. On the other hand, its assets included the popular president and a marshaling of media channels ensured by the party's greatest asset of all: money. Hall soon became the leading exponent of the belief that the party's assets could offset its liabilities and make Eisenhower's Modern Republicanism a quick reality.

Modernization did become a relatively quick reality, at least at party headquarters. Hall moved the RNC into larger facilities and expanded the staff; in the process he fired many holdovers from the Gabrielson, Summerfield, and Roberts periods.[10] To revitalize the operation, Hall brought in Clarence Adamy to head nationwide enrollment of new Republican members; Adamy's association with Hall had begun with the Citizens for Eisenhower group in 1952.[11] Dr. Paul McCaffree, a Ph.D. in political science from the University of Michigan, received increased responsibilities as research director. Bertha Adkins, who in 1958 would become under secretary of HEW, expanded the RNC women's division; assisting her was Anne Wheaton, a former news reporter who would join Press Secretary Jim Hagerty in 1957.[12] The national committee grew from around 50 full- and part-time employees when Hall began to 130 by the end of 1955.[13]

One reflection of the changes at party headquarters was the attention given the public relations division, which supervised all media functions. Robert Humphreys, a former national affairs editor for *Newsweek*, had headed public relations in 1952. In a symbolic move, Hall elevated Humphreys to campaign director, the RNC's unofficial second-in-command position, and put him in charge of the 1956 convention, because the convention was expected to draw huge TV audiences. Hall chose James Bassett, Richard Nixon's press secretary in 1952, to replace Humphreys as public relations director; Bassett served through 1954 and then returned to the *Los Angeles Mirror*, where he was an executive editor. That resignation allowed Hall to recruit L. Richard Guylay, an experienced political tactician with similar media credentials.[14] Guylay had helped manage Taft's run for the GOP nomination in 1952 before moving to New York and forming his own public relations firm. Guylay's interest was political imagery. He said in a 1967 interview, "I was always fascinated by mass psychology and how to get an idea across to a crowd." For example, Guylay was the person who anointed Taft as "Mr. Republican," a tag that grew synonymous with the Ohio senator. Another Guylay venture was a study of campaign slogans and symbols that inspired Vance Packard's 1957 best-seller *The Hidden Persuaders*.[15]

Hall was responsible for fund-raising and organization, but his element was campaign strategy. Soon it was apparent that the centerpiece of the modernized, new look at headquarters was Hall's bold embrace of television. Hall felt that the new medium could save time and money and substitute for grassroots vote-getting operations that the party desperately needed in many locales, especially the South and border states. Hall talked about television so often that *New York Times* columnist James Reston portrayed him in 1955 as a political Milton Berle.[16]

Eisenhower's interest in public relations encouraged these media efforts at the RNC, as Hall was blessed by a ring of media advisers serving in various capacities within the administration. They included presidential consultant Robert Montgomery and Eisenhower's close friend Sig Larmon of Young and Rubicam. Most important to Hall, though, were Ben Duffy and Carroll Newton, two top people at BBDO.[17] In addition, an unofficial group of New York–based media employees that was formed in the 1952 campaign and called itself the "TV Plans Board" continued to funnel ideas through White House appointment secretary Thomas Stephens.[18]

Although White House and RNC public relations activities were usually indistinguishable, there were differences. White House advisers tailored Eisenhower's communications on a continual basis, often in response to pending events and immediate political needs; in contrast, headquarters focused on short-duration, high-impact bursts of image making during campaign periods when executive branch jobs were on the line. The RNC appreciated the media beachheads already taken by those in the White House but felt the party had to penetrate much further. Photo events and TV news conferences, while giving Eisenhower regular exposure, would not be enough in a campaign. By no means had the fireside chat or its variations disappeared from councils inside the administration. If anything, the equal time snag encountered in 1954 had made this tactic more of a priority, because the guesswork had been removed. The administration now realized that it would have to pay for future fireside telecasts. Thus a new realm in Eisenhower's communications included making long-range plans and raising the money to finance them.

By 1955 the media work of the RNC dwarfed that of the White House staff in terms of sophistication and scale. It is important to note that all of Eisenhower's campaigns were directed solely from the national committee; party headquarters did not provide backup support for a candidate-only organization, as would be the rule in future elections. Hall and the RNC grew rich in insights on how the new medium was changing the fabric of the American political campaign.

Long before the 1955 heart attack, for example, Hall anticipated resistance in persuading Eisenhower to undertake any more protracted personal campaigns.[19] The president's advancing age was one reason. Equally important, with Eisenhower's familiarity and approval apparently at a peak, was that such a strategy was less appropriate. Eisenhower wanted the public to know he was above politics, not the type to slug it out on the campaign trail. In a widely circulated November 1954 interview with United Press reporter Merriman Smith, Eisenhower claimed he was not a "politician" because "a man can be classed as a politician only after he has spent his life in the political arena."[20] Hall could already see that a concentration on television in the reelection could preserve the appearance of Eisenhower as apart from the political fray.

Nonetheless, to use TV effectively, Hall faced a big job. The primary problem was money, even in the rich Republican party. The use of national television in the 1954 House and Senate races had been a disappointment, one that might have forewarned of cracks in the eventual 1956 congressional strategy had the party studied TV more closely. The GOP was not inclined to acknowledge a strategy failure in 1954; advisers still felt that a centralized campaign from Washington could rouse votes in disparate districts and states. Instead, characteristically, the Republicans blamed part of the 1954 defeats on their lack of a big enough TV bomb, a conclusion they reached after analyzing their balance sheet at the end of the election. As always after a campaign, the treasury was low, but a follow-up report by Edward Bacher, head of the RNC finance committee, showed that only 68 percent of the solicitation quota had been met, making 1954 the worst year of Republican fund-raising since 1949.[21] Hall had set aside $2.5 million for 1954, with one-quarter of it ($620,000) earmarked for television and radio; looking back, he found that $125,000 had been cut because of cash flow problems, forcing part of the media campaign in 1954 to be scuttled.[22]

It was cash flow, not the actual cash, that represented the major financial obstacle for the Republicans. Nineteen-fifty-four was tight, but over the long haul the RNC had an impeccable record of paying its bills, because of a preponderance of big-money contributors. However, the mid-1950s was a topsy-turvy period in political finance brought about by the astonishing growth of television. Financial rules of thumb that existed in one campaign were suddenly gone by the next. Because there were literally tens of thousands of new TV viewers each day, television advertising expenditures broke one record after another, tripling to more than $1.2 billion between 1952 and 1956.[23] A half-hour of low-budget CBS airtime that sold for $32,000 in 1952 cost more than $62,000 by 1956.[24] Unlike in 1952, the parties could not haggle with the networks for extra airtime or produce appeals at the last minute without incurring astronomical costs.[25] Moreover, when the Desilu studios began filming "I Love Lucy" in 1951, TV moved away from cheaper live programs toward slick and polished recorded productions. Viewers' tastes rose accordingly. By the mid-1950s a politician could no longer make a live appeal from the antiseptic but inexpensive confines of a TV studio and expect to hold an audience. Huge production costs, rising on a daily basis, now had to be considered.[26]

The actual cost of television was not the only complicating factor: beginning with the 1956 campaign a political committee's credit was no longer good at the three TV networks. This change resulted from many anxieties among TV account executives over late payments and defaults in some of the 1952 and 1954 campaigns. Now politicians either had to pay fees in advance or establish proof of their financial condition. The RNC had not been one of the culprits in 1952 and 1954. Even so, Newton of BBDO remembered the RNC in those years as a hand-to-mouth operation; he insisted that corrective steps be taken in Eisenhower's reelection effort.[27]

Hall got the message. Beginning early in 1955 Hall made repeated appearances at Eisenhower's "stag dinners." These stag dinners were not generally known to the public at the time. Eisenhower organized them as a stage for his consensus-building endeavors and as an important branch of his internal communications. Every few weeks he would invite to the White House around two dozen people representing various professions, social strata, and interests. People from small business and the working trades were featured at one of the dinners, while women dominated one or two others. Media executives appeared often at the stag dinners; in 1959, Eisenhower even held stag dinners for the press corps. Nevertheless, the people invited most often were wealthy business figures and industrialists, such as oilman-financier J. Clifford Folger, millionaire John Hay Whitney, U.S. Steel chairman Ben Fairless, Standard Oil chairman Eugene Holman, members of the Rockefeller family, and others. Individuals like these had an almost open invitation to any stag dinner; as a result, so did Hall.[28]

Ultimately, the courting of these millionaires by Eisenhower and Hall carried the GOP into one of the most opulent periods of political finance in U.S. history. A Senate investigation later revealed that two-thirds of the "official" $13.6 million the GOP raised between 1954 and 1956 represented contributions of $500 or more; the party also received 90 percent of the donations made by the 225 largest corporations, including 47 finance firms and 29 oil companies. It also got big checks from 37 advertising agencies and 10 broadcast conglomerates.[29] Not only was the GOP able to meet the rising costs of television with relative ease; at the end of 1956, there was more than half a million dollars left over according to official disclosures.

Thus Republican capital was available, and Hall's job was mainly one of shaking the money tree just prior to making commitments. Interestingly, small donors were also a priority. It was not that the party really needed their money, certainly not nearly to the extent that the Democrats did. Yet Eisenhower ordered a solicitation of these small contributions as a recruitment device. He reasoned that if a person could be roused to make even a five-dollar contribution, the gift created a sense of participation that could lead to more votes and party strength.[30] Eight million people gave money to the two parties in 1956, a dramatic leap from the three million contributors in 1952; most, though, gave to the Democrats.[31]

These increased financial burdens also forced Hall to spend more time on organization. Even though the 1940 Hatch Act had made it illegal for a committee to spend more than $3 million on a political campaign, the RNC expected to exceed that limit on television expenditures alone. To get around the law, Hall had to spread the money around among new committees formed just for that purpose. By 1956 eighteen different committees operated at the party's national level.[32]

Much of Hall's organizational work required him to do some fence-mending with two permanent GOP groups: the congressional and senatorial campaign committees, headed by Pennsylvania congressman Richard Simpson and Arizona senator Barry Goldwater. In late 1953 Charles Willis, assistant to Chief of Staff Sherman Adams, complained to Hall that these organizations "only become aware of what each is doing through chance meetings and conversations of members."[33] Although the results of the 1954 congressional elections were not pleasing, television burdens actually improved relations between the two Capitol Hill committees because neither had the resources for the needed planning. Hall coordinated a central effort of time buying and strategy.[34] He also gave the committees greater access to the RNC's public relations and research arms; when the chairman unveiled an updated organizational chart, the congressional and senatorial committees appeared for the first time in boxes at the top, to the right and left of his own.[35]

By early 1955 Eisenhower was already generating interest in his re-election plans by saying nothing about them in public. Yet Hall and most of Eisenhower's closest advisers knew he was close to committing to the race. Eisenhower's problems with the GOP's conservative wing left him with a short legislative record in 1954. The new Congress in 1955, now in Democratic control, was not shaping up much better. Eisenhower fought for school construction, tariff reduction, water reclamation projects in the West, and interstate highways, while Congress, against his wishes, introduced a tax cut and increased postal salaries. In 1956 Eisenhower succeeded with the highway program and even achieved a balanced budget. Yet Eisenhower looked ahead to better GOP results in the next congressional election, which, if they came, would not mean much to him unless he ran again.[36] Three weeks before the 1955 session began, Eisenhower held a special stag dinner that consisted exclusively of political advisers. Hagerty told in his diary of Eisenhower's pledge to do all he could, including "running in 1956."[37] Time-Life's C. D. Jackson came away with the same impression and informed Henry Luce, "I would have given odds that if the decision had to be made now, he would say 'yes.'" [38]

A "yes" decision was particularly likely because Eisenhower, by his own admission, had not groomed a successor. While he had no idea whom the Republicans might pick to replace him in 1956, nor whether his legislative goals would be supported by the eventual nominee, he was certain that any GOP candidate other than himself would be defeated. Vice President Nixon, remarked Eisenhower in May 1955, "had made some enemies and is not considered very matured. . . ." U.N. ambassador Henry Cabot Lodge was a "blueblood from Boston, and you cannot elect him." Deputy Defense Secretary Robert Anderson, "the finest candidate we could have," had no campaign experience.[39]

The guessing game about Eisenhower's 1956 plans swirled in the news media, and apparently in the White House, throughout early 1955. Sometimes it was a source of amusement for the president. Attorney General Herbert Brownell, Postmaster General Summerfield, and Hall, interested in the future of their own jobs, wanted to broach the subject with Eisenhower on February 14. As Hagerty remembered, "the President gave absolutely no indication at all of his own personal plans, and no one asked him. It was a sort of sparring match by everyone concerned to deliberately not ask him anything. I think he realized the situation and got quite a kick out of it."[40] But Eisenhower put aside his recreational attitude three days later when he met again with Hall, this time in the presence of the GOP's finance directors, and left them assured he would run again.[41] Because Eisenhower seldom joked when financial matters—especially those involving himself—were discussed, it was a sure sign of his true intentions.

Eisenhower's heart attack at the end of 1955 would renew the guessing game. Long before this point, though, it had been necessary that Eisenhower give an indication of his future plans, because of the scale of planning required for the upcoming campaign. Media considerations, now more complex and expensive than in any previous election, were a major reason why the party had to begin working almost from the day the 1954 election had ended. Eisenhower's presence on the ticket was crucial to every part of the developing strategy.

It was a dual-track strategy, where one thrust was Eisenhower's own reelection. The other, more formidable goal was returning Republican majorities in the House and Senate. Although House and Senate campaigns were run by state committees and local organizations, the national headquarters was active in them, especially in presidential years. Straight-ticket voting was still regarded as a sort of political rule of thumb. So was a notion known then as the "coattail theory," which maintained that popular presidential candidates could rally support for other candidates on the various local party tickets. Working to get the full effect of coattailing had usually impelled candidates into the hinterlands on laborious whistlestop tours with the local candidates; presidential standard-bearers had conducted at least some whistle-stopping in almost every campaign since 1900.[42]

A key reason why Hall worked through the television details was his belief that whistlestopping was not as effective as it once was. Eisenhower, who had appeared on TV several times in 1954, had spent comparatively more time in personal appearances with GOP candidates, apparently without much success. Crowds had been smaller than in previous years, and Hall surmised that television may have been a factor—that people preferred the living-room comfort of Ed Sullivan or "I Love Lucy" to crowded and noisy campaign rallies.[43] Hall also reasoned that TV could overcome limitations in whistlestopping. For example, a candidate could only attract a few hundred spectators at a personal appearance, compared to millions on TV. Moreover, on a whistlestop tour a candidate could only appear in one locale at a time. An Eisenhower appearance with a local candidate in September might be forgotten by November, a shortcoming eliminated by continuous use of television.[44]

Republican planners grew confident that TV would meet the congressional test of 1956 by converting Eisenhower's overwhelming popularity into votes in state and district races. Some of the advice to this effect came from the ad agencies, where sentiment ran high that Republican House and Senate candidates would benefit if on-air appeals revolved around Eisenhower and targeted Democratic and independent voters, millions of whom were already backing Eisenhower, according to their polling data. A massive GOP television schedule would build on Eisenhower's popularity in order to run up his vote total, a concept later known officially as the "big vote premise."[45] It assumed that a strong wave of support for the national ticket would transfer to other candidates.

If this scheme was to succeed, the Republicans would have to up the television ante dramatically from what it had been in 1952 and 1954. Thus in July 1955 Guylay went to New York and linked up with BBDO's Newton; together they went to the offices of ABC, CBS, and

NBC to begin negotiations for airtime during the 1956 fall campaign, still almost a year and a half away. Guylay brought the party checkbook. These discussions culminated in an advance commitment for network airtime at an expected cost to the RNC of $2 million, an unheard-of sum in political media buying at that time.[46]

Even with its new commitment, the party saw the potential for waste in blanket TV coverage. Newton pushed something that became known as the "piggyback," a brief five-minute spot that played at the ends of shortened entertainment programs. The GOP had done its homework prior to bargaining for these piggybacks. The half-hour speech had been the standard political TV format, but Newton had figures to show that these appeals lacked cost efficiency and did not hold the audience. For example, the highest-rated political appeal in 1954 was Eisenhower's well-promoted kickoff speech, which drew a 19.3 rating (6.5 million homes); it still ran behind "Our Miss Brooks," which stood at 22.8 (8 million homes).[47] The five-minute piggybacks played to a shorter attention span and took advantage of the often sizable lead-in audiences generated by a preceding program. Years later Guylay explained this concept: when a twenty-five-minute version of "The Bob Hope Show" or "You Bet Your Life" ended, he said, the audience "had nowhere else to go. . . . If they switched to another channel, that show was at the tail end . . . and they couldn't understand it." Logic suggested the viewer would watch the entire GOP spot.[48]

The piggybacks were instituted when, after considerable dickering, the networks backed off a demand that the five-minute spots, equal to 12 percent of one hour, be paid at the normal 30 percent rate; the networks finally cut their quoted rate almost in half, to around 15 percent. The same discounts would be available to the Democrats when they got around to finalizing their TV plans. For now, though, the Republicans thought it a steal. They immediately ordered around thirty five-minute spots in key time periods, saving hundreds of thousands of dollars.[49]

The messages these appeals were to convey likewise received advance consideration. Getting Modern Republicanism across on TV hinged on mass reverse psychology. For more than two decades, sharp ideological differences had characterized dialogue between the two parties. As the opposition party, the GOP was known for its loud contempt for Roosevelt's New Deal and internationalism at a time when print and radio were the dominant mass media. Now, through television, the public would see a different Republican party, one of compassion, vision, fortitude, and patriotism. Notably, the public would also see a Republican party that had abandoned neither the New Deal nor internationalism; indeed, with proper TV imagery, these popular themes would be assimilated into the list of GOP achievements.

Although the Republicans blurred ideological lines to enlarge their public tent, the two parties remained quite distinct operationally. While the Democratic party was built upward from its local grass roots, the GOP maneuvers of the 1950s helped define the new Republican program of seeking renewal from the top down. It was something like a pyramid effect: from their popular president at the pyramid's tip, the next step would be a Republican Congress, followed by new Republican governors and more GOP figures in local offices. Through a blanket application of mass media, these candidates would be cast as emissaries of a middle-of-the-road, forward-looking Modern Republicanism, personified by Eisenhower. With more Republicans in high places, it thus seemed only a matter of time before the party's vitality would be acknowledged by mainstream voters, causing Democrats and independents to ally with the GOP.

Winning the Congress was considered possible in 1956. In the House the party needed to retain its 203 seats and pick up 14 more to achieve a majority; the Republicans had added 22 seats when Eisenhower ran in 1952. There was even more hope in the Senate, where the party needed just 2 seats for a majority. Here the administration was already giving the national committee some help. One person Eisenhower wanted removed was Oregon senator Wayne Morse, once a staunch Republican, who had turned his back on the president and become a Democrat; Eisenhower sent Douglas McKay, his interior secretary, back to Oregon to try to unseat Morse. Eisenhower then succeeded in persuading Colorado governor Dan Thornton to enter a Senate race; he also coaxed Arthur Langlie, governor of Washington state, into challenging the state's popular senator, Warren Magnuson.

Nothing better underscored the national committee's resolve to orchestrate affairs from the top than its resistance to a separate GOP organization that might have changed the destiny of the Republican party had it been taken more seriously. This organization was Citizens for Eisenhower, the gigantic amalgam of volunteers and part-time workers that enrolled thousands of Eisenhower enthusiasts of all political affiliations throughout the country. The first Citizens for Eisenhower, formed in 1952, had been the advance guard of the "draft

Eisenhower" movement that preceded the president's entry into politics. Close to three thousand "Ike and Dick" clubs were formed that year, and 250,000 people were members.[50] The 1956 Citizens for Eisenhower would again draw thousands of participants.

Even though membership roles, organizing efforts, and the canvassing potentials of the Citizens members could have given the Republican party a start toward correcting its grassroots weaknesses, Hall and his associates at the national committee viewed the Citizens group as an irritant. In their view, the group was composed of amateurs who seemed to want to get into politics for fun and games. To join Citizens a person needed neither to have prior political experience nor to be a registered Republican. The group appeared certain to gum the RNC's precision clockwork if the two retained their ties.

Hall's determination to run a tight, professional ship, however, may not have been the real reason Citizens was left disenfranchised by the national committee. The primary organizers of the 1952 Citizens were not "balloon boys," as Hall called them, but Eisenhower's wealthy corporate friends, including one-time *New York Herald Tribune* publisher Bill Robinson, banker Howard Peterson, Continental Can chairman and former Army general Lucius Clay, and financier Cliff Roberts, who operated the Augusta [Ga.] National Golf Club, which Eisenhower frequented. Banker James Murphy headed a scaled-down version called the Citizens for Eisenhower Congressional Committee during the 1954 midterm elections. Leaders of the 1956 Citizens were businessmen John Kilpatrick and John Burr.[51] On paper the group was a loose, cumbersome, independent entity; but because it was staffed at the top by wealthy people who were closer to Eisenhower personally than those running the national committee were, it was a powerful political organization and a threat to Hall.

In no part of Hall's domain was that threat more directly felt than in his strategy planning, because Sig Larmon, Eisenhower's intimate from the advertising industry, was one of the corporate executives who ran the Citizens group.[52] While other Citizens leaders brought money, Larmon's first move after joining the 1956 Citizens was to convince Eisenhower the organization needed its own advertising agency; he offered his, Young and Rubicam, on a gratis basis. This contribution was really not necessarily so generous, because under a nonpartisan loan program, in which the networks and other agencies supplied personnel to the 1956 political campaigns, Larmon could employ outside talent and not have to pay them. Nevertheless, it was a bizarre arrangement: by the time of the 1956 election, Young and Rubicam would work alongside its chief Madison Avenue competitor, BBDO, the agency already under contract to the RNC. In February 1955 Hall was ordered by the White House to include a Citizens operation in his 1956 planning.[53] Hall grudgingly complied.

This situation with the two ad agencies showed that Eisenhower, eager to get his hands on the best media resources available, was capable of idealizing his consensus vision—in this case into a picture of different corporations spinning together like spokes on a big wheel, all for the common good, without intense rivalries. Hall, however, knew that a feud existed between BBDO and Young and Rubicam, having largely to do with their respective roles in Eisenhower politics. After Eisenhower's failed Abilene telecast in 1952, Larmon's agency found a niche in that year's fall campaign by providing TV advice as part of the Citizens movement; it was helpful to Eisenhower but played a secondary role because BBDO was already under contract to the national committee. Some Citizens organizers wanted Young and Rubicam to assume greater duties in 1952, and Larmon was not bashful in telling them his company had more television know-how than any other agency.[54]

There was some basis for his claim: Young and Rubicam handled the accounts of General Foods, Gulf Oil, and Kaiser Aluminum, pioneer TV advertisers whose programs and spots were familiar to the viewing public. However, whether Young and Rubicam had more television experience than BBDO was debatable. Both were giants of the early television industry, and their political activities were but one part of a tooth-and-nail competition for Madison Avenue supremacy. J. Walter Thompson was the world's largest agency; Young and Rubicam and BBDO battled for second place. In the category of broadcast advertising, though, both Young and Rubicam and BBDO claimed to be number one: between 1952 and 1955 they had seesawed for the top spot.[55]

Even though an agency's numerical bragging rights came from its corporate accounts, some agencies felt they could gain special status by promoting politicians, especially sure winners such as Eisenhower. Whatever Larmon's claims, in this world of candidates and campaigns, BBDO was in a class by itself in the mid-1950s, the first giant media entity to hitch its fortunes to politics. Partner Bruce Barton had been responsible for this move; he had served in Congress himself and had brought the services of BBDO to the attention of Dewey in the

1940s.[56] Barton's political interests were matched by those of agency president Ben Duffy, who had hands-on supervision of most BBDO campaign accounts. Duffy had dropped out of high school to join BBDO in the 1920s and later became president when Roy Durstine departed. In 1948 Duffy had directed media affairs for Dewey—the first time a Madison Avenue figure had had a sizable say in a presidential campaign. Although Duffy took heat for Dewey's surprise loss, Dewey wanted him back for his 1950 New York gubernatorial race. It was another milestone—the first major statewide effort to emphasize television—and a big success. During the New York City mayoral election the same year, Duffy claimed to have advised four people who wanted the job, including independent Vincent Impellitteri, the eventual victor.[57] Two years later, in 1952, while negotiating the deal that brought BBDO into the first Eisenhower campaign, Duffy began a relationship between his agency and the president that lasted the rest of the decade.

Duffy did not like his counterpart at Young and Rubicam, and the feeling was mutual. Larmon had graduated from Dartmouth, had spent time in London, and lived in the elite New York suburb of Scarsdale. Duffy, the product of an Irish immigrant family, raised in New York's Hell's Kitchen, had no formal education and was remembered for his "dees, dem, and dose" expressions. Eisenhower liked both men, but clearly liked Larmon the better of the two.

In 1955 BBDO was still under contract to the RNC, but Young and Rubicam was now in a vastly better position to challenge Duffy's agency for television turf. Besides Eisenhower's insistence that Citizens join the RNC in supervising the campaign, Eisenhower's friend Larmon had climbed in the administration, taking a post as a part-time member of the National Advisory Commission after the president had tried to get him to take a full-time position as communications director in 1954. As 1956 approached, Larmon, knowing that the main-attraction television efforts would reflect glowingly on his company, prepared to assume a major share of the campaign responsibilities. As Young and Rubicam vice president Harry Harding recalled, "We had a lot of ideas and energy to help Ike, and it was personally important to us."[58]

Guylay, the RNC public relations director, was the first person to sound an alarm. Not at all happy at the prospect of working with the competing ad agencies, he insisted that Hall delineate respective duties in order to avoid certain pandemonium later. Hall complied, deciding that BBDO would continue to represent the party in dealings with the networks, which included finalizing the fall airtime schedule, transferring the money, and collecting commissions. BBDO got most of the total television time in the 1956 campaign, including twenty five-minute spots, some fifteen-minute segments, and eleven half-hour blocks in prime time. BBDO also continued to arrange local airtime for the congressional leg of the campaign. Young and Rubicam got less airtime, but it was the richest on the Republican TV schedule: the agency was assigned an hour-long telecast on all three networks the night before the election, as well as two dozen five-minute segments in peak viewing periods. Young and Rubicam also got from Hall a blank check to defray costs; by campaign's end, Larmon's agency had spent $800,000.[59]

The national committee's assignment of duties ultimately worked; it was a rare occasion when someone from BBDO so much as spoke to someone from Young and Rubicam. "The mere matter of liaison between the agencies was formidable," recalled Guylay. "We had to see that we got our money's worth, and it took quite a bit of time and attention to ride herd on the agencies."[60] Nevertheless, irritations persisted and bad feelings lingered among participants many years later. BBDO's Newton felt that Larmon was determined to take over what was one of the best managed and organized presidential campaigns in history, although he admitted that, in addition to an Eisenhower victory, BBDO had its eyes on the commissions generated by the airtime purchases.[61] BBDO got all of the money, a reason Young and Rubicam often doubted BBDO's loyalty. "The work of Young and Rubicam was so much more effective than the work of BBDO," argued Harding. "We were all doing a personal job for Ike."[62]

Their loyalties to the president may have differed, but all hands were aware that this cooperation was something Eisenhower would demand. Less clear were Eisenhower's expectations for the Citizens group. Eisenhower continued to conceive of the organization as a vehicle for rallying Republican votes in local races and recruiting new members, even though he had been criticized for giving jobs and favors to many of the 1952 Citizens leaders. "Most of the Citizens in the last campaign were intelligent independents and discerning Democrats who adhere to a moderate philosophy," Eisenhower countered. "I think we should count them. It would be sheer stupidity to fail to do so if we want to win more elections."[63]

Even so, Eisenhower never compelled the national committee to absorb Citizens or make it a permanent unit. As it turned out, Citizens organizations started from scratch before each of the 1952, 1954, 1956, and 1958 campaigns. Eisenhower had other priorities and knew he could only push the RNC so far. It is also extremely likely that Eisenhower agreed at heart with Hall's conclusion that the group was too roguish to help the RNC tangle with the party's weaknesses. Questions about the RNC-Citizens relationship would continue, though, long after Eisenhower's reelection.

Just then in 1955, other issues were materializing in the campaign for Modern Republicanism. The national committee's goal of effecting victories at the state level was already starting to dictate many aspects of the eventual presidential television strategy. By this time campaign planners envisioned that Eisenhower, besides appearing in the five-minute appeals, would conduct some traditional auditorium rallies that would be televised. The plan was to originate these "spectaculars," as BBDO called them, from cities all around the country—not just in New York and Boston, where the 1952 rallies had originated. To get the most from these TV specials, the programs had to be scheduled in states that had moderate "Eisenhower" candidates in local races.

New constraints also affected the content of the presidential appeals. When Eisenhower whistlestopped with local candidates in 1952, his basic speech was embellished with touches tailored to please local audiences; he often got the best crowd responses when he showed he knew a community, its problems, and its issues. Eisenhower had done this especially well in 1952; by then, he had lived in every region of the country and had an alert team of advance people and speechwriters able to size up a local setting. Now localism and the precise articulation of some issues had to be deemphasized. In a campaign that sought gigantic nationwide audiences on television, Eisenhower could not delve too far into the minutiae of regional problems, which in the 1950s could have included the St. Lawrence Seaway debate, hydroelectric expansion, price stabilization for farm crops, or civil rights; these topics were not cost-effective for expensive national mass media.

The party needed a least common denominator that could bind the hopes of Republican candidates in all parts of the country to those of the administration. At work on the creative focus, the publicity agencies happily discovered that Modern Republicanism was a bonanza for the generic, one-size-fits-all television approach they had to execute.

Playing to the strength of the new medium, Modern Republicanism was uncomplicated and full of visual possibilities and could be packed with emotion. Even more, television seemed conveniently to harmonize the dual-track imperative of the upcoming campaign—that is, Eisenhower's reelection and the extension of his coattails to House and Senate candidates.

The basic technique was demonstrated in the first political TV appeal produced for 1956, a fifteen-minute BBDO television film called "These Peaceful, Prosperous Years." This production was on the BBDO drawing board in late 1955; part of it was shot at a closed-circuit TV fund-raising extravaganza in January 1956. This appeal did not focus on Eisenhower but instead followed members of an American family "going about their daily living under a Republican era of peace." To top off the family theme, the president and Mrs. Eisenhower appeared briefly with an on-camera rendition of "God Bless America" after a narrator had urged voters to "give Ike a Republican Congress." Some GOP House and Senate candidates were later invited to a TV studio set up by BBDO at the Capitol to record customized introductions.[64]

Unfortunately for the GOP, the media campaign for Modern Republicanism would merge with Eisenhower's personal campaign; in the end, according to empirical studies published later, the public could not tell one from the other. Voters connected with Eisenhower but not with Eisenhower's party. In scores of different polished TV appeals seen, according to the Nielsen ratings, by millions of viewers, the message became very similar to that of "These Peaceful, Prosperous Years," essentially a call to a voter's personal feelings of happiness and contentment. Yet this contentment theme proved to be its own Achilles heel. Things had changed since 1952, when the GOP won Congress during widespread dissatisfaction with the Truman administration. By the mid-1950s, as the GOP showed again and again in the media, the nation was back to normal; when TV plans were drawn up in 1955, Republican advisers did not foresee that tens of millions of comfortable Democrats who liked Ike would feel so content that they would stick with their own party in the congressional contests.

Nevertheless, the GOP's attempt at using national television to win Republican votes and, to some extent, manage district and state races from Washington and New York, was notable. At the 1956 Republican convention the party used much of its climactic final night to introduce dozens of local House and Senate candidates to a national audience, putting them on the same stage with Eisenhower. Later, almost every Eisenhower trip was timed so that he could appear on national television with local Senate candidates, including Everett Dirksen from Illinois; John Sherman Cooper and Thruston Morton from Kentucky; and James Duff from Pennsylvania. Centralization of the congressional effort was best indicated behind the scenes, where BBDO bargained for airtime on selected local stations and filled that time with many local segments, some as short as twenty seconds, containing slick, custom appeals produced in New York. By the end of 1956, the party's national headquarters had paid over $1.5 million to local television stations—three times the amount spent locally by the Democrats.[65]

Years later, some of the advertising agency figures remembered the RNC's strategy in 1956 and how the administration wanted to do more than return Eisenhower to office. As David Levy of Young and Rubicam recalled, "It wasn't just getting Eisenhower elected, they wanted the campaign to rub off on other Republicans."[66] According to BBDO's Newton, "The national committee's job was to elect the damn president, but [in 1956] it bore responsibility for congressional and senatorial campaigns."[67] Newton recalled that Hall's 1954 attempt to use national television in local midterm elections, which had never been done by a national committee before, was a concept that BBDO tried to perfect.[68]

To further orchestrate this nationalization of the local campaigns, on September 7, 1955, the Republicans brought the state committee chairs to Washington for a "campaign school," the first such meeting ever convened. There were panels on local time buying and video production techniques, although most of the "school" dealt with free airtime possibilities and TV cosmetics.[69]

The campaign school agenda also contained a very important piece of unfinished business, however: Eisenhower's formal decision about entering the 1956 campaign. In order to encourage Eisenhower to expedite the announcement, Hall concluded the campaign school early on September 10. Then he led members of the RNC staff, numerous assistants, and each of the forty-eight state chairs in a caravan that made its way to Washington's National Airport, where an airplane was on the runway waiting to fly them all to Denver. There they met Eisenhower, who was enjoying a long Colorado vacation, and pledged to him, one by one, total commitment to his victory the following year.[70]

The episode illustrated well Hall's flair for the lavish and spectacular, not to mention the party's imposing financial capabilities.

It was impossible to tell, though, whether Hall's feat had made any difference in speeding Eisenhower's reelection plans. Two weeks later, while still in Colorado, the president suffered his heart attack.

NO BARNSTORMING,

1955–1956

Nineteen-fifty-six marked perhaps the first occasion in which television played an important role in a presidential election. The new medium did not really make a difference in the actual outcome; Eisenhower's victory over Adlai Stevenson was certain. Nevertheless, events did not lack a mystery element. The intrigue occurred much earlier in the year during serious public uncertainty about Eisenhower's future. Acknowledging that Eisenhower could probably win the election if he chose to run, many experts nonetheless found it inconceivable that the sixty-five-year-old president, in the aftermath of a heart attack, would seek another four years in the White House.

Eisenhower's possession of television was one of the reasons he decided to do so. To continue his presidency into a second term, Eisenhower had to get past the 1956 campaign; he did not need doctors to tell him that a vigorous cross-country reelection effort could be life-threatening. Thus in his post–heart attack discussions about the campaign, Eisenhower set limitations on the amount of physical activity he was willing to offer to both his own cause and that of the party.[1] Nevertheless, Eisenhower had reason to fear that once the campaign got going, his advisers would disregard these limits and lure him into an exhausting schedule of appearances, as they had in 1952 and 1954. The weeks following the September 1955 heart attack were ones of trial for Eisenhower; the more his recovery progressed, the more he agonized about the election. When Republican party chairman Leonard Hall told the president that television could substantially ease a grueling political campaign, and then demonstrated the party's commitment to managing major television events, the assurance helped Eisenhower make up his mind. Finally, on the last day of February 1956, Eisenhower told the nation he would "wage no political campaign in the customary pattern" but would instead "inform the American public accurately, through means of mass communication. . . ."[2]

The ability to run a limited reelection campaign was not the crucial factor in Eisenhower's decision to seek another four years in the White House. More important were the opinions of his doctors, who pronounced him fit for a second term. The decision also turned on Eisenhower's conclusion that no other Republican could win the election. As White House chief of staff Sherman Adams explained, "The real reason a president wants to run again is because he doesn't think anybody else can do as good a job as he is doing."[3]

Nevertheless, it was one of the most difficult decisions of Eisenhower's presidency, and every factor was important. That Eisenhower opted to replace a "customary" campaign with one constructed around mass communication was no surprise to anyone in the administration. Still, because a television election had never been waged, Eisenhower had to be educated on the details and persuaded it would work. After this step had been taken, Eisenhower held the national committee to a media-oriented strategy; whatever his advisers did next was certain to alter many patterns in the American presidential campaign.

Prior to the heart attack, although he had not made a formal announcement, Eisenhower had given clear signals to Republican leaders that he would head the ticket again in 1956. Yet even those closest to the president may not have gauged the extent to which the sudden illness had radically changed his thinking. Stephen Ambrose explained that Eisenhower had never thought himself susceptible to a life-threatening affliction; during the recovery he was often morose and sometimes preoccupied with the subject of death.[4] Eisenhower wanted more than ever to retire and settle at his 250-acre farm in Gettysburg, Pennsylvania, something he had been eyeing almost from the moment he became president.[5]

Based on the health matter alone, there were pros and cons to serving another term. Some family members told him the demands of the presidency would agitate his condition; others, including Mamie

Eisenhower, felt he needed the invigoration of daily responsibilities.[6] What all of them feared were periods of acute strain and abnormally intense activity. Although Eisenhower's recovery was considered "total," doctors warned that a particularly stressful diversion from a regular routine could, in a heart attack victim, have fatal results.[7]

Eisenhower had enjoyed a fairly regular routine during his first three years in the White House; there had been few sudden emergencies that had caused him anxiety and long hours. Yet political campaigns were somewhat like presidential crises—stressful, consequential, and unpredictable—and they were made certain by the turn of the calendar. On paper Eisenhower liked the campaign. "Every person thinks you are waving or smiling to him," he once said. "The effect is great."[8] But Eisenhower's two previous experiences on the campaign trail had left sour, if not horrific, impressions. In 1952 his 53,000 miles of whistlestop travels and his 250 speeches had physically exhausted him; he could not even remember most of the TV appearances he had made that year.[9] In 1954 Hall had tricked Eisenhower into extending his speaking tours, not revealing until the last moment that the ten thousand miles of travels and forty appearances were record numbers for a president in a midterm campaign. Eisenhower was so weary and distressed in 1954 that he finally erupted in anger after his final campaign stop, blaming advisers who did not know when to let up. "[Y]ou sure get tired of all this clickety-clack," he fumed, then told speechwriter Bryce Harlow, "I don't see how you write a goddamned thing with so many people telling you what to do."[10]

Eisenhower did not single out specific individuals in his complaints about the campaigns, not even the wheedling Hall. Yet Hall knew he could easily become a target if he did not take steps to ease the next Eisenhower campaign. Thus, months before the heart attack, the national committee had commenced time-buying negotiations with the three national television networks and companies that represented several local TV stations. Some national radio time was also purchased in advance, although not nearly as much as in 1952 and 1954, because audiences for that medium had apparently shifted to television. Just two days after the heart attack, Hall held a news conference in New York. When a reporter from the *New York Daily News* asked him to comment on possible Eisenhower replacements, an undaunted Hall calmly announced that the GOP ticket would read "Ike and Dick." The disbelieving reporter, unable to draw from Hall a "realistic" assessment, told him, "You're completely nuts." The reporter did not know that Hall was already concocting a media plan that would relieve Eisenhower of numerous burdens during the campaign.[11]

At the time of the heart attack, Eisenhower did not know of Hall's plans either. Hall was very eager to tell him, but the chairman had to wait weeks before doing so, because Eisenhower refused to talk about the campaign from his hospital bed. The president had also made it clear that he wanted a minimum of speculation in the news media. Thus Hall stayed quiet while the White House press office, with its barrage of information on Eisenhower's condition, laid the foundation for the entire post–heart attack campaign strategy. Hall and Press Secretary Jim Hagerty found themselves in close company during the recovery phase. After Eisenhower resumed his duties and political discussion intensified, they were often seen together in public as complementary voices of Eisenhower's campaign plans. In addition, both worked behind the scenes to encourage Eisenhower to move forward with the reelection. This campaign advisory role was new to Hagerty and marked yet another step in his expanding influence.[12]

Party headquarters lowered its profile during Eisenhower's recovery in late 1955 but used this time productively. Hall followed the progress of the TV planning with RNC public relations director Lou Guylay and found that the party's early negotiations with ABC, CBS, and NBC for 1956 airtime were not only nearing completion but had also eased the party's financial anxieties. The record $2 million advance order would actually be worth more, because the networks had agreed to further discounts, which would also be given to the Democrats. This was good news, because airtime values were increasing monthly as TV continued to grow; the ad agencies were predicting that by the 1956 election, seven out of ten voters would have television. It was evident to Hall that Eisenhower would own some of the richest airtime on the TV schedule—and that the Democrats would have very little. According to Guylay, the GOP would also have money available for additional airtime if the need arose. Meanwhile, Guylay promised that this airtime would be used innovatively, not consumed by auditorium rallies as in 1952.[13] The chairman was very encouraged.

On November 28, near the end of the recuperation, Eisenhower finally agreed to lift the embargo on private campaign discussions by inviting Hall to his Gettysburg home. Importantly, Hall did not travel to Gettysburg by himself; he also wanted Guylay to see the president.[14] A flock of reporters followed the two men to this meeting and were peeved when Hall, at Eisenhower's direction, declined to discuss any of the details. Years later, though, Hall finally revealed what had taken place. "In late 1955, when we were talking to President Eisenhower about running for a second term," he explained in a 1960 *Life* article, "I told the President that he wouldn't have to travel as much as he had in 1952." Hall maintained that "four or five nationwide telecasts would be all that he would have to do." Hall stressed that with "the proper advertising build-up" for these programs, Eisenhower "would get the same impact as if he were out meeting people face to face."[15]

Eisenhower listened to Hall and Guylay but was not convinced. It was not until after the holidays, when he had moved back to the White House, that the president allowed additional discussion about the campaign. Hall now believed he had to demonstrate the power of television before the president's eyes. It was natural, particularly in the 1950s, for people performing in the hollow confines of a TV studio to wonder about the impact they were having. This was especially true for Eisenhower, who often said he was energized by crowd reactions during his personal appearances, including motorcades. Eisenhower had made dozens of TV appearances that were followed by letters and news media reaction. Except for Nixon's 1952 "Checkers" telecast, however, political TV had produced no big display of fireworks that indicated its effect upon an audience.

Accordingly, Hall invested some of the party's resources in an inventive TV production designed, in part, to stir the reluctant president. On the night of January 20, 1956, while millions of Americans were watching "Ozzie and Harriet" and "Life of Riley," a few hundred others were attending private GOP fund-raiser dinners. These fund-raisers were different from ones put on in the past because the dinners, held in fifty-three cities across the country, were equipped with giant television screens and linked by a special closed-circuit TV network. It had cost the party several hundred thousand dollars to stage this spectacle, but the investment eventually paid for itself many times over. The next day Eisenhower, who had made a rousing TV appearance, saw a river of telegrams, letters, cash, checks, and notes begin to pour into his office and that of the RNC. Ultimately, six million dollars was raised from that one night; it was the largest single fund-raising effort in U.S. history up to that time.[16] Responding to Hall's suggestion that the affair had an "electric quality," Eisenhower had to admit, "You had a grand idea and you organized its execution perfectly."[17]

This closed-circuit "Salute to Ike," as it was called, affirmed once again that the tug of Eisenhower's personal appeal was just as potent through the wires and lights of mass media as it was in face-to-face encounters. The event also removed any doubt about whether the national committee had been forthright with Eisenhower in claiming it had the talent and stamina to think big and develop an idea that had never been attempted. Eisenhower's remaining question was whether television would preserve his flexibility once the campaign got going. "Any war will surprise you," he once said; after 1952 and 1954, he was just as wary about political campaigns.

Richard Nixon became an intermediary. The vice president, whose "Checkers" telecast had lent him recognition as an authority on political television, had a lot to say about the potential of the new medium. Like Hall and Hagerty, Nixon wanted Eisenhower to end the suspense and give an affirmative decision. As he would demonstrate later that March and April when he refused to comply with the president's attempt to shake him off the ticket, Nixon realized his political fortunes for now were best kept as number two man under the popular Eisenhower.

Eisenhower and Nixon conferred on February 7 during a week when Hall was a regular visitor to the Oval Office. Eisenhower laid everything out, then asked for Nixon's sober opinion, not the arm-twisting he was getting from the national committee. "I think Hall is wearing rose-colored glasses," began Eisenhower, who did not believe "that with no more than three to five television talks [the] election would be assured." Nixon conceded Eisenhower's basic worry. "We would have to decide right off the bat," he said, "that you were not going to be pressured to come into any state for the purpose of getting a Senator elected or reelected." Then, however, Nixon turned the argument around on Eisenhower, telling him to trust Hall and show more confidence in the new modes of public communication that the president himself had done so much to urge. "The new medium of television has never been used up to its full potentialities," Nixon went on. "This is the best kind of plan. Five or six television programs, . . . but I would make it spectacular." Eisenhower wondered whether the party would lose because of his "lack of work." Nixon said no, that "the party is not so badly split." [18]

Eisenhower consented to hold more meetings with Hall during the next week.[19] Then, on Valentine's Day, Eisenhower checked into Walter Reed Hospital for a battery of medical examinations. Paul Dudley

White, the Boston doctor and mouthpiece of Eisenhower's recovery, announced to the press that "the president should be able to carry on an active life satisfactorily for five or ten years." White added that he would vote for Eisenhower "if he runs."[20] Still, characteristically, Eisenhower refused to allow the impression that his doctors had made the final decision. With interest in his future reaching a fever pitch, Eisenhower took off for two weeks of quail hunting in Georgia. After he returned, he had two more sessions with Hall.[21]

Eisenhower's announcement to reporters at a routine Wednesday morning news conference on February 29—that he had reached a "positive" decision about seeking a second term—was major news.[22] NBC correspondent Ray Scherer recalled bursting out of the news conference room and sprinting to a live unit outside so he could be first on the air with the story.[23] Eisenhower repeated this announcement in a nationwide TV address that night, when audiences were larger and when he, not the reporters, would interpret his plans.

Eisenhower's speech to the nation was filled with hidden meanings. He more or less repeated everything Hall, Hagerty, and Nixon had told him in private: that television had been underutilized and that it would bring about a major advancement in carrying issues before the American public. Eisenhower said that if nominated, he would not be able to see as many Americans as he had in 1952 because of his health and his responsibilities as president. But Eisenhower also emphasized that television would do a better job at alerting the public to the nation's great challenges; he indicated there would be "no barnstorming," as he put it—that such a practice was a thing of the past.

Actually, the traveling campaign had hardly been discarded in plans being drawn by the RNC. Nixon and a group of surrogate GOP campaigners would attend all points of the map in the coming election; Eisenhower would also make some road appearances in 1956, although on a schedule of his own design. Yet in the campaign's prelude it was essential that Eisenhower angle the eyes of the public away from the personal campaign tradition and into the new mass media arena. Without this persuasion the looming media campaign might send a signal that the president was restraining his efforts because of his physical condition. Thus, in a flurry of public statements through the rest of the spring, Hall, Hagerty, and others pressed Eisenhower's underlying theme: that the party had chosen television because it was indeed the political wave of the future, not because it was a crutch to get an infirm president past a grueling political campaign.[24] In May, for example, more headlines were generated when part of the Eisenhower fall TV schedule was announced to the news media. "President Plans TV Drive" topped a front-page story in the *New York Times* on May 14. The story quoted Hagerty as saying, "We are in a new age—an electronic age—and we have a lot of ideas and a lot of thoughts on how to campaign."[25]

The February 29 telecast had gotten this effort off to a good start. Besides stating in so many words the new importance of mass communication, Eisenhower had underscored the term "barnstorming." Before this time, "barnstorming" had been known as "whistlestopping," a different term, laden with tradition and Americana, which for average citizens evoked positive feelings about real-life encounters with great national leaders. Now Eisenhower had changed the lexicon: using the negative term "barnstorming" to discredit whistlestopping as an antiquated concept, he encouraged Americans to get used to more TV images instead.

The Republicans knew that their likely Democratic opponent, Adlai Stevenson, would insist on a traditional whistlestop strategy. As for the integrity of the GOP's mass media strategy, a lot depended on how tactfully the Democrats played it—whether they would connect TV to Eisenhower's health and galvanize the two into major campaign issues. As it turned out, the GOP had little reason to worry. Stevenson missed the health issue, while many Democratic planners took cues not from their candidate but from Eisenhower, whose administration continued to operate on the notion that heavy use of the mass media was the be-all and end-all of 1950s politics. With the election still many months away, average Americans as yet may not have cared too much. But those in the "Brand X" political party were noticeably affected by the campaign's new rules. Eisenhower and the Republicans controlled the political media playing field; they were able to sit back and watch, often on their TV screens, as media chaos unfolded among the Democrats.

MEDIA WHIPPING

THE DEMOCRATS,

1955–1956

While Eisenhower wanted Modern Republicanism and a modern strategy for effecting it, many scholars believed Adlai Stevenson was more in step with the times. By some accounts, including those of John Bartlow Martin in his *Adlai Stevenson and the World*, Stevenson was the champion of modern politics in the 1950s, the first to articulate some historic initiatives—including educational and housing aid, federal medical assistance, and a nuclear test-ban treaty—that were enacted in the 1960s and 1970s. Nevertheless, the fact remained that none of Stevenson's ideas went into law bearing his name. Stevenson's losses to Eisenhower in 1952 and 1956, his third unsuccessful presidential bid in 1960, and his failure to get more from John Kennedy than a U.N. ambassadorship suggested that Stevenson may not have been so up-to-date in all necessary respects.

Indeed, his activities in the 1950s left little doubt that Stevenson looked backward with regard to his paramount need: getting himself elected. This is not to say that Stevenson would have defeated Eisenhower with better campaigns. Yet he might have come a lot closer and built a more stable foundation for his remaining years in public life. The 1950s were a staging period more for political tactics than for ideas; Stevenson did not understand this concept. It was already known in the mid-1950s, for example, that Kennedy was priming for a presidential campaign and planned to overcome his relative obscurity with heavy use of the mass media. Stevenson assisted Kennedy by letting him steal the show on TV at the 1956 convention and then by giving Robert Kennedy, JFK's future campaign manager, a free ride on the 1956 campaign plane, from which RFK quietly observed one tactical mistake after another. In 1960 Stevenson marched into a meat grinder by trying to challenge the "modern" Kennedy TV image he himself had helped initiate.

None of Stevenson's campaigns better illustrated his problems than his second battle with Eisenhower. This subject has been amply dissected by many scholars; although it was a remarkable effort in terms of guts and substance, even Martin admitted that Stevenson's 1956 campaign was botched by organizational lapses, second guessing, and low morale. Part of the predicament resulted from internal tension over media campaign methods promoted by party leaders but knocked down in roundhouse style by the candidate. Difficulties ranged from unpaid bills that gathered at his headquarters to bungled television appearances that were frequently followed by verbal furies backstage. Personality projection, a growing requirement in politics, was a distressing task for Stevenson; the man's reputation as an erudite "egghead," which historian Bert Cochran associated with his patrician instincts, contained a measure of reality. Charles Guggenheim, a Democratic TV producer, felt that Stevenson's trouble with television was "pathological."[1] Arthur Schlesinger, Jr., another adviser, agreed.[2]

Nevertheless, the media frustrations endured at large by the Democrats in the 1950s had more to do with Eisenhower, and his control of the various outlets that reached the public, than with any breakdown attributable to Stevenson. In 1952 these candidates had engaged in virtually identical traveling campaigns, in which verbiage flew day after day, town after town; Stevenson clung to the same tried-and-true approach in 1956, giving more speeches in a single year than any previous candidate. Yet in just four year's time the Republicans had radically altered the environment of the national political campaign. While Stevenson flailed away, Eisenhower ran almost his entire 1956 campaign on television, with smooth visual images and very few words, leaving Stevenson a postage stamp of a target.

Just as many of Eisenhower's media tactics were revealed directly in his maneuvers around Congress and the press, those tactics were also visible indirectly in the Democratic party's new priorities; the president's moves stimulated the Democrats to respond to the system he had changed. The people who tried to run Stevenson's campaign were not oblivious to the importance of television in winning votes or to the benefits the GOP perceived in the new medium. Fearful but determined Democratic figures wanted to fight the administration's TV fire with electronic pyrotechnics of their own, only to preside over a mishmash of strategy and severe demoralization. They simply could not compete.

The Democrats were not just faced with an invincible president. For the first time in the electronic media age, they were up against Republican influence, money, and airtight organization at the national level. Democratic names would change as the party tried to win the White House in campaigns after 1956. Yet the gauntlet the Republicans laid at their feet in several subsequent elections had strikingly similar features.

By almost every measure besides money, organizational efficiency, and the White House, in the 1950s the Democrats were the Goliath of the two political parties. There were almost twice as many Democrats as Republicans in the party-identified electorate, and the Democrats enjoyed great strength at grassroots levels. Politics at the top had changed, but ever since the days of Roosevelt's New Deal coalition, the Democrats had usually held the thousands of precincts, wards, and individual voting districts across the country. Statehouses gave a good reflection of the Democrats' local strength. The party had 30 of the 48 governorships, and of the 5,179 state representatives, 53 percent were Democrats; the balance included 736 GOP legislators in the gigantic Republican statehouses of Connecticut, New Hampshire, and Vermont.[3] In the 1954 elections, as the Republicans were especially aware, the Democrats had won most of the gubernatorial races as well as those for the U.S. House and Senate. In the mid-1950s, the Democratic party was a model of the decentralized, confederated political organization that flexed its muscle at the local level, controlling most local governments and bedeviling Eisenhower on Capitol Hill.

When Eisenhower became president in 1953, there was disagreement as to who was leading the Democratic party, especially after the two previous standard-bearers, Stevenson and Harry Truman, fell into a feud. Yet there was unity and high morale at the Democratic National Committee. Stephen Mitchell was the popular chairman through the 1954 elections; when Mitchell stepped down, fifty-one-year-old Paul Butler became his handpicked successor. Butler, a lawyer, had risen as an accomplished, New Deal–era political organizer in Indiana and had close ties to Stevenson; he was elected against opposition from Truman, whose ongoing influence in the party depended on its machine leaders and urban factions in the Northeast. Both Stevenson and Butler were moderates who appealed to leaders in the South, West, and rural Midwest.[4] Unlike that of Leonard Hall, his counterpart at Republican headquarters, Butler's attraction was a quiet one. He was tall, methodical, and sometimes emotional; many thought him abrasive. However, Butler sustained his roots in organization politics much more than Hall. He did not have Hall's taste for the bombastic; he was unwilling, for example, to rush headlong into a personality-oriented presidential campaign.[5]

Nevertheless, Butler was one of the first Democratic leaders in the television age to be aware of the diminishing importance of party affiliation in winning the presidency. With Eisenhower the opponent in 1956, Butler realized the campaign was destined to revolve around personalities and personal style, the specialties the president displayed in his White House communications. Believing that the public would also expect quality communications from the eventual Democratic nominee, and that the nominee could comply, Butler insisted on media opportunities. Thus, not with a bold vision of new politics but rather as a defensive measure, Butler led the organization farther and farther offshore into media waters that proved over his head.

Butler had no experience in running a national campaign, and his home in South Bend, Indiana, was removed from the New York media hub. Yet Butler was ably motivated to supervise expanded Democratic TV pursuits, having become an authority on political television and the TV handicaps plaguing the party. In early 1954, while serving on the party's executive committee under Mitchell, Butler distinguished himself in a controversy over a local TV series called "Washington Calling," which was sponsored by the California GOP and carried on KABC in Los Angeles. Butler demanded that ABC, owner of the station, provide equal time for a Democratic version of the program, but the FCC overruled his claim because the Democrats could not produce verbatim transcripts. This affair strengthened Butler's resolve toward television, especially after Paul Ziffren, head of the state committee in California, alerted him to the massive media capabilities of the Republicans in that media-rich state. "Most Democratic candidates," explained Ziffren, "have no conception of what their rights are so far as radio and TV are concerned."[6]

Butler worked hard to clarify those rights, and as time went on, his attentiveness to what was available under the law became as much a part of Democratic TV strategy as anything else. Because the area was new, laws governing the use of television airtime by political candidates were spotty and incomplete. In part because Butler pressed the California dispute, on September 8, 1954, the FCC handed down several pages of rules concerning equal time procedures.[7] Attorney Harold Leventhal of the Washington law firm Ginsburg, Leventhal, and Brown became Butler's right arm in many subsequent appeals to the FCC for free airtime.[8] They also put pressure on the National Association of Broadcasters.[9] Nevertheless, Butler realized early he was at a great disadvantage. The FCC was part of the Eisenhower administration, and the NAB, an organization stocked with broadcast executives, was friendly to the president.

Equal time setbacks made up only part of the Eisenhower media shadow that hovered over Democratic party headquarters. Less known publicly in 1955, but far more aggravating, was the party's attempt to reach parity with the GOP by enlisting a major advertising agency. In a recruiting effort that dragged on for almost a year and a half, the Democrats suffered one Madison Avenue rejection after another, a source of embarrassment that left question marks behind Butler's leadership. Butler blamed Eisenhower. Madison Avenue was a trading post of the nation's corporate establishment. Not only were the big agencies themselves part of the business complex; major corporations—the General Motors, the General Electrics, and the Standard Oils, which were the lifeline of the advertising field— were even bigger and more influential. These advertisers strained to hear Butler, more tuned to their Republican clientele, which Eisenhower constantly cultivated.[10]

It was not widely known that the Democrats had actually had some experience with advertising agencies; they employed the Baltimore-based Joseph Katz group in 1952. But Katz was a regional outfit, and its work in 1952 left much to be desired. The Democrats had spent two-thirds as much as the Republicans—a little over $1 million—on television for Stevenson's 1952 campaign, but their TV appeals were not very visible. Much of the 1952 budget had been consumed by what were called "preemption charges." Preemption was another term for bad planning; if a political organization decided at the last minute it wanted more airtime, the TV networks assessed hefty additional fees to revamp their regular schedules. In 1952 the party paid $175,000

in preemption penalties to NBC alone.[11] Constrained by money short-
ages that year, Katz scaled back a series of half-hour TV speeches in
favor of a handful of one-minute spots that were hurriedly bought
and produced. Only one or two had Stevenson in them.[12]

To avoid this situation in 1956, Butler began by contacting McCann-
Erickson, the world's fourth-largest advertising agency. He got a quick
refusal. However, Emerson Foote, one of its executives, agreed to
help the Democrats find someone else; Foote began on March 14,
1955, by sending Butler information on the fifty largest agencies. The
chairman referred to this material again and again over the next few
months. At the top of the list was J. Walter Thompson, the largest
agency, which did not handle political accounts. Holding down the
second and third positions on the list were Young and Rubicam and
BBDO, already committed to the Republicans. The other companies
that rounded out the top ten were likewise unavailable.[13]

By the summer of 1955, to the delight of the White House, Butler's
hunt for an ad agency was starting to make news in national trade
publications such as *Broadcasting* and *Advertising Age*. This publicity
brought the DNC a flood of applications from small, obscure agencies all over the country.[14] Donner and Company of Detroit contacted
Butler, as did Henry J. Kaufman and Thomas Wilson of Washington,
D.C.; the Cary Hill agency of Des Moines; W. L. Gleason and Company of Riverside, California; and more than a dozen others. Some
New York agencies also applied. One of them was Doyle Dane Bernbach, destined to make political television history in the 1964 Lyndon
Johnson presidential campaign; but in 1955, it, like the others, was
tiny. Butler's discontent grew.[15]

On August 6 Butler asked Herbert Bayard Swope, a former journalist, aide to philanthropist Bernard Baruch, and a figure with numerous media contacts, to investigate some of the midsized Madison
Avenue agencies for inklings of Democratic loyalty. "I am confronted
with a very serious problem here at the Democratic National Committee," Butler began, explaining that he had contacted "eighteen or
twenty of the leading agencies in New York" without success. He instructed Swope to use discretion, "as we do not want it to get around
Madison Avenue that the DNC is shopping around for an advertising
agency and is having trouble finding one."[16]

Yet people all over New York and Washington knew the Democrats
were shopping around. For Republicans it had the makings of a crude
comedy until some in the GOP started to fear a new public relations

problem: bad publicity, if not voter backlash, from Eisenhower's pre-emptive use of Madison Avenue. Sig Larmon of Young and Rubicam was one person who anticipated this scenario. Accordingly, Larmon had an idea. He encouraged the American Association of Advertising Agencies to take some steps to ensure that the Democrats had at least some media resources—not enough to make any difference, but fully sufficient to counter any claim that Eisenhower was alone in drawing from New York image makers.

In turn, the AAAA proposed formation of an ad hoc agency for the Democrats similar to those it ran for large charities. Under this plan several large agencies and the TV networks would each contribute some of their creative people, who would volunteer for paid leaves of absence and work for the DNC at no cost to the party. At first, Butler flatly refused. He was well aware of Eisenhower's involvement in this overture and expressed appropriate resentment at a proposal that put the Democratic party on par with the Salvation Army. But the AAAA was persistent; it envisioned some good public relations for itself in helping politicians with their growing media needs. The loan program moved ahead, but only on Butler's demand that there be no ad hoc agency labeled as such and that the media volunteers be free to join any campaign.[17] Butler might have done better had he not tried to save face; the decision to open the ad agency loan program to everybody only inspired the GOP to take full advantage.[18]

Two days after his letter to Swope, Butler was informed that an ad agency called Norman, Craig and Kummel might be interested in the DNC account.[19] Eugene Kummel, who had taken control of the company from William H. Weintraub a few years before, was a Democrat, as was his partner Walter Craig. Furthermore, Norman, Craig and Kummel was an agency on the rise. Unranked in the top fifty in 1954, it had leaped to thirty-fourth place by mid-1955 after signing with the Speidel watchband company and Blatz Beer.[20] Then came this agency's blockbuster achievement, not unnoticed at the DNC: it gained the Revlon account and a quiz show called "The $64,000 Question," which within one month of its premier in June 1955 was the most popular program on television.[21] (Symbolically, BBDO stole this program and the rest of the Revlon account from Norman, Craig and Kummel in 1956.)

Negotiations with Norman, Craig and Kummel did not produce an instant resolution. The agency was leery about compensation, while Butler continued to hold out for one of the major agencies, wagering there would be more takers closer to the campaign. Finally, indirectly, the Republicans brought the two sides together. At the end of Eisenhower's heart attack recuperation in late 1955, reports surfaced in the news media that the GOP was already spending millions on Madison Avenue in anticipation of Eisenhower's reelection. Fearing his agency would get the DNC account so late in the campaign that an effective media effort would be impossible, on October 31 Kummel sent Butler part of the front page of a *New York Herald Tribune* with a story detailing the Republicans' time-buying deals with the TV networks. A nervous Kummel told Butler, "This situation is now so serious that you must take immediate action. Even if you do not choose Norman, Craig and Kummel, someone right now should be at both NBC and CBS to represent the DNC and demand equal consideration." [22]

On January 31, 1956, the DNC entered into a one-year agreement with Norman, Craig and Kummel. Butler characterized it as a historic event and, in a series of public statements, beamed over the "young, energetic and medium-sized" agency.[23] Norman, Craig and Kummel got what it asked for: control over buying and creative services, in both print and broadcast, and the standard 15 percent commission. Demonstrating its high priority, the account was placed under the supervision of partner Walter Craig.[24]

The engagement of Norman, Craig and Kummel by the Democrats was indeed historic in one respect. In previous years a political organization did not generally engage in direct battle with its counterpart until a fall campaign. This situation was changing in the 1950s mainly because of the public strategies being engineered by the Eisenhower people. To reach the masses in a fall campaign season, a party now had to settle on plans months, even years, in advance. Although in early 1956 the Democratic nominee was unknown, warfare was already taking place behind the scenes, with Norman, Craig and Kummel the party's first combatant. The agency's foe was the Republican firm BBDO, and the first piece of property for which they fought was network airtime.

The accumulation of airtime on the three television networks was critical to both parties. The concept of the "free" media, whereby candidates got their messages across by attracting television news coverage of orchestrated events, would not emerge until the 1960s; TV journalism in the 1950s was in its infancy. Prime network airtime availabilities, sold to politicians just as they were to corporations, determined whether a candidate or party would be seen and heard on television. These stakes were high, because an anticipated two of three voters would be using TV by the 1956 election.

Every step in this airtime contest was an uphill fight for Norman, Craig and Kummel. By the time the Democrats sat down to negotiate seriously with the networks in early 1956, they had already been walloped by BBDO, which had locked up the best segments on the dominant CBS and NBC networks, including almost every available time slot in the crucial final week of the campaign. After all, the Republicans had begun their talks with the networks in July 1955, almost a year and a half before the election.

Another potential menace was the five-minute piggyback format that the Republicans had now standardized. The primary TV device in the 1952 campaign had been the half-hour telecast, best for someone like Stevenson whose forte was long speeches. Even so, there had been recurrent timing problems in 1952 and 1954. For example, time often ran out before Stevenson had finished; viewers saw him simply fade to black in midsentence. During the final half-hour telecast of the 1952 campaign, a costly extra minute of airtime had to be arranged so that Stevenson would not be cut off.[25] It was frightening for the Democrats to envision what might happen if Stevenson was confined to only five minutes. In July 1955, when Butler asked Deputy Chairman Clayton Fritchey to think about this matter, Fritchey told Butler of a "continuous argument" in 1952 about the best way of putting Stevenson on the air.[26]

Butler had already taken some steps before the arrival of Norman, Craig and Kummel, by appointing Jack Christie as head of a new DNC Television-Radio Division, which operated under Fritchey and Publicity Chairman Sam Brightman; also on staff before moving to the agency was Reggie Schuebel, the DNC's expert on time buying.[27] At the same time in 1955 that the RNC's Lou Guylay and BBDO's Carroll Newton were contracting for time with network officials, Christie and Schuebel were visiting the same people.[28] The two were assisted by Leonard Reinsch, the DNC radio director from 1944 to 1952, now the executive director of WSB radio and television in Atlanta. In 1957 Christie would dispute the GOP claim that Guylay and Newton had by themselves pioneered the five-minute piggybacks.[29]

Yet this time-buying competition was a prime illustration of how the administration had forced the Democrats to expend resources on a media war they had no hope of winning. Norman, Craig and Kummel succeeded in pinning down more piggybacks than the Republicans, but the time slots were vastly inferior. In the first half of the campaign the Democrats had a preponderance of daytime and late-night segments; after the halfway point there were almost no windows on them at all. Smitten by a TV bug, the Democrats were blind to any media alternative. On January 9, 1956, Butler received a letter from ABC Radio vice president Don Durgin that suggested some realistic advantages in foregoing television and investing in his medium instead. Butler was unmoved, even after Durgin revealed some of the wizardry behind BBDO's time-buying techniques, most of it the brainchild of Newton. They went after "the most valuable and expensive television time, which . . . came to at least two times the cost per unit." By doing so, though, the Republicans would be "repaid by a four-to-one audience advantage," which, according to Durgin, even the most astute corporate advertisers seldom achieved.[30]

In the end the GOP's big weapon was money. While the networks refused to extend credit to the political parties, BBDO's promise to pay was good enough. Norman, Craig and Kummel lacked this clout, and its client, the DNC, was an unlikely source of collateral. When television planning was turned over to Norman, Craig and Kummel, the agency assumed a base TV budget of $2 million—even though there was only $100,000 in the Democratic treasury at the time.[31] Money usually came into the Democratic party in waves during the primary season, around the time of the convention, and at the peak of the fall campaign. For that reason the term "budget" actually referred to something like a gas gauge that constantly rose and fell. Unlike the Republicans, the Democrats had a reputation on Madison Avenue of spending money ahead of time in a campaign, then trying to stay one step ahead of the bills.[32]

Butler's financial course of action was obvious. While Eisenhower and Hall milked millionaires, Butler turned to the grass roots of his party—first, to educate the disparate elements on the added financial demands of the next presidential campaign and, second, to encourage them to come up with added donations. He had used this approach on June 14, 1955, when he notified the hundreds of Democratic state and county committees, "One of the big problems in '56 will be the high cost of television time."[33] He had more ideas as the campaign progressed. One was called "Teas for TV," in which county committees organized teams of women, who held get-togethers in their homes and invited other neighborhood women at a dollar a head.[34] Later there was a plan known as "Teenagers for TV," geared toward party organizers in urban wards and precincts. Young people were equipped with signs, boards, and placards and sent to train stations and shopping centers to publicize upcoming TV programs and ask for donations.[35] Finally, there was "Dollars for Democrats Day," in which party members across the country were asked for small donations somewhat like church offerings. The initial plan of calling it "D-Day for Democrats" ("D" for "dollars") was understandably scrapped.[36]

Ultimately, these efforts fell far short. Although the total number of donors dramatically increased over 1952, as did the proportion of total fund-raising in amounts of $500 or less, the Democrats wound up with a $750,000 deficit at the end of 1956, even though almost $6 million had been raised. The deficit would have been worse had the Democrats not found some big-money contributions. Organized labor gave almost $700,000, while another $860,000 was received in amounts larger than $5,000.[37]

"If we are going to get the job done," Butler emphasized in a memo in August 1955, "we are going to have to 'out huckster' the GOP."[38] Stevenson did not agree. Not only had Stevenson followed the evolution of Eisenhower's political communications for three years; he was one of the first people in the 1950s to bring critical attention to it. He had repeatedly complained about the presence of BBDO in Eisenhower's 1952 campaign and was even more repulsed by Eisenhower's communications from the White House. Stevenson was alarmed when Eisenhower hired Robert Montgomery in 1954 and felt that the televised cabinet meeting and TV chats were political gimmicks.

To little avail, Stevenson tried to turn his critique of Eisenhower's communications into something that would help him with the voters. In his first formal 1956 campaign appearance on February 1, he charged that Eisenhower was substituting a media-driven "cult of personality" for intelligent leadership.[39] Stevenson later enlarged the attack to include BBDO and the White House press office. He exclaimed, "The huckster's art of salesmanship, misbranding and exaggeration have enveloped the government and its communication with the people like never before."[40] Stevenson often used a "cornflakes" analogy, likening Eisenhower to a product peddled to voters. On March 28 he demanded an end to "huckstering and merchandising" and "this selling us instead of telling us."[41] In Stevenson's acceptance speech at the 1956 Democratic convention, Eisenhower's communication efforts would again be a theme. Although Stevenson coined a number of memorable phrases, he was never able to convey to listeners specific reasons why Eisenhower's communications represented a threat to them. As a result, some timely observations about Eisenhower dissipated into a campaign issue that had no pull.

Eisenhower was not the only political figure of the period who had learned to project a favorable image through the mass media. Another was Tennessee senator Estes Kefauver, Stevenson's rival in the 1956 primary campaign. The primaries were still a relatively new approach to winning a presidential nomination. Thomas Dewey's primary campaign was decisive in his 1948 GOP nomination; Eisenhower entered politics by deciding to enter his name on the 1952 New Hampshire primary ballot. Stevenson had been handed his party's nomination in 1952 but now needed a primary campaign to repair his loser's image. Although Stevenson succeeded in his goal of becoming the first Democratic nominee to have run an active campaign in the primaries, the personable Kefauver almost did him in.

In the beginning Stevenson felt he could brush past Kefauver. Stevenson's main worry was Averell Harriman, a former Moscow ambassador and coordinator of the Marshall Plan, who seemed to be rising fast after his 1954 election as New York governor; Harriman had Truman's backing and would control the back rooms in the eastern states where convention delegates were concentrated.[42] Kefauver won the leadoff primary in New Hampshire, where Stevenson, no doubt mindful of Kefauver's 1952 victory there, had not put his name on the ballot. Then, however, in their first direct confrontation, Stevenson suffered a humiliating loss to Kefauver in Minnesota on March 20. Not only was Minnesota a midwestern stronghold; Stevenson was invited there by the state committee and leading officeholders, including Governor Orville Freeman, Senator Hubert Humphrey, and Congressman Eugene McCarthy.[43] Kefauver got little help from the state organization, and his charge that it had tried to railroad Stevenson bothered the masses in Minnesota.

Kefauver, and the assaults he leveled at Stevenson, looked good on television, not just in Minnesota but throughout the primary states. Neither candidate could afford many paid appeals, but this was not a major stumbling block; unlike in 1952, when the TV freeze was just ending, in 1956 every important city had one or more television outlets eager to offer free airtime as a way to lure big-name national candidates into their studios. Kefauver took these TV opportunities very seriously. He had no muscle in the party machinery, and leading Democrats had little regard for him; some experts thought him doomed after he broke with the southern coalition in Congress and favored desegregation. But with a law degree from Yale, and widely known for his coonskin cap and simple manner of speech, Kefauver seemed to appeal to average Americans. His pleasing personality had come through to TV viewers in 1951 when he chaired hearings on organized crime, the first congressional hearings ever televised.

Stevenson labored almost two months to regain his front-runner status; he accomplished this goal by increasing his speaking schedule. His rebound came on May 18 in Oregon, where this heavy schedule paid off; Stevenson made dozens of appearances, compared to only a few for Kefauver, and this visibility impressed Oregon voters. Stevenson also increased his television schedule, setting the stage for some political history on May 21, when he and Kefauver met in the studios of Miami station WTVS for the first televised debate between two presidential contenders. The debate, part of the Florida campaign, was carried nationally on ABC. *New York Times* television critic Jack Gould called the affair "a new experience for a voting viewer," but complained that it "bore no resemblance to the give-and-take of the old rough-and-ready era of American politics." With the eyes of millions of television viewers upon them, noted Gould, "[t]he two candidates agreed too much and didn't really say enough to make much of a show."[44] Nevertheless, Kefauver came away with a moral victory as the favored Stevenson claimed an indecisive 14,000-vote margin: this low margin represented another surprise, because Kefauver had gone into this southern state affirming his support for integration.

The showdown came in California, a raucous affair in which Kefauver again tried to cast Stevenson as a friend of party bosses and segregationists. This time his strategy did not work; Stevenson's backroom support from leading party officeholders and committee figures helped here, because California was split between different constituencies in different regions. In addition, Stevenson's advisers resourcefully brought Eleanor Roosevelt to California to defuse Kefauver's popular appeal. On June 5 Stevenson won with 63 percent of the vote; it was the first time a California primary had decided a presidential nomination.[45] Harriman finally entered the race three days later, but Stevenson already controlled almost half of the needed 686½ delegates and had unstoppable momentum.[46] Kefauver did not give up, though, until July 31.

The 1956 primaries had been the fiercest to date—even more of a reason for the national committee to have TV plans in order for the convention and the fall campaign. To create and sell an image of party unity, the Democrats now faced a bigger task because Stevenson, the loser to Eisenhower in 1952, had proven himself vulnerable to the weak Kefauver.

However, just as they trailed the GOP in time buying, the Democrats had to play catch-up in this creative area. Democratic television concepts showed little originality but instead emulated devices the GOP had previously introduced. For example, what emerged as the focus of the Democrats' five-minute spots was a content-packed series known as "The Man from Libertyville"; Stevenson's home was in Libertyville, Illinois. "Libertyville" had a nice ring, but the Republicans had used "The Man from Abilene," Eisenhower's hometown, in 1952 and had now abandoned this theme for more advanced concepts. In addition, after it became known that Eisenhower would orient his travel schedule in order to appear on TV from several remote locations, the Democrats adopted the same strategy for Stevenson—at almost crippling expense to the party. The Democrats even planned a closed-circuit TV fund-raising dinner in October identical to the one the Republicans had premiered in January.

The individual planners were not so much uncreative as they were constricted by factors beyond their control. First Eisenhower, then Stevenson worked against them. A noteworthy example was Butler's hope for a nationwide televised debate between Stevenson and Eisenhower.

The opportunity for a 1956 debate was on the table as early as May 1955, when CBS proposed the idea and NBC agreed in principle to such a telecast.[47] The networks said they would make the arrangements and provide the airtime only if the debate featured the two major-party candidates. Plans thus hinged on Butler's ability to persuade Congress to suspend the FCC's equal time provision that would have forced the networks to give free airtime to several minor-party candidates. Because Democrats controlled Congress and presumably knew the advantages of having their candidate debate Eisenhower, Butler confidently pursued equal time suspension with his party's leadership.[48] Butler's problem was that Eisenhower likewise knew of these maneuvers, was also close to key Democrats on Capitol Hill, and was far from naive about the possible consequences of a TV debate. Eisenhower simply leveled with Democratic senator John Pastore by explaining that he had nothing to gain should he "give exposure to a man who is not as well known as I am."[49] While Eisenhower choked the debate idea on Capitol Hill, Republican chairman Hall played dumb and ignored Butler's plea that they work together on a joint TV appearance by the candidates.[50] Equal time suspension would not make it to the congressional agenda until four years later.

Butler might have won points for his party by publicizing this GOP indifference, but interestingly, after a February 1956 exchange with Hall, he never pressed for a debate. The reason was apparently Stevenson, who let it be known privately that he did not want to debate either, claiming such an affair would be another television gimmick.[51]

Nothing reflected the administration's hidden grip on the media better than Butler's fruitless attempts to gain access to the nation's public channels under the same equal time rule. On many occasions the Democrats made what seemed thorough arguments for equal time, only to have their momentum diverted by some loophole in the law located by an Eisenhower figure. With their profit margins at stake, Eisenhower's associates at the TV networks knew all of the loopholes, including the one that exempted equal time when TV facilities had been used to cover bona fide news events. George C. McConnaughey, Eisenhower's FCC chairman, listened to Butler's pleadings but seldom found them sufficiently persuasive.

Within minutes after the networks decided to carry Eisenhower's reelection announcement on February 29, for example, Butler fired off requests for equal time. NBC's answer by telegram the next morning was a firm denial on grounds the speech was a news event; CBS vice president Sig Mickelson gave the same response that day, and ABC president Robert Kintner did the same on March 6. The only favorable response came from Mutual Radio president John Poor, who gave 1952 vice presidential candidate John Sparkman an opportunity to speak for the Democrats on March 7. Butler was flabbergasted, wondering how a predictable presidential address that discussed nothing but a political campaign could be considered a "news event," particularly when Eisenhower had made the same announcement at a news conference earlier in the day.[52]

The fuss started again when CBS announced it would televise a

White House birthday party for First Lady Mamie Eisenhower on March 22. This time Butler ordered an investigation. "Is this a Robert Montgomery show," he asked, "planned and placed on the TV facilities by BBDO?"[53] It was, but CBS president Frank Stanton defined Mamie's birthday party as a nonpolitical entertainment program and thus exempt from equal time rules. Because Mrs. Eisenhower's birthday was November 14, not March 22, and because most of those who attended were the wives of presidential appointees, not personal friends, Reggie Schuebel fumed to Butler, "It smells very much like Republican politics."[54]

To add to the Democrats' problems, Press Secretary Jim Hagerty had now joined Hall in issuing public statements about the campaign; this meant that Butler was fighting not only the RNC but also the formidable White House press office. The barrier this development created for the Democrats was seen in Eisenhower's second hospitalization, this time for an intestinal flare-up known as ileitis, which struck the president in the middle of the night and required emergency surgery on June 8. There was nothing in the news media to indicate Eisenhower was thinking twice about election plans. Subsequent positive reports by Hagerty were accurate; unlike after the heart attack, Eisenhower rebounded immediately.

Still, the public reacted as if the president's latest illness had never occurred. Butler found this so maddening that he blasted the administration, in an interview published in the *New York Times* on June 13, for having "propagandized" Eisenhower's health, claiming that the Republicans had created a "new science of political medicine." His targets were Hall and Hagerty, who he said had "done a terrific job of trying to convince the American people that a man who had had a heart·attack," and now this intestinal problem, was "a better man physically."[55]

But the people did not believe Butler. They believed, as ABC correspondent Edward P. Morgan recalled, that the Republicans "weren't concealing anything, they were just accentuating the positive."[56] The Democrats were to learn still more from the administration about promoting the positive when the 1956 political conventions got under way.

Milton and Mamie Eisenhower listen to Ike's radio message on June 6, 1944, announcing the Normandy landing. Milton introduced Eisenhower to professional public relations; the plan he gave Franklin Roosevelt for the OWI did everything but name his brother supreme Allied commander. (The Bettmann Archive)

Eisenhower's first "right arm" was Harry Butcher, a vice president at CBS who managed with great distinction Eisenhower's media relations in World War II. Butcher became persona non grata in 1946 when he published headquarters diaries that impugned the British. Eisenhower remained in the public eye after the war in part to repair the image he felt had been tainted by Butcher's betrayal. (Courtesy Dwight D. Eisenhower Library/U.S. Army)

Actor Robert Montgomery, hired in 1954 as the first presidential television consultant, was as well known to Americans as the president was. Montgomery coached Eisenhower and helped stage photo opportunities. "As far as television was concerned," Montgomery recalled, "no authority was to supersede mine." (Courtesy Dwight D. Eisenhower Library/ National Park Service)

Few were closer to Eisenhower than Sig Larmon, the president of Young and Rubicam, the world's third-largest advertising agency. Larmon urged corporate principles in Eisenhower's communication strategies, but his presence complicated matters because the GOP retained the agency BBDO, Young and Rubicam's fiercest rival on Madison Avenue. (Courtesy Dwight D. Eisenhower Library/source unknown)

Eisenhower's single most significant media advancement was putting the presidential news conference on television. Remembered as a breakthrough in TV news, it was actually created as a means of circumventing press interpretations. "To hell with slanted reporters," Press Secretary Jim Hagerty said. "We'll go directly to the people. . . ." (AP/Wide World Photos)

Eisenhower with his signature self-confidence, Press Secretary Jim Hagerty with his signature cigarette, and Assistant Press Secretary Murray Snyder return to the White House after a televised news conference in 1955. (Courtesy Dwight D. Eisenhower Library/National Park Service)

This photo shows what Eisenhower saw when a live telecast was scheduled in the Oval Office. Part of Montgomery's job was eliminating logistical hardships so that more broadcasts could be scheduled. (Courtesy Dwight D. Eisenhower Library/National Park Service)

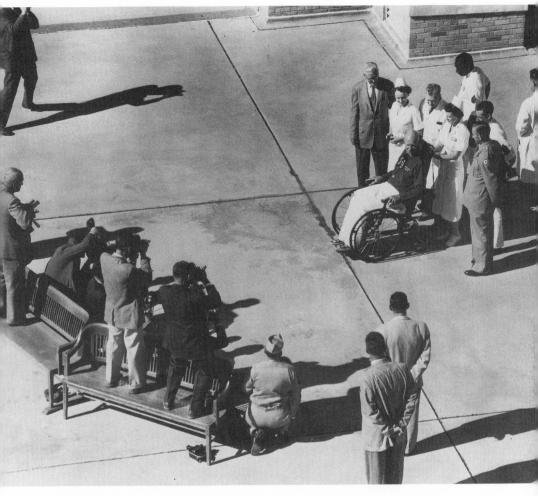

One of the most consequential of Eisenhower's many photo opportunities was his wheel-chair "stroll" on the Fitzsimons Hospital roof after his heart attack in 1955. These photographers provided pictures seen all over the world and helped convince Americans that their popular president was fit for a second term. (Courtesy Dwight D. Eisenhower Library/source unknown)

Eisenhower's arrival in Washington after the heart attack produced a scene reminiscent of his return after VE Day. The White House arranged both a motorcade and national TV coverage that allowed millions from coast to coast to participate. (Courtesy Dwight D. Eisenhower Library/National Park Service)

Leonard Hall, who chaired the Republican National Committee, talked about television so much that columnist James Reston called him a political Milton Berle. Hall took seriously Eisenhower's call for "Modern Republicanism"; he believed a heavy use of television was the "modern" way to win elections. (Courtesy Dwight D. Eisenhower Library/ National Park Service)

The GOP's centennial convention in 1956 testified to a new era of television politics. Because delegates had nothing to decide, Hall generated excitement through staged events, including a TV-orchestrated balloon drop. Although every event was timed with a TV clock, Eisenhower and Mamie supplied a few looks of surprise. (Courtesy Dwight D. Eisenhower Library/source unknown)

BBDO vice president Carroll Newton, a protégé of the agency's founder, Bruce Barton, and president, Ben Duffy, masterminded much of Eisenhower's public outreach. Through Newton and BBDO, Eisenhower became the first president to use professional "tracking" research. Newton's wizardry with the TV networks enabled Eisenhower to dominate the airwaves in the 1956 campaign. (Courtesy Carroll Newton)

Before earning recognition in the entertainment field for "The Addams Family" and other popular TV series, David Levy was the creative engine of Eisenhower's reelection effort. Levy diverted from the hard-sell advertising used by Rosser Reeves in 1952 and pioneered "responsive chord" appeals. "We were not writing the Gettysburg Address," Levy insisted. (Courtesy David Levy)

Adlai Stevenson was known as a great public orator, yet respondents in voter surveys complained of his "poor speaking ability." Voters increasingly formed impressions of candidates through television, a medium that gave Stevenson endless difficulties. (The Bettmann Archive)

It looked like a TV news conference but wasn't. Determined to convey Eisenhower's informal charm and sincerity, Levy designed this prime-time "people's news conference" as a paid political broadcast in 1956. Average citizens addressed the president, and the presence of Hagerty, seated on Eisenhower's left, enhanced the effect. (Courtesy Dwight D. Eisenhower Library/National Park Service)

Another media innovation that promoted Eisenhower's warm personality and affirmed his popularity among women was the series of televised "coffee klatsches." Used for the first time in the 1956 campaign, this type of broadcast reached millions of viewers on NBC in 1960. (Courtesy Dwight D. Eisenhower Library/National Park Service)

Eisenhower and actress Helen Hayes rehearse for "Ike Day," a televised birthday party created by BBDO and carried live on CBS on October 13, 1956, three weeks before the election. Eisenhower received this card bearing the names of 125 Hollywood celebrities. He also received a birthday cake baked by Hayes and Irene Dunne according to "Mamie's own recipe." (Courtesy Dwight D. Eisenhower Library/National Park Service)

Eisenhower went on TV in late 1957 with this nose cone from a suborbital rocket launch; an adviser unacquainted with aerospace equipment had called for him to refer to the large cone as "the object here in my hand." Although Eisenhower was a master at public relations, he did not apply his knowledge effectively after the Soviet Union launched Sputnik, and thus contributed to the national inferiority complex. (Courtesy Dwight D. Eisenhower Library/source unknown)

Eisenhower delegated duties; he regularly reserved this airplane seat for Vice President Richard Nixon, seen here with his wife Pat as they embark on a campaign trip in 1956. Nixon had little contact with the ad agencies and media specialists Eisenhower had assembled. What he hadn't learned from Eisenhower caused him to lose the 1960 election. By 1968, though, Nixon had mastered the main lessons well enough to prevail in a campaign celebrated by Joe McGinniss as *The Selling of the President, 1968.* (Courtesy Dwight D. Eisenhower Library/National Park Service)

Eisenhower implemented one of the most cordial cross-party transitions in U.S. history. Yet his smile here hid his true feelings about the young John Kennedy. In Eisenhower's words, Kennedy's win over Nixon felt "like being hit in the solar plexus with a ball bat." Eisenhower's contempt for the Kennedys only intensified as the 1960s careened forward. (Courtesy Dwight D. Eisenhower Library/National Park Service)

Eisenhower remained cozy with the TV cameras in his postpresidential years. One of the most pleasing TV encounters of his life was his return to Normandy in August 1963 for a CBS special marking the twentieth anniversary of D-Day. Eisenhower played jeep driver for Walter Cronkite, one of the few journalists he genuinely respected. (Courtesy Dwight D. Eisenhower Library/source unknown)

CONVENTIONS

A GOP REDEFINITION,

AUGUST 1956

Since the 1830s national party conventions have been vortices of the nation's political process, even though after World War II, as more and more contenders conducted primary election campaigns, the conventions only technically served their original function of nominating presidential candidates. Scholars feel the mass media helped account for the longevity of the conventions as well as for the irony that these affairs actually grew larger and more complex as their decision-making roles diminished. With television the major parties were able to transform their conventions from nominating devices into crucial components of their election-year publicity efforts.

A key motive in this transformation was pressure brought on politicians to remove tedium from these events and generate interest among home viewers when key outcomes were already known. This need was first encountered in 1956, one of the few occasions in U.S. history up to that time, and the first occasion in the TV age, when the nominations of the two presidential candidates had been decided before the conventions actually convened. When the Republicans formally chose Eisenhower that year and the Democrats selected Adlai Stevenson, the process was vastly different than in 1952, when these same figures had emerged amid great uncertainty and excitement on the convention floor. The rapidly expanding size of the potential viewing audience in 1956 gave politicians further incentives to orchestrate and manage convention activities.

Televised conventions were not introduced in 1956. The 1948 conventions, beamed to a small audience in the Northeast, were the first to appear on TV. Most existing studies on the early TV conventions have focused on the 1952 meetings, the first seen coast to coast. Kurt and Gladys Lang saw the 1952 conventions as a "proving ground" not just for politicians but also for producers, reporters, and camerapeople.[1] The Langs also discussed TV's role in the "fair play" issue that year, which helped Eisenhower snare the GOP nomination from Robert Taft. Political scientists James Davis and Judith Parris addressed this issue also and believed the 1952 affairs marked the beginning of the video image making that would soon surround the conventions. "Because of television," Parris noted, "conventions must not only be fair, they must look fair."[2]

While politicians took steps in 1952 to have their conventions "look fair," getting them to look interesting, appealing, and meaningful was the new challenge in 1956 and in most of the conventions that followed the Eisenhower era. Not only did the politicians have to consider tens of millions of additional TV viewers; more important was the public's expectation that these conventions mark genuine political twists and turns with a melodramatic plot, as was seen in 1952. Melodrama now had to be planned in advance.

Like hand in glove, this new convention requirement was ideally fitted to the capabilities of the Eisenhower administration. While the Democrats had difficulty following their 1956 script, the Republican convention that year was a masterpiece of television timing, precision, and innovation. Although this convention has long been forgotten, it is historically important precisely because little of consequence actually occurred when the GOP met in 1956. Many observers at the time marveled at the order and sparkle created by the Eisenhower people, and some considered it the best-organized political convention since the first was held in 1832. The convention also had a long aftermath. In one week's time the 1956 Republican gathering became the model for the type of convention that political organizers in both parties would aspire to create, and later achieve in creating, as the TV age continued to evolve.

Because the 1956 conventions were the second ones telecast coast to coast, politicians, writers, scholars, commentators, and network promoters hailed their coverage, with no shortage of superlatives, as another breakthrough in American democracy. As they had in 1952, commentators often referred to audience members not as "viewers" but as "participants." "The political actors will be kept completely conscious of their roles," explained Columbia University historian Richard Hofstadter in a viewer's guide put out by the National Broadcasting Company. "Television audiences will see the candidates, convention bigwigs, and on NBC, the individual delegates as they make up their minds on the convention floor."[3]

The press was also inspired. With combined audiences for the conventions expected to reach record levels, there were numerous analyses of TV's enormous growth since 1952 and follow-up reports on the impact of the FCC's decision that year to end its freeze on television station licensing. When this decision was announced on April 14, 1952, television was available on only 108 stations in 62 cities, covering parts of only 35 states. Ten weeks later, that was still the extent of television's broadcast range when the 1952 GOP convention opened in Chicago; only five additional stations had taken to the air in time to telecast the election results in 1952 and Eisenhower's inauguration in 1953. But by the end of 1953, the number of stations had almost tripled, to 309, and TV was seen for the first time in 119 cities. Now, in 1956, 459 stations broadcast from 243 locales in all 48 states. As a result, the number of TV homes more than doubled between 1952 and 1956, from sixteen million to thirty-five million; thus, the potential audience for the 1956 conventions was close to two-thirds of the voting public. In the New England and Northeast states, television penetration was up to 88 percent; in the Mountain and Southwest states, which had minimal TV service in 1952, penetration had quadrupled to 62 percent by 1956. During 1956 an average of more than sixteen thousand sets were being purchased every day.[4]

Partial completion of the Bell System's landline interconnection system in 1951 made it possible for the 1952 conventions to be the first televised to audiences on both coasts. Yet in 1952 there were not nearly enough TV stations and receivers to make these conventions the national experience that wide-eyed observers anticipated in 1956. The differences between the 1952 and 1956 conventions were well indicated by the forces mobilized to cover them. In 1956, when the Democrats finished in Chicago and the Republicans adjourned in San Francisco, the three networks together had spent close to $17 million—twice the amount they had invested in 1952. Much of the money was paid to an estimated 2,700 people—double the number of delegates in either party—who executed the coverage, ranging from technicians to executive producers; only around 1,000 people had been used by the networks in 1952. Even the equipment reflected the increased scale of convention coverage in 1956. Sixty tons of cameras, cables, switching panels, totalizator boards, and microwave gear were hauled to the conventions in 1956, compared to twenty-five tons used in 1952. *Newsweek* rightly declared that the 1956 conventions were, for television, "the biggest show in its history."[5]

Planners in both parties sought such a show, but they were not alone in spurring this escalation of TV coverage between 1952 and 1956. At the time logic seemed to dictate that the networks should either keep their investments at 1952 levels or reduce them, because the nominations of the candidates had already been decided and, more important, because the networks had lost money on the 1952 conventions. Quite to the contrary, the 1956 conventions became as much a showcase for the networks as they were for the two parties. Thirty years later this "showcase" theme had not disappeared from the TV industry's conception of these events—an affirmation of the conventions' use as publicity devices for the politicians.

A number of concerns that dogged the TV field in the mid-1950s had put this trend in motion. The dominant concerns were political anxieties that had swarmed around broadcasters since the TV freeze had ended in 1952. A huge amount of private-sector economic energy had been unleashed when the freeze ended, but this explosion proved to be tightly controlled, with limited participation. Curiously, the 197 television sponsors in 1952 had decreased right after the freeze and had risen to only 255 by 1956. The iron grip wielded by the networks—mainly CBS and NBC—had become much more apparent. The third network, ABC, was kept alive only by a 1953 merger with United Paramount Theatres. A fourth network, begun in 1949 by Allen Dumont, never had a chance and folded in 1955.

CBS and NBC were the subjects of one investigation after another on Capitol Hill, and one of them gave John Bricker an opportunity to continue in the national spotlight. Just weeks after the defeat of his Bricker amendment in 1954, the Ohio Republican began nosing into the plight of UHF television stations, licensed for the first time after the freeze, and turned up evidence of predatory practices on the part of their older competitors, the VHF stations, almost all of which were either owned by or affiliates of CBS or NBC.[6] Bricker lit a fire among

Democrats, who probed even further when they gained control of the Congress in 1955 and began to bring allegations of network antitrust violations. Eventually CBS president Frank Stanton and NBC president Robert Sarnoff were called to Washington to testify. Although these executives documented much red ink rather than enormous profits, because of staggering startup and overhead costs, ferment persisted.[7] The House Small Business Subcommittee studied charges that CBS and NBC were influencing personnel decisions at the FCC through their close ties to the Eisenhower administration.[8] Emanuel Celler's House Antitrust Subcommittee discovered that NBC, apparently with the complicity of the FCC, had forced Westinghouse to give up its TV station in Philadelphia in exchange for an NBC outlet in Cleveland, a smaller market.[9]

The conventions kept the political sharks away. Heavy investments in these unprofitable conventions were proof that the networks were not bent on reaping fortunes from their profitable and maligned entertainment shows. Investing in the conventions was also an ideal way for the networks to score points and increase their political leverage, because most of the nation's leading legislators would be attending one of the two events.

The TV industry was also looking to impress the wider audience. By 1956 executives were fidgety for the first time about the viewership of their regular TV news efforts. The CBS network, for example, did not deliberate long before removing Edward R. Murrow's acclaimed "See It Now" series when its ratings dropped in 1955. Even more scrutiny was given to the networks' nightly news programs, particularly NBC's "Camel News Caravan" with John Cameron Swayze and the CBS broadcast "Douglas Edwards with the News." These broadcasts were only fifteen minutes in length but nonetheless appeared in prime time. The net billing of these programs was glaringly low by prime-time standards—around $13,000 for the "Camel News Caravan" and $14,000 for "Douglas Edwards," compared with $36,000 for fifteen minutes of "I Love Lucy."[10] This desire to increase revenues was in harmony with the goal of each network to be number one in the news, and 1956 shaped up as a pivotal year. Swayze's long-dominant "Camel News Caravan" had slipped in the ratings; by summer its lead over Douglas Edwards's broadcast was two-tenths of a rating point.[11] News warfare between CBS and NBC was already being waged before the conventions had even started.

Some of the early skirmishes were in news releases, such as one in May on a special "Campaign '56" letterhead, in which CBS touted its colorful team of news veterans. Walter Cronkite was named anchor, with Murrow, Eric Sevareid, Charles Collingwood, and Richard Hottelet among the two dozen reporters.[12] Edwards would host the newscast live from the convention. NBC then fired its opening volley with descriptions of some never-before-seen technology, including high-speed film processors and split-screen picture devices produced by engineers at RCA, NBC's parent company. And for the first time, three people would be in the NBC anchor booth: Chet Huntley would be joined by veteran Bill Henry and young Washington correspondent David Brinkley.[13]

Promotional efforts continued. On the Fourth of July, NBC began a preconvention version of a series called "Home," in which Arlene Francis dropped in on female delegates in a manner similar to that in Murrow's "Person to Person" program.[14] Later, when NBC detailed more new gadgetry, including an "ultra portable" camera known as a "creepie peepie," writers at "The Today Show" poked humor at their own front office in a skit that featured a "Mr. Seymour Blitz," a "renowned TV engineer" whose seven-ounce camera had a built-in compartment for "cigarettes, change purse, and nail file." The front office got the final laugh, however, as the skit itself was written up and distributed in another news release.[15]

More typical of the networks' buildup was a July 3 statement by Sig Mickelson, the CBS vice president in charge of news and public affairs. "When some future historian sits down to write a history of the 1956 political campaigns," he predicted, "he will build his history around the revolution in campaign methods brought about by the new importance of electronic communications." Mickelson held 1956 up as "the first campaign year in which television has become the dominant medium in the thinking and planning of the national committees."[16]

Television did indeed dominate the planning of the two committees, and the networks were included in their planning. Each side had something to gain from the other; the industry anticipated an attractive TV spectacle, the politicians a huge national audience.[17] The importance each placed upon the other was illustrated when the networks backed away from a dilemma that initially put the relationship on a crisislike footing. The problem was scheduling. The Democrats met in Chicago the week of August 13, while the Republicans opened in San Francisco on August 20; thus, the conventions convened in successive weeks, two thousand miles apart.

Although both parties were criticized, the awkward schedule was the work of the Republicans. San Francisco, Chicago, and Philadelphia had been the finalists for the GOP affair; on February 17, 1955, Eisenhower personally selected the West Coast site because he wanted short, early sessions. This decision was one of the easiest Eisenhower ever made. Advisers had explained to him that a San Francisco setting would allow a convention session to conclude by seven o'clock locally and still be seen on prime-time TV in Eastern, Midwestern, and Mountain states.[18] Moreover, with opinion polls showing him the clear favorite over any Democratic candidate, Eisenhower wanted to reduce the fall campaign to the shortest possible period. For the Republicans, long accustomed to early summer conventions, this meant a major break with tradition; 1956 was the first time since 1888 they would meet after the Democrats. Their August 20 gavel was, at that time, the latest start ever for a major party convention. The GOP actually wanted to meet in September but was unable to because of general election filing deadlines; the party cut it so close in 1956 that papers placing Eisenhower on the New Hampshire fall ballot were filled out on the convention floor and given in person to the secretary of state, a GOP delegate.[19]

The television networks protested, naturally assuming that the two conventions would be held in the same city as they had since 1944. The GOP's choice of San Francisco was a double blow because of its distance from Chicago. These Republican moves seemed irrational to the broadcasters; indeed, only one other convention had ever been held on the far-off West Coast, that in 1920. But the Republicans refused to budge. When the Democrats proved equally resistant, the arguing ended, and cooperation began to characterize the planning.

Republican National Committee chairman Leonard Hall and Paul Butler, Hall's counterpart at the Democratic National Committee, had smoothed over some of the tensions by coordinating pooling arrangements with ABC, CBS, and NBC.[20] However, the expected throng of television people represented another problem, especially for the Republicans. San Francisco's Cow Palace was miles from the city's handful of downtown hotels, which were filled immediately. Because the TV advantages of a West Coast convention were irresistible, though, the GOP acted innovatively. It rounded up rental housing and converted a horse barn adjacent to the Cow Palace into an electronic press room, with a TV screen large enough to be seen by the overflow crowd.[21]

Putting a party's best face before the public required another detail: instructing the thousands of delegates on how to behave in front of the dozens of portable TV cameras. Neither national committee feared what a delegate would say as much as a sloppy appearance. They had had the same fears in 1952, when the National Association of Broadcasters provided a pamphlet advising delegates to make friendly conversation, sit on the edge of their seats, and walk about slowly so TV cameras could keep up.[22] The same information was circulated in 1956, but with more stringent instructions. Bertha Adkins, deputy director of the RNC, and India Edwards, a former vice chair of the DNC, had wardrobe guidelines for the women. Edwards cautioned her Democrats, "Light colors add to a woman's size, small prints are apt to jump on the screen. And big hats are taboo—they obscure the woman as well as block out others." Adkins insisted on no striped dresses or shiny jewelry.[23]

The management of CBS was likewise interested in taming the delegates, and its solution provided another show of harmony with the Republicans and Democrats. The network held special convention preview programs strictly for delegates and committee members. CBS ran it on afternoons when network lines were not feeding regular programs. The networks invited the delegates into the studios of the 167 CBS affiliates across the country, where they received personalized greetings from Cronkite and others, as well as more instruction on television fundamentals. The Democrats saw the presentation on July 23, the Republicans on July 25.[24]

The finishing touch to the arrangements came a week before the delegates arrived, when each party's rules committee met and overhauled long-standing procedures for roll-call voting. Previously, a state could challenge a floor vote on any matter by having its delegation "polled," a time-consuming procedure in which each delegate came to the microphone before the full house. This practice created problems in 1952, because a number of the challenges were apparently motivated by delegates who simply wanted to get on television. The Democratic rules committee enacted new procedures by which delegates were polled privately off the floor, and the Republican committee soon passed an almost identical provision. This change—the end of another tradition in American political conventions—did not sit well with some of the veterans. Maryland's Republican governor, Theodore McKeldrin, protested that the party could no longer claim, "if anybody wants to stand up and be counted, he can." Nevertheless, the polling debate in both parties was brief.[25]

Creating a well-ordered TV affair out of a national convention, even when outcomes were known in advance and planners had their 1952 experiences to draw upon, was not a simple matter, as the Democrats discovered.

When they gathered at Chicago's Amphitheater, things looked different than they had four years before. Gone were the traditional red, white, and blue decorations, replaced by a panorama of solid blue, which transferred better to black and white TV. Gone, too, was the center aisle, sacrificed in favor of a television platform that allowed cameras to shoot directly at the rostrum. Aisles were constructed to the right and left of this platform, making it impossible for delegates to stage unified candidate demonstrations in the middle of the floor, a tradition of past conventions. The rostrum, expanded in size and design, consumed much of the space. Because of the awkward floor layout, state delegations were seated based on their size, and some were unable to see all of the rostrum because of the television paraphernalia.[26] To ease the visibility problem, the upright delegation markers on the floor were redesigned so that state names appeared vertically up the pole, rather than horizontally as in past years. The GOP layout would be similar.

Far more important than the decor was the timing of the big pre-planned events. Because of the persistence of Sam Rayburn, the Speaker of the House, who ran the convention as permanent chairman, most of the Democratic sessions began promptly, but thereafter schedules unraveled and the party missed key TV windows. On the first day a rousing keynote address by Tennessee's Frank Clement ran almost an hour and a half and pushed a stirring appearance by Eleanor Roosevelt well back on the schedule. When the session ended, it was midnight on the East Coast.[27] There had been other contretemps as well. At a cost of $35,000, Norman, Craig and Kummel had produced a half-hour film documentary that was supervised by Dore Schary of MGM and narrated by Senator John Kennedy.[28] The documentary was seen by delegates and by viewers of ABC and NBC, but not by those of CBS, which claimed it was not a legitimate news event.[29] Delegates began a chorus of "throw 'em out!" when Butler took to the podium and charged CBS with a breach of trust.[30]

Some important activities in Chicago eluded the television cameras, even with roving bands of floor reporters, because they happened either behind closed doors or at odd hours. On the third day, the midpoint in the convention, the Michigan delegation held a morning caucus and officially assured Stevenson's first ballot nomination by pledging him forty-four votes—but the event was not reported until that afternoon.[31] The same afternoon, viewers saw Harry Truman attack Stevenson and make a last-ditch attempt to kindle support for Averell Harriman by campaigning for the New York governor's version of the Democratic platform. Yet the actual debate on the platform did not begin until after midnight; when a defeated Truman spoke, it was almost 2 A.M. Eastern time.[32] Harriman forces conceded defeat on NBC at 3 A.M.

A turning point also escaped TV view when Stevenson surprised his campaign advisers by telling them he was leaving the vice presidential nomination to the delegates. He had heated exchanges with Rayburn, Butler, and Senate majority leader Lyndon Johnson, who claimed that such an ill-timed move would deadlock the convention and throw the TV schedule out of kilter. In his biography of the candidate, John Bartlow Martin revealed that Stevenson wanted Kennedy as the running mate; Stevenson figured that if this choice was made not by him but by the delegates the Democrats would be free later to accuse Eisenhower of railroading Richard Nixon's vice presidential nomination.[33] This move was also a good way to steer around the "Catholic issue" that confronted JFK in 1960.

Thus the well-composed final day envisioned by planners turned into a scene of hurried and unorganized activity over the vice presidential battle. Almost everybody lost. Stevenson alienated many party officials, but they were no more shaken than the TV networks; even though a vice presidential balloting was the sort of spontaneous event they really wanted, the networks by then were more concerned about their weekend scramble to San Francisco to set up for the Republican convention.[34] Meanwhile, Stevenson did not get Kennedy as a running mate; Estes Kefauver, Stevenson's foe that spring, was chosen instead. Worse yet, the nominee's acceptance speech came at the witching hour for most of the nation's viewers. The networks signed off after Stevenson, Kefauver, and several of the vice presidential contenders appeared for closing farewells, well after midnight in the East.[35]

Evaluations of the convention took many forms. Interest centered on audience size; although there were early indications that viewership was low, judgments were delayed until the major TV rating services released reports weeks later.[36] As their coverage concluded, NBC's Huntley and Brinkley thought the convention had been a success because of enthusiasm among the tired delegates during the final session.[37] However, *Time* said the coverage lacked substance: "The show hardly lived up to its press agentry. . . . The relentless camera magnified the trivia and underlined the fluffs."[38] John Crosby of the *New York Herald Tribune* was similarly distracted; it was difficult, he complained, "to keep NBC from pushing those buttons." Lucia Carter of the *Chicago Sun Times* felt that the technical "sideshows" obscured the main events.[39] Jack Gould of the *New York Times* concurred, calling it "vapid fare" and noting that "journalistically, TV does not have a newspaper's advantage of flexibility to adjust its behavior to the course of the news."[40]

Scores of TV people had left Chicago before the convention was over, but the cameras, switching controls, and cables, as well as the directors and on-air personalities, could not be transferred until the last minute. CBS accomplished the move by placing all of the remaining equipment and people aboard a single chartered transport plane. The lumbering takeoff from Chicago's Midway Airport was a memorable experience for Douglas Edwards. "We used every inch of the runway," he recalled. "It was like moving a circus."[41]

During the week of August 20–23, at its centennial convention, the Republican party established the art of staging a political gathering, with stopwatches ticking and cameras trained in the intended directions. The affair offered a bold contrast to the Democratic efforts the previous week. The Chicago mishaps had contributed greatly to the GOP's final arrangements; the Republican planners had watched avidly. "We built our 1956 convention around television, and we learned a lot from the Democrats," Chairman Hall revealed years later.[42]

Eisenhower, who had also watched during the previous week, was unimpressed by the Stevenson-Kefauver ticket.[43] What did impress Eisenhower was the visible mismanagement of the Democratic affair, including the unrestrained oratory and late hours. Convinced that the home audience likewise had to force itself to stay tuned, Eisenhower was determined for the public to see a better performance in San Francisco. He wired Hall a "gratuitous" list of ideas "based on reactions from typical television viewers":

a. Allow no, repeat no, long dreary speeches from anyone.
b. There is no reason why the tremendous television audience should become so weary as to turn dials in search of relief, even to find a good commercial. Every speech should have some intellectual content.
c. Change of pace is desirable.
d. Don't be afraid of a suggestion merely because "it has never been done before." A dedicated and genuine independent on your program for a few minutes should be really helpful.
e. By all means get *some* speakers to mention the welcome that we extend to all independents and Democrats.
f. Be firm in enforcing the rules you lay down so that events happen as scheduled.
g. No "steam rollering."
h. Lastly, I repeat the first, *no long and dreary speeches.*[44]

Hall was ahead of Eisenhower, though, already having adopted all of the president's ideas and more. Strict time limits were placed on speeches, and most of the introductions by the presiding chair were eliminated. Instead, speakers paraded to the microphone in tag-team fashion and introduced themselves, thus eliminating time and tedium for home TV viewers. While the Democrats required ten sessions over five days, the GOP compressed its affairs into five short sessions between Monday and Thursday; all but one took place in prime time.

Each day had a theme. Monday was "ceremony day," as Hall called the convention to order. A fifteen-minute keynote address was delivered that night by Washington governor Arthur Langlie, put in the national spotlight because he was seeking an important U.S. Senate seat. Tuesday was "arrival day," as the White House party traveled to San Francisco. Wednesday was "coronation day," with Eisenhower and Nixon receiving the formal nominations. Thursday's theme was "hail to the chief," featuring Eisenhower's triumphant appearance at the Cow Palace.[45] The main events were interspersed with side attractions, including a placard pageant by Republican women and an appearance by Emmet Hughes, a White House speechwriter but an independent, "genuine and dedicated," just as Eisenhower had specified in his message to Hall. And as Eisenhower had predicted, Hughes's introduction as the first independent to speak before a GOP convention had a touch of the dramatic. To no one's real amazement, though, Hughes went on to cheer Eisenhower as the best choice for non-Republican voters.[46]

All of the activities were arranged according to the television clock. Closing the convention on Thursday was important because according to Nielsen there were significantly more TV viewers on Thursdays than on Fridays. Furthermore, the Republicans took pains to use the three-hour time difference between the East and West coasts. None of the "evening" sessions started later than 4:05 P.M. Pacific time; main events that occurred in the 6 to 8 P.M. period locally offered good viewership in the West and a prime-time audience everywhere else in the country.

On Tuesday, for example, Eisenhower's plane touched down at 6:53 P.M. in San Francisco, 9:53 P.M. in the East. The West Coast daylight not only made it possible for television viewers to witness the First Family walking off the plane; they could also see enthusiastic spectators at the airport, along parts of the downtown motorcade route, and at the St. Francis Hotel where the president was quartered. All three networks carried these festivities, preempting routine activities timed for the Cow Palace.[47]

The only episode that threatened to disrupt the order of the convention was a late attempt by Harold Stassen to oust the vice president. Yet it, too, was blocked by a well-orchestrated, if not sudden, TV maneuver. The Wednesday of the convention, when Stassen appeared at the St. Francis for a scheduled conference with Eisenhower, he was stopped in the lobby by Hall, who told him the president refused to see him. To regain favor, Stassen had to not only end the anti-Nixon effort but also second Nixon's nomination.[48] Peace again prevailed in the GOP, and minutes later this peace was beamed to the nation as Eisenhower came downstairs and held the first live presidential news conference to affirm his support of Nixon.[49]

Viewers around the nation got the message, but some of the delegates did not. The result that night, when the nominations got under way, was a strange incident that attracted the many TV floor reporters starving for any sort of newsworthy angle. After word circulated that someone planned to submit a new name for vice president, network crews flocked to the Nebraska delegation to interview Terry Carpenter, the move's apparent organizer. NBC's Randall Jessey reported that Nixon's new opponent would be Interior Secretary Fred Seaton, but when the roll call came around to Nebraska, Carpenter placed in nomination the name of "Joe Smith." NBC stayed with the story. Viewers saw correspondent John Chancellor quiz Carpenter on Smith's "pedigree and fingerprint," and Huntley and Brinkley attempted to locate the mystery candidate through telephone calls from the booth.[50]

There was no Joe Smith, and Nixon officially had the approval of all 1,323 delegates, as had Eisenhower when the presidential roll was taken earlier in the evening. As delegation chairs rose to read their votes and extol their home state virtues, many took time to praise Nixon. As if to eradicate any leftover anti-Nixon stigma, Chairman Joe Martin allowed this praise to continue unabated, and the session did not end until 12:05 A.M. Eastern time.[51]

The closing session on Thursday, however, was a monument to convention organization and TV timing. The gavel fell at 4:01 locally, 7:01 P.M. in the East, to give the networks time to sign on and make introductions before the proceedings began. Interestingly, it was not the candidate coronations but the ninety minutes preceding them that were considered of greatest tactical importance. This time period was used to publicize the congressional races, a GOP concern in the upcoming elections; scores of Republican candidates were introduced one by one to the nation's viewers. At 8:40, as the band played "California Here I Come," Nixon appeared and delivered a fifteen-minute speech. Then, shortly after 9:00, Eisenhower entered the Cow Palace and made a slow walk to the rostrum while balloons fell from the ceiling, the band played, and delegates celebrated in the aisles. They were back at their seats on cue by 9:20 when Eisenhower began a twenty-minute speech, pausing for numerous ovations. After more jubilation, the convention ended at 10:03 on the East Coast—enough time for the delegates in San Francisco to return to their hotels and have dinner.[52]

In 1952 observers had been exhilarated by the first nationally televised conventions. Typical of the comments that year had been those of Professor David Williams, who felt that viewers "saw more of the convention than the average delegates."[53] But four years later, after the second nationally televised conventions, the enthusiasm was restrained, suggesting not only that the novelty of TV conventions had already worn off but also that television had brought some adverse side effects to these affairs. Criticism accompanying the 1956 conventions would be echoed again and again in the years that followed, with calls later for convention reform.[54]

As they would in the future, analysts focused on the staging measures of the two parties and a by-product of these tactics: a change in the role of the news media. Instead of covering the conventions, it appeared the media now participated in them. "TV critics from coast to coast were almost unanimous in their judgment that the blanket coverage was at best over-thorough, at worst downright tedious, and in large part unnecessary," *Newsweek* reported.[55] Writing in *The Reporter*, Marya Mannes claimed the home viewer was drawn to the conventions by pomp and promotion, only to be a pawn of vote-minded politicians and a TV industry in search of rating points. She likened the TV personalities to "modern Laocoöns, struggling to make their voices heard through and above the constricting coils of their electronic gear." Mannes also questioned whether conventions "warrant complete and continuous reporting" and maintained that TV coverage may constitute "a time killer and a strength waster that far exceeds its prime purpose of presenting news."[56]

Besides voicing concern about the integration of party and press in staging the conventions, critics were also bothered by the public's response. Television ratings figures, which had shown a meager average viewership of 40 percent during the 1952 conventions, had scarcely been reported that year. In contrast, Nielsen's release of its 1956 viewership report on September 19 generated much attention. Although average viewership in 1956 was only slightly less than in 1952, the word "tuneout" was a topic in many 1956 accounts.[57] The underlying theme, with TV now in two-thirds of U.S. homes, was that indifference had descended on a much larger cross section of the American public. Ninety percent of the nation's homes tuned to at least one convention session between August 13 and 23, but the average viewer saw only ten of the thirty-five convention hours telecast from Chicago and eight of the twenty hours from San Francisco.[58] *Newsweek*, summarizing findings of the Sindlinger and Trendex services a week before the Nielsen survey, reported that the number of sets in use had dropped to 27 percent the first day of the Democratic convention, from 46 percent the week before. The national radio audience had reached a ten-year high, and movie theaters had seen their best two weeks of the summer. In large cities independent stations enjoyed an influx of viewers.[59]

On the other hand, television had created some critical bright spots. Observers hailed the appearances by Kennedy. Having hosted the film and nominated Stevenson, Kennedy also delivered a gracious concession speech after losing the vice presidential nomination. Within weeks after Stevenson's loss to Eisenhower in November, Kennedy was at work on his 1960 campaign.[60] Brinkley was also recognized for his success in livening up the conventions while serving as an NBC anchor. Suggesting that Brinkley "quite possibly could be the forerunner of a new school of television commentator," Gould of the *New York Times* was fascinated by his humor, "on the dry side and rooted in a sense of relaxed detachment from all the political and electronic turmoil around him." According to Gould, Brinkley's teamwork with Chet Huntley gave NBC an edge over the galaxy of news personalities seen on CBS.[61] The ratings-conscious management at NBC agreed. That fall, the network fired Swayze as host of the evening news and made Huntley and Brinkley permanent dual anchors; they would top the television news ratings for most of the next fourteen years.

As politicians looked ahead to future conventions, their concerns did not match those of the 1956 critics. Eisenhower, for one, had been delighted with the outcome of his party's meeting in 1956.[62] Moreover, Republican planners had a much different interpretation of the ratings figures. Overall viewership may have seemed low, but Eisenhower's arrival in San Francisco was seen in 53 percent of the nation's homes. The GOP attracted 50 percent of the homes during its compressed nominations and another 51 percent during the acceptance ceremonies. Clearly, the GOP's advance planning around "big" events and the tactic of short speeches and lively, thematic organization could pay off. "It isn't just the speech that attracts attention to your candidate," GOP chairman Hall explained. "[I]t's the film of him leaving one airport, arriving at another, 20 miles of motorcade, an audience of 15,000 people shouting and cheering, and all the other added advantages [of television]."[63]

In addition to demonstrating an ability to generate large audiences at key time periods, perhaps more significant to the TV conventions' future was sentiment in 1956 that overall monotony was an end in itself. Lou Guylay, the GOP's public relations director at that time, spoke of the image of stability at the 1956 convention and in the campaign, which he called "the best organized in recent history."[64] Guylay's point was that incumbents seeking renomination, and clear front-runners in elections with no incumbents, benefited from convention tuneout. Tuneout reflected trust in the favored candidate and the expectation that there would be no change in the existing order.

Peter Dailey, the stage manager of Nixon's renomination in 1972, concurred with Guylay, emphasizing the importance of running a convention "with a degree of precision and organization that added to the impression that the President was a man who was able to . . . control the destiny of the country."[65]

The 1956 conventions had not produced the formula that would enable this control to be exerted on every occasion. The Democratic gatherings in 1968 and 1972 were landmark illustrations that the presence of television not only failed to ensure positive publicity but could also contribute to the tendency for events to get out of hand. Even the Republicans would discover this danger at their stormy meeting in 1964. Still, if not redefining the political convention, the 1956 Republican affair had at least redefined what the two parties wanted it to become. Ordered spectacle was now the standard.

The conventions marked the beginning of the 1956 fall campaign for the politicians, but not for network journalists. For TV reporters the big show was over. The television industry had neither the financial resources nor the technical mobility to cover the campaigns on a daily basis the way it had scoured the political world at the conventions.[66] Of the fifty journalists who traveled with Stevenson at the beginning of the fall campaign, only three were from television.[67]

Even so, the marriage of politics and television did not end, especially for Eisenhower. No longer limited by the needs of TV journalists, he advanced to a different field of television orchestration, in which he paid for the airtime and had complete control.

8

TELEVISION VERSUS THE NEW AMERICA, FALL 1956

The 1956 Eisenhower-Stevenson contest generated intense interest for about seven weeks of the eight-week campaign period; the election week itself was overshadowed by the Suez Canal crisis and the Hungarian uprising, which hit just days before the voting and determined Eisenhower's eighteen-point margin of victory. Voting research later showed that Eisenhower's use of the media during the official campaign, as elaborate as it was, made little difference. By the time the campaign began, according to these findings, a majority of voters were convinced Eisenhower was acting in their best interests.[1] The president validated this impression on the eve of the election by keeping the nation out of war—a decision that might have gone either way.

Yet the significance of 1950s politics continued to be the means, not the ends. Although largely unrecognized as such even at the time, 1956 was in many ways a defining moment in twentieth-century electioneering, marking both the point at which television was fully injected into the process and a major showdown between the video campaign and the system it replaced. On one level the campaign was a laboratory in paid political advertising; the Republicans revised concepts they had pioneered in 1952 and introduced the first "soft sell" devices, a standard feature in future elections. While the GOP was well equipped to advance this evolution of political spot announcements, and scholars would persist in studying them, 1956 offered even more profound insights as to how TV affected votes. Far more important than brief campaign spots had been the steady accumulation of positive impressions during the preceding three and a half years of Eisenhower's presidency. Early in the TV age the advantages of incumbents' daily visits in homes across the nation were obvious, especially if these incumbents could manage appealing images over a long haul.

Indeed, advancements in campaign ads in 1956 were important purely because they supported a more enduring lesson about television and its application by office seekers: the medium was there to be marshaled, not used with caprice. Television worked best when a political organization could think big but stay flexible; wire itself to the public pulse; keep money in reserve; trust its judgments; and commit to a media master plan, without panic, until the last day of the campaign. In the 1950s, television at the national level was tailor-made to the Republican style of campaigning. The same control exhibited in Eisenhower's campaigns was recognized in many Republican campaigns that followed; it was noted in the two victories of Richard Nixon (1968, 1972) and Ronald Reagan (1980, 1984) and to a lesser but definite extent in the defeat of Gerald Ford (1976), who initially trailed by thirty points in public opinion polls but then lost to Jimmy Carter by only a slim margin.

Eisenhower had not had as much control as he wanted in 1952 or 1954. In 1956, however, he demanded flexibility and precise organization as a condition of his entry into the race. Working in harness, White House advisers, researchers, press aides, fund-raisers, the national committee, and the ad agencies answered Eisenhower's call with heavy emphasis on TV. Satisfied and remarkably fit after two hospitalizations, Eisenhower decided to make several traveling appearances after all. When these travels were cut back because of the foreign hostilities, TV was still available to finish the campaign and, as it turned out, underscore his role as peacemaker in the crucial period just before the voting.

The result was the first truly national TV campaign, particularly noteworthy because the race was also a match between new and old politics. While Eisenhower left Washington eight times that fall, Stevenson wound up covering 75,000 miles in 1956, with up to half a dozen speeches in a single day. For the first time ever, Madison Avenue was pitted against itself, but with Eisenhower drawing from two agencies and ten times as many media specialists as the Democrats. Money constantly changed hands. Even after extracting discounts from the TV networks, the GOP spent more than $3 million on the medium, almost double its spending in 1952; the Democrats' $2.3 million was an increase of 130 percent.[2] In terms of media use and contrasting styles of the candidates, there had never been a campaign quite like it.

By summer's end, opinion research had given the GOP a green light for its electronic strategy. Voters did wonder about Eisenhower's health.[3] Yet the nation was calm and prosperous; if the public wanted anything, it was someone in Washington to worry about the Russians and assure increasing personal comfort. Eisenhower was that person. Furthermore, evidence continued to indicate that TV would be important; for the first time, according to one BBDO study, a majority of voters would be basing their decisions primarily on information that came from television.[4]

A "big vote premise" and an effort to draw new members into the party were the main provisions of the official GOP campaign plan. The document spoke of individuals, namely Eisenhower, who were "welcomed visitors in almost 100 percent of the living rooms of America. . . . [The] vital importance of television in the 1956 campaign is readily indicated by tracing its remarkably swift expansion," it said; accordingly, "[t]his campaign plan calls for maximum utilization of television during the stretch drive. . . . It breaks completely with past experience by placing first importance on effective use of the television instead of the traditional emphasis on personal appearances." For the first time, "employment of television, instead of personal appearances, [is] the principal approach."[5]

David Levy, at age forty-three a sixteen-year veteran at Young and Rubicam and vice president of its television department, felt that a new vision in political TV was needed to help Eisenhower and the party. Levy had served in the military during World War II and was one of the first Madison Avenue figures ever to work with Eisenhower. Through Sig Larmon, Levy stayed in contact with Eisenhower during his tenure at Columbia University and was part of Citizens for Eisenhower in 1952. Only days after Larmon enlisted Young and Rubicam in the 1956 campaign, he named Levy as television supervisor.[6]

Armed with research, Levy decided that the creative focus of the campaign would diverge sharply from the 1952 path. The first campaign had relied on speeches—a problematic strategy, because Eisenhower liked to list programs and philosophies point by point, sometimes listing more than a dozen points at a time. Levy accepted this Eisenhower trait much as TV adviser Robert Montgomery had accepted other Eisenhower idiosyncrasies. Levy was determined, though, to sift Eisenhower's rhetoric into something better adapted to TV's emotional theater.[7] Early in the year, after analyzing a major speech that outlined eight principles of leadership, Levy devised catch words, such as "integrity," "honesty," "peace," and "prosperity." "I wonder if we might not think of the eight principles as Eight Signposts on the Eisenhower Road. You can see the visual application of this for posters, advertisements, television and the like," Levy proposed. Later the "signposts" were abandoned and Levy sought to promote the leadership principles more simply as the "Eisenhower Eight." Finally the eight principles were reduced to three: "peace, prosperity, and progress," the slogan of the 1956 Eisenhower campaign.[8]

Because speeches were difficult to reduce in this way, Levy and others wanted to deemphasize them. They succeeded, too; a final tally at the end of 1956 showed that Eisenhower had made only fourteen formal speeches the entire year.[9] Some oratorical drone was inevitable, because the GOP was committed to several half-hour rallies, the remote "spectaculars" that Hall had used to persuade Eisenhower into the race. Attempts to dress speeches up by reducing their length and highlighting crowd reactions had proved effective in 1952; these methods were stressed even more in 1956.

But to Levy, even a dressed-up televised speech seemed backward. He felt interest and emotion could be pushed to the furthest extreme by film production, a standard format in entertainment TV but mostly untapped in politics. Levy wanted entire programs done on film; in July 1956, he dispatched camera crews to the White House and other locations and had aides stockpile an assortment of file footage.[10] Film was more expensive than live TV, but money was no obstacle.

Film had been used during 1952 in the appeals produced by Rosser Reeves, a creative specialist loaned to BBDO by the Ted Bates Agency. Reeves was known for ad campaigns that repeated, often to the point of distraction, a "unique selling proposition." Reeves's goal had been to drill into the public's mind the failings of the Truman administration. To achieve this effect, he had Eisenhower record a series of carefully worded "answers" by reading off cue cards; Reeves filmed forty of these answers in one sitting, then hired some average-looking citizens to record the "questions" at a different sitting. The questions and answers were then spliced together.[11] Known as "Eisenhower Answers America," these productions made an impression on the public and helped humanize Eisenhower. By 1956, though, there were few White House disciples of Reeves's contrived hard-sell ads. According to Levy, Eisenhower would never have allowed himself to be used in such appeals again in 1956. These ads did not transmit the "genuine" Eisenhower, including his smile and friendly personality. In addition, a hard sell was not a good way to achieve one goal of the GOP media work—dispersing the health issue. Much the way political advertiser Tony Schwartz described his "responsive chord" concept two decades later, Levy surmised that hundreds of written words about Eisenhower's good health were far less effective than a single televised scene with the same message, such as a picture of Eisenhower working, playing, moving, walking, or smiling. "We were not writing the Gettysburg Address," Levy recalled. "Eisenhower was a natural, and he had charm. This is what impressed people when he was on TV."[12]

Assisting Levy at Young and Rubicam were talent coordinators Mildred Fox and Walter Bunker. They headed a "star committee," an offshoot of Levy's "Ed Sullivan project." Sullivan, whose Sunday night variety show was the third highest rated program on television, was Levy's choice to emcee a star-studded election eve gala. To get him to accept, Levy urged assistants "to impress upon Mr. Sullivan that very high personages [among them the president] are desirous of having him participate"; if Sullivan refused, Levy agreed to use Bob Hope or William Holden as an alternate.[13] The star committee compiled a list of eighty-five entertainers and popular figures; forty-seven agreed to work for Eisenhower in public capacities. Many had also helped Eisenhower in 1952. Among those who appeared in 1956 were James Cagney, Nat (King) Cole, Irene Dunne, Eddie Fisher, Helen Hayes, Howard Keel, Gordon McCrea, Jane Powell, and James Stewart.[14]

Eisenhower was apprised of these activities through Larmon; not only did he like the inventiveness, he even added what he thought was a clever idea of his own. On September 19, using a film projector in the Oval Office, Larmon and Levy screened some rough-cut appeals, in which Eisenhower saw scenes of college students, blue-collar workers, and black leaders. After viewing a segment that featured housewives, Eisenhower suggested a spot that focused solely on his wife Mamie and her duties as First Lady. He reasoned that millions of people would quickly connect this ad to Stevenson's 1949 divorce from his wife. Eisenhower did not know that Levy had already sketched a "Mamie" spot that had been rejected by Larmon, who felt it was in bad taste. After the meeting, though, Larmon and Levy returned to Madison Avenue and began a "Mamie project" at Young and Rubicam. It did not matter that the First Lady declined to take part directly; newsreel footage of her was used instead.[15]

A few blocks up Madison Avenue, BBDO media plans were resembling those of Young and Rubicam in their heavy emphasis on informality, feeling, and emotion. The BBDO staff had read the research also and knew the only trouble spot was Eisenhower's questionable health. In a Gallup poll on August 24, for example, only 58 percent of the respondents who intended to vote for Eisenhower felt he was physically able to execute his duties. In submitting his plans to the White House, BBDO president Ben Duffy felt it imperative that Eisenhower be shown moving about and spontaneously interacting with crowds. During the auditorium rallies, BBDO insisted that Eisenhower walk slowly to the main stage, stop, and talk to people; floor directors would make sure there was continuous applause while Eisenhower made his entrances and exits. "The whole idea here is to bring the President's communications a little closer to the public. It would give the viewers a more informal picture of the President [because] when he is doing this, he is at his best."[16]

The Republican plans moved ahead, but an annoyance began in September, when Tennessee senator Albert Gore decided that his Subcommittee on Privileges and Elections would investigate party finances concurrent with the campaign. To the GOP it looked like a political trick, another Democratic attempt to draw attention to Eisenhower's media extravagance. Leonard Hall and Paul Butler, the two party chairs, were the first witnesses when hearings began on September 10; sure enough, there was a ripple in the press when it was revealed that the Republicans had cash reserves of $647,000, compared to $35,000 for the Democrats.[17]

What the Republicans most feared was the disclosure of something the Gore Committee apparently never unearthed: a money transfer scheme ensuring that the GOP would not exceed the campaign spending limits imposed by the 1940 Hatch Act. Apprehensions peaked when BBDO's Carroll Newton was summoned to Washington to explain reports that the agency's television spending was above the $3 million allowed for a single committee. BBDO was actually paid from the bank accounts of several committees legally indepen-dent of the RNC; yet the arrangement looked questionable and could easily reinforce Stevenson's charge that Eisenhower was a pawn of the wealthy. The night before Newton appeared, Hall outlined the dilemma to Nebraska senator Carl Curtis, the ranking Republican on the committee.

The next day, October 8, the Republicans got past the problem not through public relations legwork but through their good luck. Newton was the leadoff witness when the hearings opened at 11 A.M.; Curtis stalled by asking him general questions about the TV industry. The first part of Newton's testimony lasted only an hour before the com-mittee recessed to watch game five of the World Series between the New York Yankees and the Brooklyn Dodgers, when Yankee pitcher Don Larsen threw the only perfect game in Series history. After seeing that, the Democrats returned to the hearing room in no mood to grill Newton, and they also wanted to hear from their own witness, Eugene Kummel, who had also been brought down from New York to testify. Thus, the matter was buried.[18]

Kummel, who had been hired by the Democratic National Commit-tee, was not in a position to tell the senators very much. He never did confer with Stevenson, who by the time of the hearings had comman-deered DNC office space in Washington before beginning a whirlwind schedule of speaking tours.[19] Butler, who had enlisted Kummel's ad agency and put millions of dollars of mass media work into motion, yielded all control to Stevenson's Jim Finnegan and was left with the mundane tasks: leaflet distribution, mail communication, and promo-tion of the national television appeals.

Even so, most hailed the Stevenson campaign organization as more formidable than in 1952. John Kenneth Galbraith provided guidance on economic matters, while former ambassador George Kennan and former Air Force secretary Thomas Finletter assisted in foreign policy and military affairs. Harvard historian Arthur Schlesinger, Jr., Ober-lin president John Tufts, and journalist John Bartlow Martin formed the core of Stevenson's speechwriting staff. Most of the major cam-paign decisions were made by the traveling staff, which was headed by Willard Wirtz and included Newton Minow and William McCormick Blair, law partners of the candidate.[20]

Stevenson's media staff, though, generated curiosity. When Clayton Fritchey crossed over from the DNC to become press secretary, the

New York Times said the move "emphasized what had been a major weakness of the Stevenson campaign this year as in 1952"—that "Mr. Stevenson's press secretaries have not enjoyed full rapport with the candidate." Fritchey had reported for the *Cleveland Press* and the *New Orleans Item* and had contributed to WDSU TV and radio, stations owned by the New Orleans paper, leaving little uncertainty about his solid media background.[21]

The same could not be said of George Ball, Stevenson's choice as public relations coordinator. The forty-seven-year-old Ball, later an under secretary of state and U.N. ambassador in the Kennedy and Johnson administrations, had known Stevenson during World War II; they grew extremely close after Stevenson became governor of Illinois. Ball had headed the Volunteers for Stevenson group in 1952 but had had little contact with the media. He traveled with Stevenson so extensively during the 1956 primaries that many were surprised when the candidate assigned him to a desk job that fall. Ball himself felt his appointment as public relations director was illogical, although he agreed to help his friend and "learn on the job."[22] Ball had a mild reputation, inside the organization and out, as a television pundit. It was Ball who created many of the phrases that Stevenson used to condemn Eisenhower's advertising tactics, including the "cornflakes" comparison.[23] At first Ball played down the media in Stevenson's second try against Eisenhower. "The most accepted theory of 1956 is that television is the magic key to the coming campaign and that the election will be won or lost on the airwaves," Ball asserted. "The facts bear out the claim that television has added a potent dimension to campaigning, but, at best, it is an important supplement rather than a substitute for everything else."[24]

That a person who criticized political public relations and bad-mouthed television would end up supervising the operations of Norman, Craig and Kummel was an irony symbolic of Democratic affairs in 1956. The relations that later developed, beginning with Ball's first contact with Kummel shortly after the convention, were unexpectedly warm and productive.[25] Still, though, Ball could not avert what Butler had feared the previous spring: a hybrid Stevenson campaign divided between the candidate's serious personal agenda and Norman, Craig and Kummel's polished television appeals aimed at selling Stevenson as an alternative to Eisenhower.[26]

In early September, as Ball worked closely with the agency, Stevenson was on the campaign trail hundreds of miles from Washington.

The candidate had already crisscrossed the country before his official kickoff, timed for TV, on September 13 in Harrisburg, Pennsylvania. Ball was unsure whether Stevenson even knew about the television planning.[27] Everyone knew, however, that Pennsylvania was of strategic importance, trailing only New York in electoral strength, with its capital both a base of Democratic blue-collar support and a center for many farmers who were mad at Eisenhower. With research indicating that millions of voters would choose between Eisenhower and Stevenson at the beginning of the campaign, the Democrats used 10 percent of their entire 1956 television budget, around $200,000, to televise the Harrisburg rally on all three networks.[28]

As the Stevenson entourage arrived, the reception was so enthusiastic that little attention was paid to problems in the auditorium. Because of bad weather, the NBC crew assigned to the broadcast arrived late. After lights were hurriedly installed, technicians found they were insufficient to illuminate the speaker's stand. To compensate, outriggers that supported the two teleprompters were swiveled a few feet to each side so they would not darken the picture. Then it became evident that the ventilation system was not adequate to cool the platform because of heat from the lights. As this discovery was made, word also came that Stevenson was not sure whether he wanted to be introduced by Estes Kefauver, the vice presidential candidate, or by Pennsylvania governor George Leader. This last problem fell into the lap of Bill Wilson, Stevenson's twenty-five-year-old media consultant, who had seen the candidate disregard TV plans many times during the primaries. Wilson scrambled to devise and circulate a contingency lineup. The new task diverted Wilson's attention from his checklist; as a result he was unaware that crowd microphones had not been installed. Stevenson followed the original plan on speakers but decided to make his entrance in the hall forty-five minutes early in order to have more time to chat with local dignitaries already assembling.[29]

That night viewers saw a scene that looked like the Chicago convention, a packed auditorium with signs and banners. But though Stevenson was already on stage, there was no spontaneous opening demonstration, but rather an odd-looking welcome in which many spectators waved to the cameras. Applause was almost inaudible. Stevenson delivered an assault on Eisenhower that culminated in his outline for "The New America." As he spoke, his head darted from left to right because of the extreme positioning of the teleprompters, and he uncharacteristically stumbled numerous times. At one point viewers heard Stevenson stutter, "The tide, the tide, the rising tide"; and just as he began an attack on Nixon, Stevenson had to stop so he could pull a handkerchief out of his vest pocket and wipe perspiration from his forehead. Even though he had a reputation for speaking past allotted times, Stevenson finished this speech five minutes early. The rest of the half hour was filled with more muffled applause and scenes of spectators reacting to the cameras instead of to Stevenson. A surprised announcer had to ad-lib a long request for viewers to send money to the "Stevenson victory fund."[30]

Backstage, Stevenson was furious and launched into a tirade about the "damn lights"; Blair and some of the others had to cool him down.[31] Wilson had been his main target. The young TV adviser grumbled later that a large share of the difficulties that night were created by Stevenson himself, because for months he had refused to familiarize himself with teleprompters and had kept television co-ordinators guessing until airtime.[32] Wilson explained this situation, in his mind to no avail, when he and Kummel were summoned to Washington to reconstruct the mess before Finnegan, the campaign manager.[33]

Although the campaign was just beginning, Stevenson's Harrisburg speech endured as one of the great fiascos of early political television. In the 1950s politicians remembered it alongside Eisenhower's Abilene telecast in 1952 until both were topped by Richard Nixon's poor showing in the first presidential debate of 1960. Many factors beyond Stevenson's control conspired against him, as did some he conceded were his own fault; he told author Gerald Johnson, "The whole thing was a frightful failure."[34] *New York Times* writer James Reston, a friend of Stevenson's, embarrassed the candidate with a harsh critique of the telecast, noting that "he even mispronounced the name of his running mate."[35]

The Republicans liked what they were seeing. Young and Rubicam workers in New York took turns monitoring the Democratic broadcasts, and their reports sometimes sported a comical tone. One report detailed Stevenson's troubled Harrisburg speech, and another dealt with the premier episode of "The Man from Libertyville" on September 24. A summary of the first "Libertyville" segment picked up on the Democrats' attempt to personalize their man, but noted that Stevenson's air of informality lapsed into long-winded "straight talk directed at the viewer. His remarks were of a rambling nature." After a "Libertyville" segment on September 29, Young and Rubicam spotted more bad technique as Stevenson delivered another long and serious speech, this time in a business suit "with a large bag of groceries in his hand."[36]

On September 28 the Republicans and millions of other Americans saw a nationally televised speech in which Stevenson proposed more federal aid to education but missed his time cues and composed a hasty conclusion about the importance of American mothers. Blair recalled "wild signals." "They would hold up all sorts of things in front showing you had eight seconds to go, and time and time again Stevenson said he didn't even see them."[37] It may have been that Stevenson did not want to see the signals because he was too wound up in the content of his speeches. He spent countless hours "beavering" or revising drafts of his speeches, leaving Fritchey beset by reporters' complaints that the speeches did not match advance texts.[38] Professor Russell Windes later studied fifteen of the speeches and found that the candidate alone had made 976 changes.[39] Actually, it was not uncommon for the first TV-age politicians to exceed these strict time limits; Nixon had done so in his "Checkers" speech. Yet this problem never plagued Eisenhower.

Nor did Eisenhower battle, like Stevenson, the tricks and gimmicks designed to shape a "leader of the people" persona. According to Schlesinger, Stevenson had wanted this reputation but "felt the kinds of things he was asked to do were false."[40] Many examples came during a series of northeastern stops in early October, added to Stevenson's schedule in order to gain free news coverage in New York. He appeared at the second Yankees-Dodgers World Series game at Ebbets Field, but refused to circle the field in an open automobile, as Eisenhower had done in game one, and thus got less notice. Stevenson's advisers, wanting to tease out his wit and informality, arranged an appearance on NBC's "Today Show"; they were astounded when the candidate showed up in the green room with notecards intending to make a speech from the interview set.[41] Stevenson was even slated to be the "mystery guest" on the popular CBS "What's My Line" program; advisers at the New York Democratic Committee, including media supervisor Mel Helitzer, had toiled for days in sculpting this CBS appearance, and they envisioned a deluxe occasion for convincing the public their candidate was wholly able to mix serious themes with charm and self-deprecating humor. Several people on Stevenson's traveling staff liked the plan and persuaded Stevenson to agree to it, only to see him cancel the day of the show.[42]

Immediately after this aborted appearance, Democratic fund-raising stalled and the party treasury dropped again to almost zero. To keep Stevenson's traveling campaign afloat, all of the party's day-time spots after October 15 were canceled.[43] The most painful scene came on October 18, when a closed-circuit TV fund-raising dinner, set for two nights later, was eliminated for lack of funds. The party had promoted the event heavily; the same day it was scrubbed a news release had gone out describing advanced interactive TV and the covey of celebrities expected to attend, including Orson Welles, Oscar Hammerstein, Mitch Miller, and Marlon Brando.[44] By late October so many telecasts had been canceled that many media advisers were sitting around with nothing to do.[45]

Eisenhower, counting on victory while concentrating on events abroad, had been willing to let his TV strategy unfold as planned. But a Stevenson TV broadcast on September 25 suddenly made the president eager to exceed the eight- to ten-point margin of victory indicated in the polls. That night, while attacking the administration's foreign policy, Stevenson had incorrectly stated that Eisenhower had loaned millions of dollars to Argentine dictator Juan Perón. Perón did get U.S. loans, but all of them were approved by President Truman. The vindictive side of Eisenhower blasted forth. He regarded this statement as a calculated TV "mistake" that could not puncture his image so much as heap disgrace on his brother Milton, a Latin American affairs adviser. Even though Stevenson never repeated the charge, Eisenhower would not forgive him.[46] Once content with a respectable victory, Eisenhower now wanted a rout. "[U]nless I win by a comfort-able majority," Eisenhower wrote Swede Hazlett, "I would not want to be elected at all." He added that "the Stevenson-Kefauver combi-nation is . . . about the sorriest and weakest we have ever had run for the two top offices in the land."[47] Soon after Stevenson's speech on Perón, the White House announced several previously unscheduled road appearances, including a three-day trip to the West Coast. The tours provided more media opportunities; they had headline value in the press, and BBDO staged two additional remote telecasts.

Moreover, Eisenhower's anger at Stevenson inspired more dialogue between the president and his aides as to how the media could be used. Eisenhower was contemplating a TV tactic that might, he be-lieved, go a long way toward decimating his opponent. It pertained to Stevenson's pronouncements on foreign policy, particularly his call for a nuclear test-ban treaty with the USSR. While Nixon and other surrogate GOP campaigners attacked the treaty idea as absurd, Eisen-hower had so far let Stevenson have his way; at an October 11 news conference, the president dodged comment on the treaty.[48] Indeed, the candidates's own advisers had pled that Stevenson stick with The New America and stay out of foreign affairs, because the public knew them as Eisenhower's domain; with world tensions heating, the treaty was especially ill-timed. Eisenhower kept silent because he believed Stevenson's venture into foreign policy would self-destruct. Finally, in mid-October, after hearing that the Democrats planned to put Stevenson on TV to discuss the H-bomb treaty, Eisenhower was ready to speed up the process. He had his staff draft a speech that implied merit to a test ban but in a way that made Stevenson seem an ap-peaser of the Soviets and uninformed in matters pertaining to Cold War defense.[49]

Eisenhower preferred not to deliver this speech. Instead, he wanted to pursue a test-ban treaty after the election; and his wish was fulfilled, in part because Stevenson's attempt with the H-bomb issue on Octo-ber 15 was another TV flop. This broadcast was so important to the Democrats that they sacrificed a scheduled TV fund-raising program featuring John Kennedy in order to free up a network time slot. They also convinced Stevenson to appear in a talk-show setting, hoping that an informal telecast would better reduce the horrors of nuclear war to gut-level terms. Yet viewers saw Stevenson glance quizzically around the studio for floor cues and seldom make eye contact with the camera. Little of his emotion or concern was evident, and again there were timing problems. According to Nielsen data, two-thirds of the TV audience turned him off before the telecast concluded.[50] Eisenhower learned of this tuneout in a BBDO tracking report in-dicating that voters still did not know what the terms "test ban" and "moratorium" really meant.[51] Delighted with this news from BBDO, Eisenhower kept his response locked in his desk.

It did not hurt the GOP that Stevenson's communicative lapses made news in the press and that Eisenhower was the yardstick by which he was compared. Columnist Drew Pearson noted on Octo-ber 10 that "Mr. Stevenson's campaign managers route him on a hand-shaking tour of a supermarket where he can greet at most 900 people, but don't give him enough time to rehearse for television where he greets nine million people." In Pearson's estimation Stevenson needed somebody like Eisenhower's Robert Montgomery. Pearson said the candidate "failed to come through as a person over TV as effectively as he did in 1952."[52] *New York Times* TV critic Jack Gould agreed. "The qualities of idealism and inspiration that were detected by his partisans in 1952 have not been as evident in this campaign," Gould wrote. "He has seemed remote and frequently ill at ease; his sense of timing has been very poor."[53] Some network news personalities had tried to coach Stevenson, including Edward Murrow, Walter Cronkite, and Eric Sevareid of CBS, and John Daly, ABC news anchor and the host of "What's My Line."[54] "I thought Murrow was the one person Stevenson would respond to," related Ball. "[But] Adlai sort of resented the exercise."[55]

Besides providing a negative comparison for Stevenson's TV image, Eisenhower's well-ordered media operations were indirectly disposing of Stevenson's primary message. The heart of Stevenson's New America was domestic policy; he was certain his plan would prompt the nation to remember the Democratic party's reputation as the champion of prosperity and progress. The New America thus included health insurance for senior citizens, expanded aid to education, resource conservation, and urban renewal. It tried to convince voters that Eisenhower had done little more than drift with the flow of New Deal liberalism; the administration's Social Security reform, minimum wage, and Department of Health, Education, and Welfare were essentially Democratic visions; so was Eisenhower's Interstate highway project, the largest public works undertaking ever, approved in June by a Democratic Congress. Stevenson produced hundreds of position statements and white papers that cast Eisenhower as a pretender to a Democratic party cause.[56] Still, in the mid-1950s it was hard for Americans to heed such a charge when they saw with their own eyes, on Republican TV programs, blue-collar families in nice homes with new automobiles that sped down four-lane superhighways.

Stevenson did have one wedge he could more realistically drive between himself and the GOP's alleged theft of New Deal prosperity: Eisenhower's close association with big business. But again Stevenson's assaults on the "millionaires" in Eisenhower's cabinet got him nowhere. The matter hardly seemed urgent, when the working classes had a media-promoted mental image of high and rising standards of living. Moreover, BBDO put many of the cabinet members on TV in a series of five-minute appeals called "You and Your Government." These appeals used the trusty fireside chat format; through the informality viewers could see that Eisenhower's cabinet members were not the insensitive, opportunistic capitalists Stevenson made them out to be.

Some of Stevenson's own campaign workers understood the impact of Eisenhower's communications as well as anyone at the time. Walter O'Meara, one of the top New York advertising figures who had volunteered his services to the Democrats, complained to Ball in early October that the more Stevenson talked, the more Eisenhower emerged as the "man of peace."[57] When the blitz of GOP TV appeals hit the air late in the campaign, Wilson recalled watching them in dejected fascination.[58] Wilson's sentiment was echoed at Stevenson headquarters in Washington. One adviser told Ball after an Eisenhower TV special from Pittsburgh that "the president responded beautifully to the adulation of the crowd," that he "grinned and waved and had a fine time looking the very essence of a vigorous leader. . . . It was impossible not to be impressed with the excitement he produced." This note concluded sarcastically, "God bless Robert Montgomery."[59]

Almost everything in Eisenhower's public dialogue, campaign or otherwise, boiled down to the mnemonic phrase "I Like Ike." It is uncertain who coined "I Like Ike"; the slogan had been synonymous with the Citizens for Eisenhower movement in 1952. "I Like Ike" may have revealed nothing about programs, policies, and ideas, but it was an advertiser's delight. While Stevenson produced a torrent of words, "I Like Ike" said everything for the Republicans; it was simple and had emotional value. The GOP used it incessantly in 1956: in direct mailings; on hundreds of thousands of red, white, and blue campaign buttons; in traveling "bandwagons" that showed up at Eisenhower's campaign stops; and especially in the television appeals.

Young and Rubicam's advertisements for the GOP exploited the simplicity of "I Like Ike"; they seldom showed Eisenhower speaking on camera. Average Americans who liked the president got the message across instead. One appeal featured a lively scene at a university campus, with hearty pro-Eisenhower reactions both from teenagers and from veterans attending college on the G.I. Bill. Notre Dame football coach Frank Leahy proudly appeared and summed it up by calling Ike "an experienced quarterback."[60] Very similar in concept was the eventual "Mamie" spot, which showed a woman at home, tending her family, then moved to the White House and the First Lady. A female voice announced, "Women will decide the election, and they like Ike. . . . and here's something else they like—Ike's be-loved Mamie."[61]

More subtle and emotional was a dramatization that featured a Washington, D.C., taxi driver walking his dog at night in Lafayette Park. Pausing by a lamppost, the cabbie spied a single lighted window across the street at the White House and soliloquized, "A neighbor of mine lives there. Yep, Dwight Eisenhower, a man with the most important job in the world. What do you suppose he's doing tonight?" As portentous music swelled, a narrated film montage took viewers to a school, a farm, and, finally, to troops in the Middle East. The cab driver reappeared and concluded, "I need him, don't you?"[62] More direct was a stock tag line on each production: an appeal to "all thinking voters regardless of party." This tag reminded viewers that "I Like Ike" also meant Modern Republicanism.

Another device was a half-hour travelogue, which Levy had conceived as a "swiftly moving cavalcade of the four years," showing such things as "the comeback of Judy Garland, a Mickey Mantle home run and Mary Martin as Peter Pan." This telecast had elements of both the movie *Knute Rockne—All American* and an episode of the World War II documentary series "Victory at Sea," then popular on TV.[63] After plumbing the depths of the stalemate in Korea and the corruption in the Truman administration, the film rose to a swell, with excited narration, loud background music, and spinning newspapers, to herald Eisenhower's election in 1952. His successive achievements were treated with similar flourishes. Happy soldiers home from the Korean War embraced their wives, a scene that looked every bit as momentous as the end of World War II. They returned to new highways, cures for dreaded diseases such as polio, and weekend football games.[64]

Other programs did include Eisenhower. On October 12 a "people's news conference" was telecast over NBC, preempting "The Big Story." One hundred participants from around the country were flown to Washington and invited to ask the president questions; Eisenhower called on them much as he fielded questions from real reporters on TV. The show was not genuinely "random," though, because participants were handpicked by the national committee and had rehearsed questions before the show with Hagerty and Montgomery, who in turn told the president exactly what to expect.[65] On cue, Eisenhower welcomed "Democrats and independents," made an opening statement on the Middle East, and looked almost dazed as each question was prefaced by a long, glowing testimonial. "There are things going out over the air," he chimed in, "that warm my heart."[66] Though this period in his administration was marred by setbacks abroad, Eisenhower was exuberant. Peter Lisagor wrote in the *Chicago Daily News*, "President Eisenhower look[ed] as pleased as a kid at a candy counter," while Russell Baker of the *New York Times* commented, "The President's answers seemed as spontaneous as they normally do in his regular news conferences." Eisenhower congratulated Young and Rubicam and passed along a sheaf of commendatory telegrams.[67]

On October 24 Duffy's agency carried the concept further by holding a White House "coffee klatsch" that featured Eisenhower and several women. The program did not have all of the informal effects that BBDO wanted: Eisenhower insisted on standing during the entire half hour, and the First Lady would not appear. Yet it got a respectable afternoon audience of over a million homes by preempting the CBS quiz show "The Big Payoff."[68]

There were other innovations as well. The night after the people's news conference, BBDO celebrated Eisenhower's sixty-sixth birthday with a TV party at Washington's Statler Hotel. Actor James Stewart hosted the affair, which reminded *New York Times* critic Gould of "This Is Your Life."[69] Near the conclusion Helen Hayes and Irene Dunne cut a cake baked according to "Mamie's own recipe," and a large piece was delivered to the president, who watched the show with the First Family at the White House.[70] Eisenhower loved the originality. Never before had the public seen serious national leaders associated to this extent with familiar, everyday situations; the offbeat nature of these programs found its way to the heart of middle America. After his years with Eisenhower, Levy would carry the offbeat effect further and distinguish himself in the entertainment field as creator-producer of several popular TV series, including "The Addams Family" and "The Pruitts of Southampton."

But the innovative programs were too much for George Ball, who in mid-October went before the Women's National Democratic Club and tore into these Republican television tactics. "During the last two weeks," he said, "I've been developing a bad case of television eye. It's been a great fortnight for the soap business." After ridiculing the people's news conference and the birthday party, Ball insisted the Republicans had substituted "a cult of personality for an earnest debate on the great issues of our times." Ball exclaimed, "[Some people] like Elvis Presley, and I like Marilyn Monroe, but I doubt that is sufficient reason for electing either [as] president."[71]

In fact, Presley may have been on Ball's mind for an interesting reason. Ball had just seen an appeal sketched by Claude Traverse, a producer on loan from NBC, that dissected the images made by BBDO and Young and Rubicam and cautioned voters against emotional involvement in the theatrics. The ad was to have Orson Welles, Henry Fonda, Bette Davis, and other entertainers loyal to the party team up for a course in Hollywood staging techniques. At the end Presley would appear and plead, "I'm young and I admit to knowing very little about politics—some say I know very little about singing. . . . [But] from what I've learned in a short time about advertising and promotion, I certainly would hate to see us make the mistake of choosing a president on the basis of a popularity contest." [72]

The Democrats could not afford to put Presley on the air and have him take a swing at Eisenhower. The timing also would have been very bad, because the Suez and Hungarian crises finally peaked in late October. Americans learned on October 24 that thousands of Soviet troops, with tanks and artillery, were rolling into Hungary to crush the revolution; thousands of Hungarians were killed, and streams of others fled to the West. Meanwhile, there was news of massive troop movements in Israel.

Administration maneuvers at the U.N. foundered, helping Stevenson for a time. On October 26 the Gallup poll showed that Eisenhower's lead had dropped from twelve points two weeks before to ten points (51–41); in the West Central and Far West regions Stevenson had sliced Eisenhower's margin to six points, close to the margin of error. A Burns W. Roper poll released October 29 showed that Stevenson trailed the president by nine points nationwide, at 52–43. The same day, an estimated 100,000 people, Stevenson's largest crowd of the year, turned out in Boston to greet him; receptions the previous day in California had been equally enthusiastic. Eisenhower was unmoved, though. Maintaining that he was more engrossed in his foreign diplomacy than in Stevenson's small gains, he refused to alter his homestretch campaign schedule, which consisted of nighttime TV broadcasts and some one-day airport stops. Remaining travels included an October 29 visit to Florida and Virginia; an October 31 excursion to Texas, Oklahoma, and Tennessee; and a tour of New England on November 5, the day before the election.

Nevertheless, before Eisenhower had completed his first trip, he received news that gave the campaign a final twist and cleared the way for a television conclusion to his first term. As the presidential plane *Columbine* hopped between Miami, Jacksonville, and Richmond on October 29, the onboard teletype machine spewed State Department intelligence about a massive Israeli thrust into Egypt. Eisenhower and his staff could barely believe this news, because all along they had expected Israel to attack Jordan. The move on Egypt was a certain signal that Great Britain and France were about to invade the Suez Canal; Egypt's seizure of the canal from these two countries in July had precipitated the crisis. Indeed, British and French troops poured into the region less than forty-eight hours later. Fears were compounded by rumors that the Soviet Union was going to ship troops to the canal to help Egypt defend it. Returning to Washington that day, Eisenhower ordered that all of his remaining road appearances, except for a BBDO telecast in Philadelphia on November 1, be canceled. Most of what was left of his campaign would be carried out on television.

The Hungarians pleaded for assistance, as did the Israelis, while the French and British were furious at Eisenhower, first for his failure to support them and then for making them back off. In his memoirs Eisenhower admitted he had placed himself in an "anomalous situation" by siding with the Soviet Union against U.S. allies in the Middle East, with the opposite alignments in the Hungarian crisis. Several anxious Republicans told Eisenhower that for the first time ever, they felt he might not win reelection.[73] These were rash predictions; Eisenhower did not rethink his decision against deploying troops.

This situation set up a media climax to the campaign—a television "duel" between Eisenhower and Stevenson on the nights of October 31 and November 1. On the morning of the thirty-first, Hagerty ordered airtime for a presidential address; the president delivered a fifteen-minute speech at 7 P.M. Eastern time and, following Montgomery's cues, reiterated what was already known: there would be no U.S. military involvement either in Egypt or Hungary, no special session of Congress, and a continuation of efforts at the U.N.[74]

Then, in one of the most confusing episodes in early political TV, the Stevenson organization requested and received equal time. Minow, who had watched Eisenhower's speech from Washington, flew to Pittsburgh that night to meet Stevenson. The candidate was tired and reluctant to make another TV appearance, but Minow was adamant. He felt that Eisenhower had left himself vulnerable to an equal time request by perking the ears of the electorate and not saying anything new. Because the party was limping along with little money, the prospect of free saturation coverage five days before the election had magnetic attraction.

With Minow in a Pittsburgh hotel room and Ball and Finnegan in Washington, party officials worked until early morning contacting network executives and FCC officials by phone. At first the networks said they would not comply unless the FCC amended the equal time rule in a way that would protect them from similar requests by a dozen minor-party candidates; commissioners agreed to consider the matter at an emergency meeting the next day.[75] Nothing was decided. The networks, under pressure, now had to act without FCC guidance. As Stevenson traveled from Pittsburgh to Buffalo on November 1, he got word that one by one, each network had consented to give him equal time and that a broadcast was being arranged for 7 P.M. that night. Angry Republicans filed their own equal time request; it was refused, though, the day before the election, when the FCC reconsidered the whole affair and told the networks they were in error in helping Stevenson.[76]

Voters, knowing little of this, were interested only in Stevenson's response to Eisenhower's address the night before. Speaking from WBEN in Buffalo, Stevenson failed to answer the salient question of the hour: whether he would have sent American military forces to either trouble spot. Television, an image medium, was ideal for conveying a simple "yes" or "no"; but instead, Stevenson reviewed past events and concluded, "[T]here are many things which might have been done."[77] Besides the question of military involvement, Americans wanted to see someone who looked like a leader. They saw instead a tense Stevenson in another unprofessional studio appearance. Harrison Salisbury of the *New York Times* reported that Stevenson, who had campaigned all day, arrived at the studio six minutes before airtime with his speech half-completed.[78] Minow later confirmed this report; he blamed it on the short notice and the fact that Stevenson did not know officially that the airtime had been granted until two hours before he spoke. Minow also recalled that this affair was the beginning of his personal interest in television, which led to his chairmanship of the FCC under John Kennedy. From this position, for other reasons, he would refer to the medium as a "vast wasteland."[79]

Viewership, though not spectacular, was sizable; audience estimates were complicated, because 7:00–7:15 P.M. was not technically defined as prime time in 1956. Nielsen did show an influx of viewers at 7:15 on both October 31 and November 1, with the combined three-network audience representing close to 30 percent of the nation's homes. These figures suggested that millions saw part of Eisenhower's address on October 31 and Stevenson's response the following night. Blair felt the Buffalo broadcast was the end for Stevenson.[80] Based on the substance of the Eisenhower and Stevenson addresses, even the *Washington Post*, friendly to Stevenson, seemed to agree. "Adlai Stevenson stated the essential consideration well," the editors stated, but they still perceived a "need for leadership."[81] In a *New York Times* article, reporters analyzed the two speeches and concluded that the crisis would "help the President more than it hurt him."[82]

A Gallup poll conducted immediately after the two speeches and published the day before the election spelled out Stevenson's decline in numerical terms. Eisenhower's lead had soared to eighteen points (57–39), while Stevenson had dropped below 40 percent for the first time; the "undecided" column, at 8 percent on October 26, had shrunk to 3 percent, suggesting that uncertain voters were choosing Eisenhower. The British and French scored decisive victories over Egypt before the U.N.-imposed cease-fire. The Soviet Union, with its army strung out over eastern Europe, made no move in the Middle East. Eisenhower knew that the election was over and that his opponent, as he had hoped, was about to get clobbered. Two days after Stevenson spoke to the nation, Eisenhower sent a confidential cable to NATO commander Alfred Gruenther in Paris, forecasting the final results. The cable predicted 403 electoral votes for "E" and 128 votes for "S."[83] As it turned out, Eisenhower had shorted himself by fifty-four votes.

Stevenson's final appearance, on November 5, haunted him until he died in 1965, partly because he used this election-eve telecast to awkwardly roll out the Eisenhower health issue. "I must say bluntly," he announced, "that every piece of scientific evidence . . . indicates that a Republican victory tomorrow would mean that Richard M. Nixon would probably be president of this country within the next four years."[84] Even Stevenson's closest advisers were stunned. For eleven months Stevenson had brushed aside every adroit tactic for maneuvering into the health issue; to address the matter now in such a clumsy way was a sure sign that he was crushed and that the Democratic presidential campaign was back to where it had begun almost two years before: against a solid Eisenhower-based brick wall.

While an Eisenhower landslide was in the offing, the Republican campaign for Congress had reached a cliff-hanger stage. George

Gallup reported that Eisenhower's clear statements about the Middle East crisis were helping in some key House and Senate races where Republican candidates had trailed; a fraction of Eisenhower's increasing margin, if it converted, would be sufficient to bring them into office. A survey conducted by Paul Hoffman indicated that in several regions, independent voters already favoring the president were starting to move to the Republican column elsewhere and that they needed some final assurance from Eisenhower.[85]

This assurance appeared primarily on television. Eisenhower went to Philadelphia for the final BBDO rally, then he and Nixon and their wives appeared in an hour-long election-eve program from the White House on all three networks. Because of the crisis atmosphere, it was decided that Ed Sullivan would not be an appropriate host; newsman John Cameron Swayze was recruited instead. Viewers saw one of early TV's most elaborate displays of fiim, live broadcasting, and production razzle-dazzle, which attempted one last time to mix the national and local goals of the GOP campaign. Scenes shifted from coast to coast, where "reporters," most actually hired actors, detailed crescendos of support for Eisenhower and local candidates as if returns were already coming in.[86] Hagerty and Levy had labored on preparations, with facilities so crowded that Levy wound up directing the show from the first-floor ladies' room at the White House.[87]

Eisenhower never knew the true extent to which he vanquished his Democratic opponent in 1956. Stevenson's prospects in government were now postponed until the Democrats regained power. When the Democratic ticket won four years later, the victorious Kennedys were not at all keen on giving Stevenson a Cadillac position, especially that of secretary of state, the post he had yearned for. His 1956 campaign was one of the reasons. Robert Kennedy had been with Stevenson throughout the fall campaign as an observer. Though he had professed admiration for Stevenson in the beginning, RFK revealed in 1967, two years after Stevenson's death, that he had voted for Eisenhower instead.[88]

Almost thirty-six million other Americans did likewise. Eisenhower carried all but seven states and attracted 57.4 percent of the popular vote; only Franklin Roosevelt, Warren Harding, and Herbert Hoover had won larger popular vote percentages. Yet the Republicans wound up with a .500 batting average. Eisenhower fumed about the congressional results. Although the election had actually been a standoff—

the Democrats had kept their 49–47 margin in the Senate and gained only two seats in the House, increasing their majority there to 234–201—Eisenhower went down in history as the first victorious president since Zachary Taylor in 1848 to yield both houses of Congress. He was especially perturbed to see that numerous Republican moderates, including Senate candidates Jim Duff in Pennsylvania, Douglas McKay in Oregon, Arthur Langlie in Washington, and Dan Thornton in Colorado were all defeated. Still smiling, Eisenhower claimed victory before 2,300 onlookers and an estimated seventy million TV viewers—and privately spoke of bolting from the GOP and advancing the moderate cause in a new political party.[89]

Eisenhower did not weigh this idea seriously. To the contrary, having failed in three elections to locate a moderate base with a GOP identification, Eisenhower's interest in party salesmanship and electioneering began to recede. Eisenhower took more stock in the scale of his personal victory, validated by a Gallup poll at the end of the year showing that 79 percent of the public approved of his conduct as president. This approval rating was the highest Eisenhower would ever receive. Preserving the president's public standing became increasingly important, and much more difficult, in the second term, as challenges to his expert public relations multiplied.

STATIC FROM
HOME AND ABROAD,
1957–1959

Eisenhower's public outreach after 1957 was not the energetic, often indulgent pursuit it had been through most of his first term. Efforts to sustain Eisenhower's positive image became more labored beginning the night of the 1956 election, in part because the multi-million-dollar campaign was over, and also because numerous lifetime Republicans were grumbling that the president had been the only beneficiary. The first victim was Leonard Hall, the GOP's national chairman. Though his 1956 national campaign had been a masterpiece, Hall nonetheless offered his resignation; that Eisenhower accepted it was surprising to some but not to those who were close to the president.[1] Eisenhower needed to make a blood offering to GOP figures who wondered whether the president had exploited rather than led the party. Meade Alcorn, Hall's replacement, followed up by announcing that the RNC would get back to basics, with less stress on mass media and more shoe-leather cultivation of the party's grass roots, which were in many ways weaker than ever before, despite the Eisenhower landslide.[2] Even so, Hall's media-centered voice did not disappear from the administration. And in almost the same stroke that brought Alcorn on board, Eisenhower renewed the RNC's retainer contract with BBDO through the 1960 campaign.

Hall's departure from party headquarters left the White House as

Eisenhower's lone mass communication workshop. There, too, interests shifted. Advisers put much of the "I Like Ike" imagery back on the shelf and once again used public channels to support Eisenhower's initiatives, but now without the incentive of a reelection campaign. Although some advisers found the second term less satisfying, it was more urgent to Eisenhower, who initially shot high and hoped to finish his presidency with legislative breakthroughs. As was the case with Modern Republicanism, the results were mixed.

Yet as time went on, a pattern of communications emerged that departed from the political and legislative endeavors, eventually shaping the public's basic perception of Eisenhower in his final years as president. Rather than as a forward, ground-clearing device, Eisenhower was impelled to use the media as a reactive shield against a flood of insidious developments that placed one crisis after another at his doorstep. These crises threatened the viability of the administration as well as Eisenhower's postpresidential reputation, both internal concerns at the time. Less inclined to drink in the peace, prosperity, and progress themes, the public began to demand more unembellished information. While Eisenhower calmly handled the various crises, and some historians later applauded his actions, his advisers at the time had a difficult task in giving this period a tidy outward look.

In front of them at almost every turn was a new public relations problem: the Soviet Union. Eisenhower himself had anticipated a resurgence of Cold War trouble. He had blamed the Soviets, not the Egyptians, for the Suez crisis; thus, in his January 1957 inaugural address, he attempted to put the public in a watchful but assured frame of mind. He spoke of a "shaken earth" where "harshly blow the winds of change."

A new and unexpected element, though, was the appearance of Nikita Khrushchev, now in full control in the Kremlin, as a figure who could match Eisenhower in the image-making game. Like Eisenhower, Khrushchev understood the importance of public relations in a world becoming enveloped in mass communication. He also understood, better than Eisenhower, that at the time the world could not care less that the USSR trailed the U.S. economically and militarily; what mattered in the Cold War was the image of a Soviet Union about to take the lead. To Eisenhower's surprise, Khrushchev conveyed exactly that image to millions of Americans with his launch of Sputnik on October 4, 1957. Eisenhower's landslide reelection was one dividing line in his presidency, and Sputnik, less than a year later, provided another. Through the first term, speechwriter William Ewald recalled, "[a]ll, or almost all [was] light," including the "euphoria of the campaign of 1956." After Sputnik, Eisenhower came to symbolize "an America grown complacent, fat, and unconcerned."[3] Eisenhower's next three years in office were largely an attempt to pound out the dents in his 1956 peace, prosperity, and progress framework, which had been mangled by Sputnik in 1957.

In addition to sharpening the public's appetite for news from the White House, Sputnik was responsible for an ominous national cloud of fear and uncertainty, a dilemma Eisenhower brought upon himself by trying to maintain that a space race did not exist. This "hysteria," as he termed it, created new communication factors for Eisenhower, who had to concentrate on calming the people while abandoning his characteristic attraction to corporate-style promotion. Fear management was a backward public relations strategy, but one Eisenhower was forced to use repeatedly in his second term. Sputnik was not the only reason. Two weeks before Sputnik, the impact of the 1954 Brown decision had finally been dramatized nationally, with a racial confrontation at a high school in Little Rock. Then the economy stalled, plunging the nation into a recession that continued for almost a year. Abroad, there were more crises in the Middle East and the Far East, before the beginning of what appeared to be a direct showdown with the Soviets in Berlin. In the middle of these troubles, Eisenhower was back in the hospital again.

For the first time in Eisenhower's public life, observers spoke widely of a "crisis in confidence"; polling data gave credence to this conclusion. Eisenhower's on-the-job approval rating declined from close to 80 percent at the end of 1956 to 50 percent a little over a year later. Incredibly, considering the scale of his reelection, there was talk that Eisenhower should resign.

Nevertheless, as in other phases of his presidency, the second-term story had a happy public ending, at least at the end of 1959. Eisenhower was sensitive not just to the adverse events but also the public's mood and reaction. When public trust appeared to reach low ebb, he cut back his appearances, narrowing himself as a target for critics, with a trademark self-confidence that averted panic and patiently held out for a shift in the ill winds. When this shift was finally detected in 1959, his communications experts were prepared. In a series of grandstand world tours designed around further breakthroughs in mass communication, Eisenhower took the public offensive once again. As he began his final year as president, it appeared he would leave the White House the way he came in: as an American hero.

The motives behind Eisenhower's image making changed slightly as he began this second term, but the changes became increasingly more noticeable. Previously, Eisenhower's communication activities had sought an environment for his middle-of-the-road, consensus-driven political strategies; he needed public opinion to bridge a divided Congress and help GOP moderates. This search continued, but Eisenhower also began to focus more on his personal needs, while looking ahead to his ultimate image—the one to be transmitted in future history books. Through the second term Eisenhower often used his personal diary to clarify for posterity events that had occurred much earlier in his life, such as the way in which he was second-guessed by British general Bernard Montgomery and the circumstances that led him into politics.[4] Eisenhower's attention to the historical stage was an emerging factor in his communications not just during his final four years in office but also in the remaining years of his life.

For the same reason the 1953 Eisenhower could not get his consensus measures to make news, the 1957 Eisenhower feared his consensus successes would not make history. He had had an admirable record against constant opposition from Congress but no dynamic legislative achievements of the Franklin Roosevelt stripe to punch up his presidential legacy. Thus in 1957 Eisenhower set his sights on foreign policy with a series of proposals known as the Eisenhower Doctrine that were intended to solidify U.S. influence abroad through peaceful, although very expensive, means.[5] The heart of the effort was a $4 billion foreign aid program similar in concept to the Marshall Plan but aimed at Third World countries. A companion project was an expansion of American mass communication through an upgraded U.S. Information Agency (USIA). Despite a vigorous attempt to sell these projects in numerous media appearances in 1957, Eisenhower's grand plan died in its infancy.[6] Congress listened to a public uninterested in another worldwide philanthropic effort, particularly when expenditures would be offset by cuts in the military, and brutalized the foreign aid package.[7] This defeat foreshadowed much of the future.

Eisenhower still had big plans, including balanced budgets in his three remaining fiscal years. But back in the congressional trenches with time running out, he grew less averse to having his legacy, if not the "waging peace" campaign, come to rest on the certain power of his projected personality.

Besides dealing a personal blow to Eisenhower, the failure of these capstone foreign policy initiatives in Congress sent a negative signal to many Eisenhower communications experts. They had enjoyed the innovation of the first term and the excitement of the reelection, but in 1957 some were already growing weary as communications activities settled into a tedious uphill routine. One such figure was speechwriter Emmet Hughes, another Henry Luce protégé, who had written Eisenhower's "winds of change" inaugural address as well as most of the formal remarks during the 1956 telecasts. Ewald, one of his associates, recalled that by early 1957 Hughes had had enough of "press agentry" and was now interested in "the direct conduct of foreign policy."[8] Hughes walked out in April after Secretary of State John Foster Dulles told him a communications background qualified him for a policy apprenticeship and nothing more; he later became the administration's most vocal expatriate.[9]

Another adviser, speechwriter and former under secretary of labor Arthur Larson, did get promoted, only to find himself soon the denominator in Eisenhower's crumbling attempt to build up the USIA. Administered by the National Security Council, the agency had grown out of the Office of War Information in World War II; on a shoestring budget it distributed materials selected by the White House, such as TV and radio programs, to bureaus around the world. Eisenhower had gone to Congress in 1957 with a vision of turning the USIA into a foreign equivalent of the efficient public relations instrument he used domestically. He picked Larson to direct these USIA efforts, then requested $144 million for USIA operations in 1958, a one-third increase over the previous year.

Eisenhower did not understand that Larson was anathema to Democrats. In 1956 Larson had been the sage of Modern Republicanism; his popular book *A Republican Looks at His Party* expressed in steel-tipped words the features of Eisenhower's politics associated with the president only in indirect images. Larson referred to the New Deal as a "leaden era of poverty, class bickering, and repeated frustration" with residual "hypochondriac economics."[10] Among the many Democrats insulted by Larson was Senate majority leader Lyndon

Johnson. After slashing the USIA budget to pre-1956 levels, Johnson told Eisenhower he needed to recruit better management.[11]

Eisenhower got the message and by year's end had moved Larson out of the USIA and named George Allen as director.[12] Even so, Congress never went along with Eisenhower's plan for a White House–directed foreign public relations operation. The Democrats wanted the State Department to absorb the USIA—an idea unacceptable to Eisenhower, who insisted on guiding the agency with his personal hand. Secretary of State John Foster Dulles, meanwhile, agreed with Eisenhower that foreign propaganda was better left outside the State Department, with "the governmental connection concealed as often as possible."[13]

Eisenhower's failure to expand structured communication activities beyond American borders bothered him immensely. He was particularly alarmed by intelligence reports, including one in mid-1957, indicating that Soviet expenditures on foreign propaganda had now reached above half a billion dollars.[14] The issue erupted into an angry scene in the White House during the summer of 1958, when Eisenhower sent three Marine battalions to Lebanon to protect American interests that appeared threatened by a coup in Iraq. Already disappointed with America's meager propaganda capabilities in the Middle East, Eisenhower discovered that the State Department's Voice of America was augmenting its news coverage with statements opposing the landing. Enraged, Eisenhower told the VOA to stick to the facts and not provide interpretations that created questions about his policy.[15]

Although setbacks with Congress constricted a public dialogue that Eisenhower wanted to direct to all people of the world, they also made the administration more circumspect with regard to what it could continue to accomplish at home. Eisenhower had run for president in 1952 in part because he saw himself as a doctor able to cure the nation of its isolationist tendencies; in his second term he planned to focus on international awareness, using all the persuasive means at his disposal. By the middle of 1957, though, these hopes seemed dashed. That July, Eisenhower lamented to Swede Hazlett about "the apparent ignorance of members of Congress in the general subject of our foreign affairs" and the public's misguided belief that the nation "would greatly prosper by withdrawing" into what he condemned as "a fanciful 'Fortress America.'"[16] Eisenhower's communications, as considered and deliberate as they may have been, failed to sway public opinion. Having fulfilled a personal goal of becoming an effective communicator, Eisenhower would increasingly wonder how his achievement was benefiting the general public.

Hughes and Larson had not been the only communications specialists to grow restless. In February 1957 Assistant Press Secretary Murray Snyder told Eisenhower that he too was tired of presidential public relations and was looking for a new job. Especially grateful for the relentless work of the press office, Eisenhower helped him find one as an assistant secretary of defense.[17] Robert Montgomery, the president's special consultant for media affairs, did not fare as well. Problems began lacing his relationship with Eisenhower around the time of the Sputnik launch that October; they suggested to Montgomery that Eisenhower was not entirely immune to the "hysteria" that ensued.

Because of Sputnik, late 1957 saw one of the heaviest concentrations of free airtime requests in the eight Eisenhower years. The president did not deliver a nationally televised Oval Office statement immediately after the October 4 launch, but instead discussed it for the first time at a TV news conference. That 1955 innovation proved its versatility again: With the public clamoring for guidance from the White House, Eisenhower was able to express a "no big deal" first-wave reaction without interrupting regular programming to broadcast an emergency announcement that, in itself, would have made a tranquilizing appeal impossible to convey. Eisenhower then waited until the Sputnik fever had died down a little before talking about it on live television.

Ultimately, the networks turned over their facilities to Eisenhower on five occasions that fall, starting on September 24 with an address near the end of the Little Rock crisis.[18] The other four dealt with Sputnik. Eisenhower insisted that Soviet rocketry neither jeopardized American defense nor symbolized a catastrophic erosion in American education, as many claimed. Nevertheless, he laid groundwork on TV for what went into law a year later as the National Defense Education Act. Eisenhower was candid about the big question in late 1957: when would the U.S. match the Soviets in space? Not for a long time, said Eisenhower, although he had an explanation he hoped would make the public feel better. The Soviets' lead in space was not because of their own efforts, he explained, but because they had captured most of the German rocket scientists after World War II.[19] Thus, said Eisenhower, it was only a matter of time before the U.S. caught up.

What irritated Montgomery was Eisenhower's sudden concern about the staging of these broadcasts. Eisenhower had not been seen on live TV in anything but the address format since the 1956 campaign; events had not allowed for fireside chats. Whenever Eisenhower appeared from behind his Oval Office desk, it sent a visual signal that bad news could be on the way—a perception Eisenhower desperately wanted to avoid in the aftermath of Little Rock and Sputnik. Senior advisers seemed to be taking TV matters into their own hands, and Montgomery felt obliged, though reluctant, to concur.

One of the advisers' TV ideas created a humorous moment before a November 7 telecast for which Larson had proposed that Eisenhower use a visual aid: a nose cone recovered by U.S. scientists from a suborbital rocket launch. Larson was unaware that the device was so big and heavy that it would take a crew from the Pentagon most of the afternoon to muscle the object and its accompanying pieces into the Oval Office. A thoroughly amused Eisenhower watched for a while, waited for an opening, motioned to Larson, and then said, "Let's go over the paragraph about this thing. . . ." The paragraph had begun, "The object here in my hand . . . has just been to outer space and back."[20] A different staging gimmick was used a week later when Eisenhower flew to Oklahoma City to discuss new technology on national TV with a group of supportive scientists and futurists who were meeting there.[21] This rather hastily arranged telecast created a great strain among many White House staff members.[22]

The next telecast was Eisenhower's worst TV experience since the Abilene debacle in 1952. Two weeks after visiting Oklahoma, Eisenhower suffered a stroke. It was mild and he recovered rapidly. To display his renewed physical fitness, Eisenhower elected to make another trip, this time to a Sputnik-related NATO meeting in Paris in which he traveled in tandem with Dulles. Montgomery was prepared when Eisenhower returned on December 20 and requested yet another block of network airtime. He was not ready, however, for Eisenhower's next TV idea—having Dulles appear on the same program. It was not an Eisenhower whim. From the beginning of his presidency, Eisenhower had felt he could help himself with the public, and with historians, by giving exposure to people he had recruited. Still, Montgomery never appreciated having to coach cabinet members and the rest of the entourage, particularly Dulles, who, in the actor's words, "was not noted for his inspirational effect on audiences."[23]

Montgomery explained his hesitation to Eisenhower, and they reached a compromise. Eisenhower wanted to make some opening remarks before handing the telecast to Dulles, but Montgomery, sensing trouble in the Dulles phase, persuaded Eisenhower that the broadcast would have more life if both men appeared together through the entire program. Montgomery outlined a talk-show format and assumed there would be interaction. Instead, Dulles wound up delivering a twenty-minute speech; and because of a communication breakdown in the control room, almost all of it was captured in a "two shot." While Dulles spoke, viewers could also see Eisenhower fiddling with his glasses on the desk, adjusting his suit, and looking around the room.[24] The broadcast illustrated the Hollywood bromide that the toughest act in show business is listening to somebody sing. In this case the TV camera had created the impression that Eisenhower was bored and unable to follow important discussions—a bad message to send just weeks after the stroke. Eisenhower was agitated but forgiving after he watched a recording of the telecast; it was the only occasion in their seven years when Eisenhower blamed Montgomery for fouling up.[25]

The timing of these problems was especially bad for both Eisenhower and Montgomery. The overseer of White House television was still a voluntary staff member, an arrangement that had worked because of the sizable paychecks Montgomery drew from NBC and the sponsors of "Robert Montgomery Presents." However, beginning with the 1955–56 TV season, the program began to tumble in the ratings. NBC decided in early 1957 to cancel the show; the final episode was seen the following July. Although "Robert Montgomery Presents" was one of many live dramatic programs to lose favor with the audience, some critics noted a decline in the show's quality beginning about the time Montgomery began working for Eisenhower.[26] Montgomery now needed full-time work, and Eisenhower was not sure what to do.

At first it appeared Eisenhower would come through for the actor. In January 1957, shortly before Snyder moved to the Pentagon, Montgomery's name was placed on a list of candidates for the post of assistant secretary of the Navy. Few rallied on Montgomery's behalf, many feeling it was wrong that a Hollywood leading man had even been considered for such a position. "This news," stated one letter writer, "is shocking indeed."[27] Later in the summer, Montgomery was listed again, this time when George McConnaughey's retirement created a vacancy on the FCC.[28] Montgomery was not a serious candidate for this position either. Eventually, Montgomery did win a part-time post on the Advisory Commission on the Arts and helped the FCC as an adviser during the quiz-show scandals in 1959 and 1960.[29] Yet as 1958 began, Montgomery sensed clearly what Eisenhower never told him directly: that a TV adviser was not qualified for a policy-making position.

In mid-1958 Montgomery moved back to Hollywood and commuted only infrequently to the White House while he began work on what proved to be his final, and eventually unsuccessful, attempts at a major film credit. Not surprisingly, Montgomery pinned these hopes initially on Eisenhower. On the drawing board was a feature-length motion picture biography of the president, to appear in early 1960. Not opposed to a cinematic hurrah just before leaving the White House, Eisenhower provided some early support for this idea by offering Montgomery "literary and dramatic" rights to his life story.[30] Later, when Eisenhower opted to keep the literary rights for himself, Montgomery turned to another World War II hero, Admiral William "Bull" Halsey, for a film entitled *The Gallant Hours*. Montgomery directed and narrated the production, which starred Academy Award–winning actor James Cagney. The film was critically acclaimed but did poorly at the box office.

It was not difficult for Montgomery to live on the West Coast and still serve as TV consultant, at least through 1958, because the actor perceived a slowdown in White House television activities that year. Indeed, while the second year of Eisenhower's first term had witnessed an acceleration of presidential media appearances, the second year of his second term saw them reigned in. Eisenhower made only four requests for live airtime during the entire year, and his twenty news conferences in 1958 were the fewest of any previous year except 1955, when he had met the press nineteen times prior to the heart attack. The twenty-three White House photo events in 1958 compared to thirty-one in 1957. There was a good reason for this: Eisenhower simply had few positive matters to talk about.

Eisenhower's difficulties in 1958 were reflected in his news conferences, some of the most heated of his entire presidency because of the space race, the arms race, and the economy. They were also reflected in his Gallup poll public approval ratings. Still above 70 percent through early 1957, the ratings had slid into the high fifties after Sputnik and continued to drop in early 1958. In February 1958, 54 percent of respondents approved of Eisenhower's handling of his job; only 50 percent were satisfied in March. Although the March reading was his all-time low, Eisenhower's ratings remained in the low fifties through most of the year.

Eisenhower's drop in popularity might have been inevitable. Pollsters showed that public confidence in presidents tended to wane the longer they had been in office; a second-term decline in the numbers had also greeted Harry Truman, Eisenhower's predecessor. Yet Eisenhower took a different approach from Truman, who in the face of turmoil had stepped up his news conferences and talked more and more.[31] As Truman prepared to leave office, his approval ratings were in the 20 and 30 percent range, a lesson not lost on Eisenhower.

Interestingly, the reduction in Eisenhower's public appearances created more work for the White House press office. Anne Wheaton, who moved from the Republican National Committee to the White House as assistant press secretary after Snyder's departure, recalled having to deal with angry reporters when Eisenhower, in her words, "ditched them" on his way to the golf course.[32] In response to heavier requests for reactions and background information, Wheaton and Press Secretary Jim Hagerty were forced to conduct multiple daily news briefings, with a schedule that reminded Hagerty of the period after the heart attack in 1955. "This is a rough job down here," Hagerty complained in April 1958, "and it certainly keeps the one who sits at my desk very busy."[33]

Hagerty, and to a lesser extent Wheaton, became increasingly visible to the American public. The more visible they became, the more closely critics inspected Eisenhower's communication practices, with themes similar to Stevenson's "merchandising" assaults years before. Oklahoma senator Mike Moroney, a Democrat, delivered a speech in March claiming that it was Hagerty, not Eisenhower, "who speaks for the Western Free World to answer Khrushchev."[34] Some outlets of the news media carried the same idea in a harsher vein. Douglass Cater of *The Reporter* charged that Hagerty "holds the lens over the White House" and that "too much of the news that should come out of the White House is blocked [and] distorted." Cater assembled his observations in a book called *The Fourth Branch of Government*, which appeared in bookstores in early 1959.[35]

Hagerty tended to Cater and other print reporters, but he also expended much effort in meeting the needs of television journalists. By 1958 almost 80 percent of American families had television; the evening newscast, although still only fifteen minutes long, had apparently found a permanent niche. The Chet Huntley–David Brinkley combination on NBC, besides setting news ratings records, was one of the most talked-about programs on television. As the networks grew richer, their news-gathering capabilities expanded. For example, the news divisions phased out their practice of buying material from newsreel companies and relied on newly hired staff members and production crews outfitted with small, portable field cameras.

Many of the pictures these TV cameras conveyed in 1958 did not flatter Eisenhower. The 93 percent of Americans who had jobs saw on TV the plight of the other 7 percent, put out of work by the recession. Civil rights unrest in the South—including bombings of churches, synagogues, and schools, which were blamed on white resistance— continued to create stark impressions on home screens. Meanwhile, television had become sufficiently sophisticated that it was able to beam live pictures from very remote locations, including the sands of Cape Canaveral. Millions had tuned in the previous December to watch a launch of a Navy Vanguard rocket, the apparent U.S. answer to Sputnik, only to see their screens fill instead with images of white smoke and flame after the booster exploded three feet off the ground.

The U.S. space program was an intense behind-the-scenes public relations concern for the White House throughout 1958. Americans would have been baffled had they known this at the time, because they were hit between the eyes by one Soviet space adventure after another. Yet White House advisers spent innumerable hours on strategies that could bring credit to the U.S. space effort, if not give Eisenhower the sort of surge that Khrushchev had enjoyed after Sputnik. With the public now captivated by space, it even seemed possible that a string of American successes, combined with the proper promotion, could offer a break in negative affairs and ease the nation out of its 1958 doldrums.

The space program was a policy matter, not a study in mass communication. Yet it was an area in which policy and public relations were virtually inseparable. As such, space exploration wound up as one of the two biggest public relations miscalculations of Eisenhower's career. (The U-2 incident in 1960 was the other.) It was true that because of the Soviets' clear lead, the U.S. program did not have all of the necessary image-making parts. Still, while many advisers talked excitedly about space, Eisenhower sat back. The only part of the Soviet space program that interested him was the coordinated work on the huge missiles that had orbited, or in his words "hurled," the large Russian payloads. Even these missiles did not scare Eisenhower inordinately. Although Sputnik had woken Eisenhower up to the U.S. military's lack of coordinated development, the Army's Redstone missile and the Air Force's Atlas and Titan boosters were sufficient for delivering the compact U.S. nuclear weapons package; these missiles, combined with B-52s and short-range missiles in Europe, allowed the U.S. to tout a basic "first strike capability" against the USSR. The only value Eisenhower could ascribe to a satellite program was in scientific research and development, not usually an urgent priority. Thus Eisenhower was content to allow the Navy to work methodically and "in the clear" on the Vanguard satellite, even though the Army's secret Redstone project could have orbited a U.S. satellite in 1955.[36]

After Sputnik, Eisenhower was still slow to realize that the payoff of a space program was not so much in science as in vital Cold War publicity. In early 1958 Nelson Rockefeller, an adviser working on military reorganization, discussed some possible U.S. feats in space, such as launching nuclear-powered rockets to the moon. Ann Whitman, Eisenhower's secretary, noted that Rockefeller "sincerely wants such an accomplishment to take place during the time the President is in office."[37] Soon after this discussion, Eisenhower mused to legislative leaders that "he would rather have a good Redstone than be able to hit the moon, for we don't have any enemies on the moon."[38]

Indeed, Eisenhower had a tendency to make fun of those who felt that outer space was now a major concern. Eisenhower's comic relief before the "nose cone" telecast had been one example. At a news conference rehearsal later, after the Soviets had followed their launch of a lunar device with word they had given Russian names to features on the back side of the moon, Hagerty urged Eisenhower to prepare a response in case a reporter quizzed him on territorial claims. When someone suggested the president point out that the front side of the moon had Latin names and that "we are not worried about it belonging to the Romans," Eisenhower chuckled nonstop for five minutes.[39]

Actually, Eisenhower used humor to underscore his very serious personal belief that space was far too expensive an undertaking for the federal government. Eisenhower traded off space in his effort to balance the federal budget, a pursuit bred more from principle than public relations. He last gave the nation a balanced budget in 1960; a generation later, Eisenhower's success in balancing the budget would seem almost as momentous as an interplanetary expedition.

Nevertheless, Eisenhower was oblivious to the true shape and certainty of the space race. He missed many opportunities while he was president to communicate the success stories the U.S. program was able to achieve. As a result, Eisenhower added to the national inferiority complex. Ironically, many space-related events that Eisenhower could have pushed were developments on which he had been forced to spend badly needed money. When the U.S. did finally orbit the Explorer satellite on January 31, 1958—less than four months after Sputnik—the triumph was applauded by Hagerty, not Eisenhower. "Let's not make too great a hullabaloo over this," Eisenhower instructed.[40] That April, Eisenhower was dragged by public opinion and a unified Congress into creating a civilian National Aeronautics and Space Administration (NASA). After seeing NASA take shape and consume almost a billion dollars of his 1959 budget, Eisenhower wrote, "Personal feelings are now so intense that changes are extremely difficult."[41] This may have been the reason Eisenhower never held a photo opportunity with the seven astronauts picked for Project Mercury in early 1959.

Eisenhower's reluctance frustrated Hagerty, who continued to see public relations potential in giving the U.S. space program more of a winner's image. Though he had been as unmoved as Eisenhower before 1958, Hagerty held ongoing meetings that year with James Killian, the White House science adviser, and Alan Waterman of the National Science Foundation, even ordering from Killian a list of books on space topics.[42] Through this research Hagerty became a widely quoted futurist, discussing, as he did in a *TV Guide* article, the use of communications satellites.[43] The first communications satellite was launched in December 1958; the first voice heard from space was Eisenhower's.[44] The U.S. also launched the first weather satellite. But because of the Soviets' superiority in big promotion as well as big missiles, and because of Eisenhower's general lack of interest, the U.S. space ventures usually had the appearance of a white flag.

Public heartburn continued into late 1958, with two new international crises followed by a weak Republican showing in the 1958 elections. After the Lebanon landing in July, Eisenhower made one of the year's few nationally televised addresses. Then he appeared two months later to repledge U.S. support to the Nationalist Chinese after the Communists shelled two tiny Nationalist islands known as Quemoy and Matsu.[45] Neither affair was suited for the rally-around-the-flag effect Eisenhower sought; the Lebanon action was a response to turmoil hundreds of miles away in Iraq, while Quemoy and Matsu did not seem to warrant another Korea-like conflagration in Asia.

The 1958 campaign had gotten off to a messy start for Eisenhower, who painfully accepted political pressure in September and fired Chief of Staff Sherman Adams, following allegations that Adams had accepted bribes. Eisenhower held no news conferences during the entire month of September and made only three trips during the campaign. The election, a GOP disaster which took forty-eight House and thirteen Senate seats away from the party, had nonetheless been a foregone conclusion; Eisenhower had apparently just wanted to get it over with. The president's difficulties, including the Adams problem, hurt the Republicans; Eisenhower blamed the successful efforts of the AFL-CIO in defeating statewide right-to-work referendums and the GOP candidates who supported them.

Then, on November 10, with Eisenhower at 52 percent in the Gallup poll, Khrushchev again commandeered the world stage to announce that the USSR, fourteen years after World War II, would sign a peace treaty with East Germany within six months; according to the Soviet leader, this treaty meant that the U.S. was now legally bound to end its postwar occupation of Berlin. Eisenhower publicly said no, and for the first time in the Cold War, the superpowers appeared headed for a full-scale confrontation. For millions of Americans, Khrushchev's May 27, 1959, deadline contained eerie, end-of-the-world connotations.

The year ended not just with the Berlin deadline but with an uncertain Fidel Castro about to take power in Cuba, more labor unrest and a major steel strike on the horizon at home, increased concerns about civil rights, and looming tangles with Congress over the administration's budget-balancing demands. Eisenhower felt he had reached the lowest point in his public career, with "I Like Ike" a distant twinkle from the past. He had told close friend Ellis Slater that "all hell broke loose" during 1958 and that it had been the "worst year of his life."[46] He said essentially the same thing to Hagerty.[47]

Hagerty, though, was already at work on a strategy, another go-to-the-people effort that borrowed from tactics honed during the more buoyant days of the first term; this effort would represent the most ambitious White House publicity undertaking yet. If all went well, this effort could submerge the adverse images and mark a favorable "last stand" for the president with the American public.

Hagerty began outlining this strategy in a series of lengthy memoranda to Eisenhower beginning in December 1958. He referred to his concept as a "Tribune of the People," a revival of the "Roman idea" in which leaders, whatever their political demons, rose up and placed "repeated public emphasis" on working "for the welfare of the . . . people without regard for partisan politics." On various issues, Hagerty said, "[p]eople are confused by conflicting claims" by the Soviets, the Democrats, and the news media. "The President should take the whole subject directly to the people." Hagerty conjured up images of the 1952 and 1956 political campaigns but conceived of something more dramatic. "[T]he President should, in my opinion, personally participate in more foreign affairs. . . . [W]e should gamble more with the office of the President." "By 'personally,'" Hagerty emphasized, "I mean trips by the President outside of the United States."[48]

The desired break that allowed Hagerty to proceed with this planning was Eisenhower's handling of the Berlin crisis—an "absolutely bravo performance," according to historian Stephen Ambrose's assessment. Eisenhower's firmness forced Khrushchev to postpone the treaty and, thus, stop talking about Berlin. All the while, Eisenhower behaved in public as if a crisis did not exist, satisfying the nervous nation, in the words of Ambrose, "that his response was appropriate."[49] By spring, as the May deadline was about to pass without incident, Khrushchev was retreating in a way that provided some needed public relations opportunities both for himself and for Eisenhower. A thin but significant shaft of light was detected in February, when the Soviet leader quietly hinted through unofficial channels that Eisenhower should visit his country.[50]

It was not the first time an informal Khrushchev-Eisenhower exchange had been discussed. Hagerty had been pushing such a meeting since mid-1958, but always against great opposition in the White House.[51] Eisenhower wanted more than a high-profile publicity splash; he sought something in writing with the Kremlin, specifically a nuclear disarmament treaty, and knew that a formal agreement depended on normal diplomatic channels and meetings among foreign ministers.[52] Eisenhower remained committed to substantive talks. Yet by May 1959 Secretary of State Dulles was dead of cancer, and a four-power ministers' meeting in Geneva had collapsed. With the clock winding down on the Eisenhower era and Khrushchev still hinting at cordiality, Hagerty's ideas looked better and better.

With Adams and Dulles now gone, there was no one in the administration closer to Eisenhower than Hagerty. Given the restive feelings in White House communications circles after 1957, Eisenhower had reason to fear that Hagerty, too, might leave. Herbert Hoover, Franklin Roosevelt, and Harry Truman had each trained four different press secretaries. Like Eisenhower, Hagerty had health problems and often complained about the stress and burnout his complex job produced. Hagerty accepted his government pay, although he was not getting ahead financially; he had joined the White House staff at a starting annual salary of $18,000.[53] Hagerty could have done better in government had he wanted to; for example, Eisenhower had helped Murray Snyder, the press office assistant, into a Defense Department position. It was more likely, though, that Hagerty would be lured back into the journalism field. Few were surprised when Hagerty was snapped up by ABC News in 1961 and remained there as a vice president until his retirement in 1975. Two weeks before leaving the White House and joining ABC, Hagerty told his family, "I'll be glad to get out."[54]

It is to Eisenhower's credit that he kept Hagerty happy until the end, even admitting him to that exclusive club made up of his golf partners.[55] Yet many factors besides Hagerty's low golf handicap continued to make this president–press secretary relationship fluent and unique. Hagerty never swerved from his one-dimensional loyalty and his "get the job done and go home" attitude, which Eisenhower appreciated as he looked ahead to his retirement. In addition, Eisenhower relied on Hagerty's insights on foreign and domestic events. Hagerty was an encyclopedia of knowledge on current happenings, because he read dozens of newspapers and regularly tuned in to news programs on radio and TV. Like a newsroom editor, he presided over newswire tickers installed in the press office. Because the Kremlin specialized in surprise announcements, Hagerty's sources often gave more expedient information than the intelligence services. For example, Eisenhower had learned of Stalin's death in 1953 from Hagerty.[56]

It was again through Hagerty's channels that the president was informed, in early July, that Khrushchev had finally gone public with his proposal for a series of informal contacts, beginning not with an Eisenhower trip but with a Soviet tour of the United States in the fall.

Against a hundred warnings that a Khrushchev visit would weaken the Western Alliance and damage the president's reputation among Americans, Eisenhower responded days later with a secret invitation to the Soviet leader.[57] This decision had not been easy for Eisenhower, who told his new secretary of state, Christian Herter, that he "had fumbled around with the question" but saw the Khrushchev visit as a "break [in] the logjam" that might lead to talks with the Soviets.[58] Hagerty had pushed hardest for this overture and wanted it made public as soon as possible in order to cement Eisenhower's return invitation to the USSR.[59] These steps were precisely the type of public relations gamble the press secretary had been describing all year.

At least in terms of Hagerty's stalled public relations designs, a logjam was indeed broken. With Khrushchev's visit set for September, the timing was right and the need great for a presidential trip to western Europe; Eisenhower wanted his meeting with Khrushchev to leave no sour taste in the mouths of the Western allies. Then, in rapid-fire fashion, plans sprang forth for yet another Eisenhower trip, following the Khrushchev visit, which would take the president through southern Europe and into the Near East.

The reason Hagerty campaigned for these foreign travels, and in turn softened Eisenhower's inhibitions about them, had little to do with the press secretary's own wish for a disarmament treaty. Instead, Hagerty had his eyes trained on the huge captive audience Eisenhower would have at his fingertips back in the United States. Never before, not even in the earlier years of the Eisenhower presidency, could such a calculation have been made, due to technical constraints in overseas communications. The United States may have trailed the USSR in rocket technology, but by the late 1950s American capabilities in the television field were opening unprecedented possibilities. No matter where Eisenhower went, he would not be far from the cameras of the three domestic television networks. The CBS and NBC networks had bureaus in most European capitals, and now, through an improved transatlantic cable, they could provide same-day coverage of events there, with a favorable five- to six-hour time difference. Another new tool was videotape technology, a three-year-old invention. The greatest step of all was transportation technology. Boeing's two-year-old 707 could not only expedite the movement of TV cameras and reporters; in addition, films of Eisenhower appearances could be shuttled to feed points and shown to American audiences within hours.[60]

One of the most inviting features of these worldwide tours was

Hagerty's virtually gilt-edged guarantee that the news media, if per-suaded by buildup and exhaustive advance planning, would go to historic extremes to cover the various events. The accumulation of TV technology had thus far exceeded its need; the networks were in search of history in the making, an impetus for demonstrating their technical and logistical magic. While the news media showed off, Eisenhower would have an open stage for reaching the masses. This plan essentially used the 1955 TV news conference strategy in a more concentrated form. For Hagerty the prospect of taming the media with foreign travels was not exactly like plucking an apple from a tree. "Any press secretary who has gone through that experience could very easily handle the Barnum and Bailey circus any place in the world," he recalled.[61] Yet the payoff to Eisenhower from these efforts was enormous.

The western European trip began on August 26, 1959, and lasted two weeks. The departure alone was newsworthy, as it marked the unveiling of a 707 that went into service as *Air Force One*. The trip was Eisenhower's first on a jet aircraft, as it was for many of the 102 reporters on board a chartered TWA 707 press plane; Eisenhower described the experience as "exhilarating."[62]

The trip to southern Europe and the Near East had Eisenhower away from the White House through most of December. As predicted, the television industry and its sponsors were enthralled. CBS invested resources in a series of prime-time specials entitled "Eyewitness to History," which had premiered during the August travels and grew in sophistication during the December odyssey. Almost the entire roster of CBS correspondents was dispatched for close-up coverage of the president, including Daniel Schorr in New Delhi; Alexander Kendrick in Karachi; Howard K. Smith in Athens; David Schoenbrun and Winston Burdett in Rome; and Robert Pierpoint in Madrid. Walter Cronkite hosted the broadcasts, usually from the network's Paris bureau; the continuous exposure Cronkite enjoyed in the "Eyewitness" series served him well when CBS went looking for a new nightly news anchor three years later.[63] NBC, not to be outdone, answered the CBS effort with an equally ambitious series of special broadcasts called "Journey to Understanding."

In scenes reminiscent of the 1956 campaign, Americans saw Eisenhower cheered during these two trips by genuine mobs of West Germans, French, British, Greeks, Turks, and Italians. In Pakistan there were signs that read "We Like Ike."[64] Viewers saw glimpses of the serious Eisenhower in meetings with the main leaders of the Western Alliance, including Adenauer of West Germany, Macmillan of Britain, and de Gaulle of France. They also saw him call on Pope John XXIII, receive a Persian rug from the Shah of Iran, tour the Taj Mahal with India's Nehru, and steam from Athens to Tunis aboard the cruiser *Des Moines*, the flagship of the U.S. Sixth Fleet. These images were seen on TV night after night, and often weeks later in recaps of the travels.[65]

As successful as the August and December travels turned out to be, they did not stir the American public as much as the tour that came in between them—Khrushchev's visit to the United States. Public skepticism prevailed until the day of Khrushchev's arrival; incoming White House mail was running three-to-one against the visit.[66] CBS correspondent Howard K. Smith was also opposed; in covering the Washington welcoming ceremonies on September 15, he told viewers the event was "an act of weakness on our part."[67] Yet from the public's perspective, the TV pictures of Khrushchev soon overpowered the negative analysis. Eisenhower saw the Soviet leader at the beginning and end of the eleven-day stay. In the meantime, in full TV view, Khrushchev traveled back and forth across the country, chatting with steel workers in Pittsburgh, farmers in Iowa, and computer engineers in the Bay Area. He also met Frank Sinatra and Shirley MacLaine at a motion picture studio in Hollywood, and he would have seen Disneyland had it not been for security problems.

Eisenhower complained that he got little out of Khrushchev diplomatically.[68] Even so, it was instantly apparent that Eisenhower was gaining a public relations windfall; interest in the Khrushchev visit increased daily, and commentary in the news media grew more favorable.[69] At the end of the visit, Hagerty remarked that he "rather liked the guy" and felt that the public at large, at least in late 1959, was less inclined to fear him.[70] It may have meant a lot to Americans that the man who could push a button and annihilate them in a nuclear exchange was toasting, laughing, and joking on their own soil. Although Khrushchev had also boasted and criticized, he had said mostly good things about average Americans.

The Khrushchev visit was considered such a publicity success that Hagerty had wanted to move immediately on Eisenhower's return trip to Moscow, perhaps adjoining it to the Near East trip. In October the press secretary prepared a memo that outlined "steps needed to get things on the right track"; eventually, Hagerty himself went to Moscow to begin the necessary planning. But Hagerty conceded a drawback in pushing too rapidly with Eisenhower's USSR tour: the frigid Russian winter, which would "affect crowds, receptions, etc., all of which are an integral part of your visit, particularly the reporting of that visit by the world press."[71] Thus the White House elected to schedule the return trip in the spring of 1960, when planning could assume warmer weather. This decision turned out to be fateful, for by spring U.S.-Soviet relations were back in the Cold War freezer because of the U-2 spy plane incident. Hagerty's dream of penetrating the Kremlin with media and having the American public participate in a presidential mission to Moscow was never fulfilled.

Nevertheless, the two presidential trips, the apparent success of the Khrushchev visit, and the general perception of positive diplomatic ventures rekindled the nation's love affair with Eisenhower. At the end of 1959, the president's approval rating had risen to 76 percent, the third highest level of his entire presidency. Largely because of the public's renewed confidence in Eisenhower, the White House exuded a vitality and optimism that had not been seen since the 1956 election. "The home stretch is upon us," Eisenhower told Hagerty on December 29. "A thoroughbred tries to make his best effort in the last furlong. . . . I have no fear that you will exert your energies to make all Americans proud, as I am proud, of the record."[72] Hagerty told his former boss Thomas Dewey, "I am ready now to go into this last year with bands playing and banners waving."[73]

This optimism was confirmed when *Time*'s first edition of 1960 reached the newsstands with Eisenhower on the cover as "Man of the Year."

DROPPING
THE TORCH,
1960

The American public, in the form of the 1,500 people in George Gallup's random sample, had its last opportunity to judge Eisenhower as president in early December 1960. Eisenhower's final on-the-job rating was 59 percent, a respectable figure; to date, only Franklin Roosevelt and Ronald Reagan have enjoyed higher measured levels of public confidence on their departure from office. Still, Eisenhower's final 59 did not compare favorably to the 76 he had going into 1960 or to the nineteen other Gallup polls over the previous eight years in which his approval rating had been above 70 percent. Eisenhower's public dialogue indeed ended with a glitch: the 1960 election.

Eisenhower's public relations advisers had a grand slam year laid out for 1960, beginning with a Latin American trip in February, to be followed by a summit meeting with Khrushchev and possibly, by mid-year, a disarmament treaty with the Soviets. Soon thereafter would come Eisenhower's reciprocal visit to the Soviet Union, a condition of the agreement that had brought Khrushchev to the U.S. in late 1959. Eisenhower would then round out his presidency with a tour of the Far East. Press Secretary Jim Hagerty told Eisenhower he could trust the press office to "keep our news media informed . . . so that they will write what we want."[1]

Eisenhower's two-week tour of Latin America, his third foreign excursion in seven months, was another media success. However, the image-making mother lode, the meetings with Khrushchev, escaped Eisenhower because of the U-2 affair. The U.S. obtained vital information from top-secret U-2 flights through Soviet airspace. Although Eisenhower planned to suspend these flights for the duration of the Khrushchev meetings, after several flights had been grounded due to bad weather he approved one last mission on May 1—the Soviet national holiday, no less. After learning that the plane had been shot down, Eisenhower tried to keep a cover on the matter, having been told that these delicate aircraft would disintegrate in an engagement, thus leaving no evidence. However, Khrushchev produced both the aircraft and the pilot, Frances Gary Powers, and made a worldwide spectacle out of Eisenhower's alleged disregard for international law. With the Kremlin charging that the flights were an act of war, days passed before Eisenhower gave comment. James Reston of the *New York Times* called it a cover-up and referred to a "clumsy administration, bad judgment and bad faith."[2]

Hagerty's theory as to why Khrushchev reacted so violently was that the Kremlin wanted a pretext for canceling Eisenhower's tour of the Soviet Union. When he had gone to the USSR to plan the trip, the press secretary had found living conditions in even some of the most developed locales to be in a shambles. He recalled that "the Soviets were not overjoyed about the visit" or the hoard of world press that would venture into the Russian interior with Eisenhower.[3] Still, the U-2 incident was a supreme humiliation for Eisenhower; it was followed by another just weeks later, when the presidential party embarked on the Far East tour. The feature attraction of this trip, a tour of Japan, was canceled at the last minute because of Communist-inspired anti-American riots there. Hagerty, who had also supervised the advance work in the Far East, escaped without injury when rioters converged on his car at the Tokyo airport.[4]

Eisenhower's final year also witnessed new cracks in his dealings with the press. Reporters criticized the foreign miscues. Of much more concern in the White House, though, was the rather sudden willingness of reporters to use unauthorized information apparently leaked to them by parties in the executive branch. The reporting of sensitive information in the news media had not been a noticeable problem earlier in his presidency. Unable to do much about the leaks, Eisenhower left office with even more doubts about the press.

Surprisingly, the public's confidence in the president was not torn apart by the troubling events in early 1960. After his surge in the fall of 1959, Eisenhower's approval ratings settled into the two-thirds range and stayed close to that level through the summer, despite a dip after the U-2 affair. It was now Khrushchev's turn to assess the malleability of American public opinion. "Despite the fact that the United States had committed an act of aggression against the Soviet Union," he wrote in 1974, "the American man in the street reacted as though it were the other way around."[5] After the U-2 furor diminished, Eisenhower used national TV to explain the importance of reconnaissance in preserving the peace.[6] Eisenhower was helped most by the continued belligerence of the Soviet leader, which led to greater solidarity among the nation's NATO allies.[7] Eisenhower went to the U.N. in September and restored his leadership aura through contrast with these new images of Khrushchev, who had come to the U.S. again and harangued the president with an ill-mannered, shoe-pounding exhibition at the same General Assembly.

Nevertheless, this U.N. appearance took place about the time that the presidential election campaign between Kennedy and Nixon began to command the public's attention, marking the start of a very unsettling period for Eisenhower. No previous setback compared with the devastation Eisenhower felt when the American public chose Kennedy as his successor. He wrote to a friend that it was like being "hit in the solar plexus with a ball bat."[8] The 1960 campaign saw the Democrats pluck, one by one, the scabs from almost every presidential blemish, including muddled farm policies, the 1954 and 1958 recessions, civil rights unrest, the "missile gap," Communist inroads in Cuba and elsewhere, and even to some extent the issues of Eisenhower's health and age. Persistent personal communication efforts had helped Eisenhower defuse these matters previously. Now, in the campaign, these questions came whizzing out of the past, and Eisenhower, confined to a spectator's role, could not act. To Eisenhower, Nixon had been Kennedy's opponent in more or less a technical sense. Eisenhower saw 1960 as a referendum on his eight years as president and felt every bit the loser.[9]

In his Pulitzer Prize–winning *The Making of the President, 1960*, Theodore H. White was the first of many authors to focus on television in explaining why Kennedy had won. What remained a more intriguing question, given the importance of TV in 1960, was why Nixon had lost. The Republicans, not the Democrats, were the masters at public relations, media manipulation, and electronic imagery. They also had a better grip on the fund-raising practices necessary to grease these procedures. Yet the tense finale of 1960 was an illusion. In terms of the kind of politics the Republican party had advanced in the 1950s, and Nixon might have applied in 1960, Kennedy's victory was decisive. Many in the GOP were surprised Nixon came as close as he did.

Eisenhower had been one of them. Watching recordings of the historic September 26 television debate between the two candidates—Nixon's death knell in the view of White and innumerable others—Eisenhower could not believe his eyes. "Dick never asked me how I thought the campaign should be run," Eisenhower told close friend Ellis Slater. Eisenhower had urged Nixon to refuse any joint appearances with Kennedy. When a stunned Eisenhower learned that Nixon had ignored his advice, he offered him Robert Montgomery, the White House television consultant. This gesture was likewise spurned by the vice president. Eisenhower fumed, "Montgomery would never have let him look as he did in that first television debate. . . ."[10]

The GOP had the coordination, expertise, and financial capacity to win a television campaign easily. But Republican minds did not merge in 1960, and as factions remained aloof, the party had a campaign task that was somewhat like fighting the Vietnam War. The 1960 outcome depressed Eisenhower and Nixon equally; they were equally responsible. After eight years as the nation's highest elected officials, they went their separate ways with opposing conclusions about the political process. Eisenhower conceived the prerequisites of leadership more as Kennedy would, a personified, consensus-building dialogue that relied on instruments of mass communication. The younger Nixon more closely resembled Adlai Stevenson, seeking strength through endless rhetoric, backroom consensus-building, public persuasion on the microlevel, and shotgun whistlestop tours. This strange turn of events for the Republicans was another study in a changing political system, curious above all because the old looked to the future while the new looked back.

The fundamental problem was an Eisenhower-Nixon relationship that had never produced mutual trust. In 1952 Eisenhower had chosen Nixon as running mate to appease the conservative wing of the Republican party; for the same reason, and to avoid an image of instability, Eisenhower kept Nixon on the ticket after the funds scandal in 1952 and let him run again in 1956. Conspicuous by its absence was any show of fierce conviction on Eisenhower's part. That Eisenhower would not or could not grant Nixon the sense of security that others in the White House typically enjoyed in the 1950s was a theme in Nixon's affairs almost to the hour that Americans began marking their ballots in 1960.

Eisenhower never doubted Nixon's intelligence and counsel; he praised Nixon's commitment to his job and to the Republican cause. What bothered Eisenhower was Nixon's rough, overly political, and malignant image; knowing the American public would not warm to having such a personality in their homes for four years, Eisenhower could never realistically conceive of Nixon as his successor. In March 1957, in his private diary, Eisenhower gave letter grades to people being mentioned for the number one and two spots on the 1960 ticket. He gave Nixon an A. But he gave A-pluses to Henry Cabot Lodge; young, up-and-coming cabinet member Robert Anderson; Illinois GOP leader Charles Percy; and White House economics adviser Gabriel Hauge.[11] Eisenhower also liked Nelson Rockefeller for a while before parting with the New York governor on the issue of military spending. Later, New York congressman John Lindsay and Oregon governor Mark Hatfield, whose 1958 victories, like Rockefeller's, were among the few GOP bright spots that year, made it to Eisenhower's "watch very closely" list.[12] These men all looked good on TV and could surpass Nixon as "men of the people."

Eisenhower and his associates were among the first to detect Nixon's hard side, which Americans by the millions saw in the 1960 TV debates. During the 1954 campaign Nixon's attacks on the "traitors" and "rats" in the Democratic party were so vicious that Eisenhower had to intervene, instructing him that such statements were "indefensible."[13] Nixon also repelled others in the White House, including the president's brother Milton, who felt Nixon was struggling "to have the public regard him as a statesman rather than as a low-type politician."[14] Moreover, Nixon seemed combatively indifferent to public opinion. The tactic used in 1956 to persuade Nixon into accepting a cabinet post was one Eisenhower naturally assumed was surefire: he showed Nixon the Gallup polls indicating that the ticket would benefit by a new vice president.[15] Nixon was unswayed.

Characteristically, though, the president had faith that Nixon's shortcomings could be corrected by better packaging, promotion, and salesmanship. Eisenhower doubted Nixon's image but never gave up on it, partly because of the availability and growth of television. Eisenhower's observations of the vice president's on-camera work suggested to him that television, an intimate medium, could level and soften Nixon's rough demeanor and make him a "new man." Just as he saw Nixon's flaws, Eisenhower was one of the first to spot what observers noticed later, in the 1968 campaign: that Nixon, given the right setting, was an extremely effective TV communicator.

Eisenhower had been genuinely impressed by the "Checkers" telecast in the 1952 campaign, in which Nixon used a personal approach to save himself against charges that he was profiting from the secret GOP fund. This TV event had generated much positive public support; Eisenhower himself proclaimed the telecast "magnificent," an interesting yet not surprising choice of words.[16] Although the telecast, topped off by Nixon's probing of matters pertaining to his family dog, struck experts as sappy and cornball, Eisenhower saw in Nixon an ability to stir the emotions of average people tactfully and bring them around to his point of view.

For this reason Eisenhower put Nixon on TV frequently. Nixon spoke for the administration during the McCarthy affair in 1954 and appeared in many photo events. By 1955 Nixon was so familiar to TV viewers, and presumably so effective, that his advice carried weight with people, including six hundred broadcast executives and politicians who heard him speak in New York on September 14 of that year. Nixon lectured on the "intimate approach" and using TV "to bring up something new" but cautioned against going to the point of using "canned news releases." "When you rehearse," Nixon preached, "you lose in spontaneity what you gain in smoothness."[17]

Nixon's awareness of political TV was at least as advanced as Eisenhower's. Only on rare occasions did Nixon have contact with Montgomery; at no time was Nixon actually coached. Until 1960 Eisenhower did not think Nixon needed a consultant. During the 1956 campaign, in fact, Eisenhower felt Nixon was underutilized. After the success of the people's news conference that year, Eisenhower informed Leonard Hall that "it might be a good idea to use another half-hour of your television time the same way," that "Nixon might do a lot of good for us on such a program."[18] Nixon's TV campaign schedule was increased in 1956, and another news conference was added, this one featuring Nixon in front of student editors at Cornell

University.[19] Another TV appearance that pleased Eisenhower was Nixon's "debate" with Khrushchev in a model color TV studio at an American trade exhibition in Moscow in July 1959.[20]

Although his maligned performance in the first debate with Kennedy made it seem otherwise, Nixon's problem in 1960 was not his television persona. Eisenhower had given Nixon ample opportunities to sharpen his TV skills and use TV to boost his reputation; Nixon considered his meeting with Khrushchev the "decisive break" that led to his 1960 nomination.[21] Instead, what collapsed was organization.

Eisenhower saw no reason why the 1960 campaign could not be a repeat of the well-organized Republican effort in 1956. Just weeks after the 1956 election, Eisenhower had put several plans in motion, and he anticipated turning his complex of political persuasion over to the party's 1960 candidate. The GOP had renewed its contract with BBDO. Then came Eisenhower's reshuffling of the Republican National Committee, in which Hall vacated the chair in favor of Meade Alcorn, a GOP organizer from Connecticut, who was more adept than the TV-minded Hall in grassroots organizing. Alcorn's talents were needed in 1957, because the next challenge was the series of congressional elections in 1958. Hall, though, was not forgotten. The former chairman resumed a law practice and stayed on Eisenhower's good side by vying with Rockefeller for the 1958 New York gubernatorial nomination. Eisenhower penciled him in as campaign manager for 1960, considering Hall superior to anyone in either party for national strategy making. In addition, the president laid plans for a 1960 version of Citizens for Eisenhower, with the new name "Americans for Modern Republicanism."[22]

The 1958 defeats had brought further steps. That election was enough to satisfy Eisenhower that the GOP was hopelessly disorganized at the local level—and that there was no time to wait for improvement. In December 1958 he initiated another shakedown at the RNC, recentralizing the party's resources and talent.[23] By January 1960 the president issued more recommendations of speakers he wanted used in the 1960 campaign; more than fifty names appeared on the list given, among other people, to GOP front-runner Nixon.[24] Inevitably, Eisenhower tended to the most important advance task of all: making sure the party's financial war chest was filled. Eisenhower headlined a GOP closed-circuit TV fund-raiser, a repeat of the 1956 affair.[25] The seed money for what eventually became Nixon's 1960 media operation was a $60,000 unsecured loan from J. Clifford Folger, an Eisenhower associate who sat on the boards of IBM, C & P Telephone, and Burlington Northern and had founded Folger Nolan and Hibbs, a prominent brokerage firm in Washington, D.C.[26] Eisenhower also generated cash from oil executive W. Alton Jones, another tycoon and member of his gang, who became one of Nixon's major financial backers.[27]

By the time Nixon was nominated that July in Chicago, the scale and direction of Republican advance planning was comparable to what it had been in 1956, with many of the same people in charge. Image specialist Lou Guylay was back, and Young and Rubicam's Sig Larmon pledged support in the form of money and talent. Meanwhile, as it had done in 1956, BBDO had been busy staking out network airtime for the homestretch, testing slogans, and mocking up televised appeals. Following Ben Duffy's stroke and retirement in 1957, Carroll Newton gained supervisory control of BBDO's political accounts; before the nomination, Newton presented a complete TV plan for Nixon that featured, in the adman's words, "production values, shifting scenes, and various things to make [real] television shows out of it."[28] Much as he had in 1956, Eisenhower discussed these TV plans with Hall in the White House.[29]

Organizationally, Eisenhower had gone to great lengths to get the 1960 fall campaign off to a rolling start. Yet he neglected two important things. First, in the period before the nomination, Eisenhower never assured Nixon that the behind-the-scenes activity at the White House had him solely in mind. Although Rockefeller's withdrawal from the race in December 1959 left Nixon the only candidate, Eisenhower refused to endorse his vice president until after the convention, sending him a strange signal. What eventually became a more serious problem was Eisenhower's second oversight: not adequately acquainting Nixon with the campaign plans in words Nixon could understand.

Hall indeed wound up as Nixon's campaign manager, seemingly an ideal match; through 1960, Hall had been one of Nixon's staunchest supporters and closest confidants. Nevertheless, when Nixon and Hall began working side by side for the first time, it was as if they were speaking two different languages, at least in the recollection of Newton, who observed repeated breakdowns in communication. Hall, who had learned to manage national campaigns under Eisenhower, believed candidates must concede to a showcase role atop an organizational pyramid. Accordingly, Hall insisted that Nixon delegate strategy and communication duties to the team of experts assembled under him and accept their expertise. This philosophy could not have been more alien to Nixon, who took charge of every detail, more so even than Stevenson in 1956.

It seemed at the time that Nixon had an inborn instinct for shrugging off campaign plans and dictating strategy. Yet it would have been odd had he reacted in any other way. It had been ten years since Nixon had run a campaign on his own. During the 1954 and 1958 campaigns, and dramatically so in 1956, Nixon was removed from the political command center, where advisers combined efforts on centralized, national, media-driven campaign tactics. Not only did Nixon lack a voice in this political war room; he rarely had a glimpse of it. Time and again, Eisenhower flew him away, weeks at a stretch, to barnstorm in hundreds of far-flung locales. In one respect this practice became a bonus for Nixon, because he wound up making friends with party leaders in counties and precincts from one end of the country to the other. Still, his fifties campaigns reinforced Nixon's conception of politics as a one-person, travel-and-handshake, gain-a-favor proposition. A decade into the television age, this approach was not adequate. Although Nixon did not realize this truth, his first set of 1960 campaign managers, willed to him by Eisenhower, clearly did.

A month after the convention, for example, the Eisenhower people running the Nixon campaign were confused about the new Citizens organization, now known as the "Volunteers for Nixon." In 1952 and 1956 Citizens groups had raised up to one-quarter of GOP campaign monies; Eisenhower considered these groups a priority. Thus it was disconcerting for Eisenhower's associates to discover that Nixon, who for eight years had been sheltered from major fund-raising worries, had not gotten around to naming a director for his Volunteers.[30] Word of this situation got back to Eisenhower, who was told that Nixon sat $3.5 million short of meeting immediate expenses of $6 million. In late August Eisenhower moved again by contacting eight more wealthy associates, including David Rockefeller of the Chase Manhattan Bank, Ernest Breech of Ford, and Harlow Curtice of General Motors.[31]

Nixon was similarly indifferent to his TV operations, which would eventually cost $5 million and consume almost half of his campaign treasury. Nixon did take one decisive step, but the Eisenhower people considered it ludicrous. Confident he would ease through the television appeals, Nixon feared Kennedy would raise the "huckstering" issue again, as Stevenson had four years before. Nixon's solution was to form the political unit at BBDO into a small independent agency known as Campaign Associates. To further disguise the connection to BBDO, and to make it more difficult for the Democrats to brand him a puppet of Madison Avenue, Nixon had the new agency set up offices a block away from BBDO, on Vanderbilt Avenue.

Nixon was nobody's puppet in 1960, though, particularly not Eisenhower's, after his acceptance speech at the convention spoke of a "brand-new strategy" for world peace. The next day, without any outside consultation, he announced his decision to debate Kennedy on television. Republican leaders were astounded. Nixon was already the best-known candidate, as Eisenhower had been when he refused to debate Stevenson, and he had previously played down the debate, even informing his campaign staff that the mere mention of a debate would result in firings.[32] Nixon changed his mind because of the Democratic Congress's June suspension of the FCC's equal time rule, a move required to implement the debates. Nixon felt that if he refused to debate after the fanfare of this decision, critics would frustrate him through the rest of the campaign.[33]

Less beset by critical fallout and more concerned about what might ultimately be seen in forty million homes, Eisenhower disagreed.[34] For this reason the president was anxious on September 25, the day before the first debate, about placing a phone call to the vice president. Nixon admitted the debates "are risky for both sides," but with confidence remarked that "people thought he was somewhat of a debater" and that he was "going to play it gentlemanly [and] let Kennedy be the aggressor." Eisenhower, pleased that Nixon grasped the seriousness of the debate, nonetheless advised that he "should not be too concerned about Kennedy looking bad."[35] Truer and more astute words could not have crossed Eisenhower's lips at that moment. Yet they failed to register with Nixon, and as a result history was made the following night. The president had been unable to view the live telecast, but upon hearing conflicting reports about Nixon's attire, makeup, and general preparation, he ordered a kinescope of the debate so he could watch it personally. Hagerty and Montgomery were with him, and all three were flabbergasted. "We didn't like it," Hagerty recalled. "It wasn't the content, it was the whole appearance and everything else."[36]

After Nixon turned down the offer to have Montgomery join his campaign, Eisenhower, in subsequent conversations with the vice president, attempted to play the role of TV consultant himself. There were three debates and a dozen Nixon TV appearances still ahead.

On October 1 the president told Nixon he needed more "zip."[37] Still bothered after the second debate on October 7, Eisenhower implored Nixon to "not appear to be so glib, to ponder and appear to think about something before answering a question."[38]

Eisenhower encouraged Nixon, also. Yet it was too late for them to begin dialogue about media tactics, particularly after Nixon was wounded by a thoughtless piece of communication from Eisenhower. At TV news conferences in August, reporters had badgered Eisenhower for an assessment of Nixon's contribution as vice president. Finally, on August 24, after *Time*'s Charles Mohr demanded "an example of a major idea of his that you adopted," Eisenhower replied, "If you give me a week, I might think of one."[39] Later that day Eisenhower was on the phone apologizing to Nixon for a poor choice of words; what he had meant, apparently, was that he would answer the question at next week's news conference.[40] Still, the embarrassing remark was seen over and over on TV in Kennedy's fall appeals. NBC's Sander Vanocur could not resist bringing it up in the September 26 debate.

As Nixon was forced to find comfort in his own self-appointed circle of advisers, Hall became persona non grata, as did Newton, the manager of a GOP advertising machine that slowed to a crawl. As Hall, Newton, and others fell back, new people with less experience—but more affinity with the candidate—rotated through Nixon's airborne command post. For a time Attorney General William Rogers was Nixon's top assistant, before former interior secretary Fred Seaton emerged.[41] Near the end of the campaign, Nixon settled on H. R. Haldeman, who began in 1960 as head of the advance team.

In late October Eisenhower finally began some previously scheduled personal appeals for Nixon. Few Eisenhower political TV broadcasts ever drew a larger share of the audience (almost 35 percent), were better executed, or generated more excitement than his appearance in Philadelphia on October 28.[42] Although the election was just days away, it was the first time in 1960 that Eisenhower had talked in public about the campaign. "The obstacle that prevented me from starting earlier," Eisenhower explained years later, "[was that] Dick wanted me to make a swing of a 'non political' character." According to Eisenhower, this was the reason that "people got the idea that I was not enthusiastic about Nixon."[43]

However, Eisenhower was in fact very unenthusiastic about Nixon, and this feeling intensified. On October 31 Eisenhower gathered Hall and other veterans of the 1956 effort for a meeting with Nixon at the White House. Eisenhower speechwriter William Ewald also attended and described how Eisenhower for the first time deferred totally to the vice president. "Tell me how I can help," he said. When Nixon declined Eisenhower's offer, apparently concerned about the president's health, the White House people were again floored. "You could have fired a gun off and he [Nixon] wouldn't have noticed," Hall fumed after Nixon left the room. "Goddammit," the president added, "he looks like a loser to me."[44]

Eisenhower made three more appearances for Nixon in the seven days that remained before the election. Still, just as he had sensed his own victories in 1952 and 1956, Eisenhower was prepared for Nixon's imminent defeat. The weekend before the election, Campaign Associates had bargained for some emergency TV airtime in Illinois and Michigan, two large states where Nixon was making noticeable gains. The agency even contacted an executive of AT&T at home, and he coordinated spur-of-the-moment technical arrangements. Nixon learned of this development while completing a tour of California; he did squeeze these broadcasts into his schedule. Nevertheless, when his campaign plane lifted off, it did not head east. Instead, it set a course for Alaska, in order for Nixon to make good on a July pledge to be the first presidential candidate to visit the fifty states.[45]

Kennedy's election by a little over 100,000 popular votes seemed like a landslide in the White House. Eisenhower expressed his bitterness to only a few people, including Ann Whitman, his personal secretary, who had to endure his complaints that Nixon's loss "was a 'repudiation' of everything he had done for eight years." Whitman told him that "the President, and the President alone, is responsible for the surprisingly good showing of the Nixon-Lodge ticket. . . . [T]hey are not entitled to it," she said, "by the campaign they put on."[46] Even Hagerty was angry at Nixon, who made the mistake of going on TV with what seemed to be an official concession speech; Nixon's actual concession did not come until later. Eisenhower prematurely released his congratulatory telegrams to the Democrats, forcing Hagerty to persuade Kennedy's press secretary, Pierre Salinger, to sit on them until Nixon decided what to do.[47] Bad feelings rose again the following April when Eisenhower learned that Nixon had not sent thank-you letters to the many financial contributors the White House had helped to round up. In a letter that began, "Knowing you wanted or needed no counsel from me," Eisenhower hinted about a lack of gratitude on Nixon's part.[48]

Thus the torch of television-age politics passed, in some ways by default, to Kennedy. By most accounts Kennedy's 1960 campaign was no better organized that Nixon's; both candidates were left with deficits approaching $1 million.

Yet there was little doubt in Eisenhower's mind that television had made the difference in the election. "One man projects well, another does not," Eisenhower concluded. "It showed again how much elections can be controlled by sentiment and emotion rather than by facts and experience."[49] Eisenhower had a good vantage point from which to make this analysis; he himself had learned to project well on television and had not shied from sentimental and emotional appeals during his eight years. That Kennedy had followed in the same pattern suggested similarities in the two men, or perhaps some indication of the type of president sought by the mid–twentieth century electorate, which knew that because of TV the leader they chose would be their living-room guest for years into the future.

Although Eisenhower and Kennedy were a generation apart, looked and dressed differently, and shared little ideologically, there were indeed background and stylistic parallels worthy of note. For example, Eisenhower had had no professional political record when he became president; Kennedy's record had not been considered very distinguished. Neither figure was as interested in the routine of politics, its closed-door dealings and compromises, as in the outreach of their views, ideas, and evolving legacies to the mass public. Like Eisenhower, Kennedy faced a divided Congress and challenges from the Soviet Union; both were consensus leaders who were helped by their public communication skills. While Eisenhower organized, delegated, and managed his communication ventures, Kennedy's communication efforts were more freewheeling, even more personality-centered. Yet both figures, while often condescending toward public opinion, held the public's confidence in high regard; both saw opportunities in the media to advance their personal reputations and records of achievement.[50]

An expanding mass media had been crucial to both Eisenhower and Kennedy in their arrivals as national politicians. Both men had to overcome imposing figures in their parties who could boast vastly more legislative experience; both seized upon television as a way to

brush these opponents aside. To overcome Robert Taft in 1952, Eisenhower's supporters had shown films of him to voters in primary election states, and his personal campaign had begun with the expensive
nationally televised appearance from Abilene. Eisenhower's control
of TV was also a factor at the 1952 convention. Kennedy became the
leader of his party by making somewhat similar calculations. His visual
appeal was already well known to his advisers, who pushed for his TV
appearances at the 1956 Democratic convention; during the vice presidential battle there, they papered the hall with a circular that hailed
Kennedy's "attractive, magnetic appeal" within the new medium.[51] In
a time span of five days, Kennedy convinced half the delegates he
should have been on the 1956 ticket. Kennedy was already the front-
runner four years later when he disposed of Hubert Humphrey in
a TV-oriented primary campaign; later in 1960, three other distinguished Democrats—Lyndon Johnson, Stuart Symington, and Adlai
Stevenson—fell at his feet. These newer means of obtaining national
political leverage also revealed a common Eisenhower-Kennedy trait
very important in a mass media context: money. While Eisenhower
cultivated numerous wealthy supporters and Kennedy relied on his
family fortune, their money spent the same way, and neither one was
hurting for it.

It was also noteworthy that one of the few direct links between
Eisenhower's and Kennedy's affairs in the 1950s was in the mass media
field: both at various times were helped by the advertising agency
BBDO. The agency's president, Ben Duffy, had ties to the Kennedy
family that predated his company's relationship to the Republicans;
he and Joseph P. Kennedy, Sr., for example, were members of Car-
dinal Francis Spellman's Committee on the Catholic Laity. Duffy had
helped in the younger Kennedy's 1946 congressional election, one of
the first district campaigns to draw from a large agency. In 1952, when
Kennedy was doubting his future in politics and wanted to be a college
professor, Duffy encouraged him to run for the Senate, assuring him
that the Kennedys would have media support, even though by then
BBDO was working for Eisenhower. Ironically, Kennedy's opponent
in 1952 was Henry Cabot Lodge, Eisenhower's campaign manager.[52]
That Duffy could cross party lines in this manner seemed like a coup
but actually was not. At the time most leading politicians did not take
the image makers too seriously. Eisenhower and Kennedy were among
a scattered few who did.

Similarities between Eisenhower and Kennedy were not confined to image building. Both understood legend building as well. Four years before he ran for president, Eisenhower published a critically acclaimed and very lucrative book called *Crusade in Europe*, which later inspired a TV series and which did much to keep him in the national spotlight before 1952. Four years before Kennedy ran for president, he published *Profiles in Courage*, a Pulitzer Prize winner, which like Eisenhower's book became a best-seller and the basis of a TV series. Eisenhower's wartime legend was boosted when the U.S. Army Pictorial Center carved its library of World War II footage into a series of programs called "The Big Picture"; this series, which contained an Eisenhower scene practically every week, aired on ABC in the mid-1950s and in reruns well into the 1960s.[53] Similar in outcome had been the Kennedy family's commissioning of author John Hersey to write an account of John Kennedy's PT-109 episode for *Reader's Digest*, the nation's largest mass-circulated magazine. A dramatic rendition of the Hersey article on ABC's "Navy Log" was excerpted for use in Kennedy's 1960 campaign; another rendition made later was a feature-length motion picture. Shortly after Kennedy's 1960 victory, Eisenhower felt that had he, too, contributed something to *Reader's Digest* on the eve of the election, it might have pushed Nixon over.[54]

Eisenhower's byline did not appear very often in the 1950s, but Kennedy's did, in diverse publications including *Atlantic Monthly*, *Progressive*, and *Foreign Affairs*. He also contributed to *TV Guide*; on November 14, 1959, an article signed by Kennedy reflected on changes that TV had brought to the political system. Although the article did not praise the administration's TV work, it suggested the Kennedys had watched a lot of political TV in the 1950s and had reached conclusions similar to those drawn in the White House. Kennedy pointed to a "new breed" of candidates who were appealing on TV, including Rockefeller and Hatfield, whom Eisenhower had listed privately for the same reason. Kennedy explained that because of the new medium, Eisenhower could "[take] his case to the people . . . without ever leaving his office." In words almost identical to those Eisenhower gave Hall before the 1956 convention, Kennedy declared that the "slick or bombastic orator, pounding the table and ringing the rafters, is not as welcome in the family living room. . . ." And as if to foreshadow Eisenhower's frustrations with Nixon in 1960, Kennedy wrote of politicians who regarded TV with suspicion. "No matter what [his] defenders or detractors may say," Kennedy also observed, "the television public has a fairly good idea of what Dwight D. Eisenhower is really like."[55]

Actually, the television public never did get a good idea of what Eisenhower was really like. The public never saw Eisenhower in his many moments of rage, overbearance, and ill health. The public never witnessed any of Eisenhower's news conference rehearsals. Nor did citizens ever see Eisenhower apply facial makeup or be fitted for one of Montgomery's "TV suits." Only occasionally was Eisenhower seen in public with glasses. The idea the public had of Eisenhower was one it created; people already knew what a president was "really like." Eisenhower found improved ways to fit this image; Kennedy, perhaps, did even better. This sort of effect created a link between the two: not a kindred bond, but a bond nonetheless.

Eisenhower and Kennedy had one of the most cordial cross-party transitions in U.S. history. Eisenhower offered few words on the media in his postelection meetings with Kennedy, stressing instead the more urgent area of foreign policy, with emphasis on Communist expansion in Latin America and Southeast Asia. Nevertheless, with the help of Hagerty and Montgomery, JFK's press secretary Pierre Salinger and TV consultant Bill Wilson moved ahead on many projects, including the regular live telecasting of the news conferences within a month of Kennedy's inauguration.[56]

In his final days as president, Eisenhower's interest in presidential public relations was fairly depleted. With the exception of a campaign debate, he had "mass communicated" in every way a television-age president could, or probably ever would, and now had had enough of the routine. The only item left on Eisenhower's media agenda was to make some closing reflections on the press corps, a subject that had him torn. He finished with admiration for a number of reporters; people like Marvin Arrowsmith, Larry Burd, Robert Donovan, Edward Folliard, Bill Knighton, and Merriman Smith—even James Reston—might have annoyed him and might have been Democrats, but they were with him every step of the way, some as far back as his World War II days.

Still, Eisenhower did not overcome his distrust of the press. He continued to see too many reporters motivated by a desire for personal prominence and influence, not service to the public. No reporter was elected, appointed, or drafted; while other public servants adhered to a system of checks and balances, reporters rejected such controls. Eisenhower had discussed this matter before; his uneasiness about the press had been an impetus for much of his communication activity over the previous eight years. Late in his presidency, however, Eisenhower came to believe reporters had established a precedent for carrying press freedom to new and dangerous extremes, for on several occasions they had published sensitive information or material clearly designated as off-limits. Inaccuracies, distortions, and faulty interpretations had always bothered Eisenhower, yet he considered them venial sins and dealt with them mildly. In contrast, Eisenhower viewed the publication of classified information as a mortal trespass; only in this situation did he single out reporters by name and actively attempt to follow up.

One of the first such episodes had come in April 1959, during the sticky disarmament negotiations with the Soviets, when CBS correspondent Daniel Schorr had leaked word that cancer-stricken John Foster Dulles had resigned. Eisenhower responded to Schorr with a statement that read, "This is about as irresponsible reporting as I know of."[57] A few months later, against express instructions to the contrary, James Warner of the *New York Herald Tribune* reported statements Eisenhower had made at a White House stag dinner.[58] Eisenhower's most vehement reaction came in early 1960: with the sensitive U-2 flights still a secret, Warner's newspaper and the *New York Times* hinted at their existence in banner stories that again used unauthorized information. Eisenhower "exploded," according to science adviser George Kistiakowsky, and referred to columnist Joseph Alsop as "the lowest form of animal life on earth. . . ."[59] The president felt similar anguish just ten days before he left office, when the *Times*, with maps and diagrams, revealed the training of anti-Castro forces in Guatemala, those used later in the ill-fated Bay of Pigs invasion.[60]

Eisenhower did not know how the reporters were getting this information, although at the close of his presidency he showed some interest in finding out. There is scattered evidence that the government's intelligence community was employed in such a pursuit. An exchange between Eisenhower and Hagerty alluded to an internal investigation of the *Times*'s E. W. Kenworthy and that reporter's sources at the State Department after several ambassadorial appointments were leaked in 1959.[61] Later, Kistiakowsky wrote in his diary that FBI agents questioned him and others in August 1960 after accounts of a National Security Council meeting appeared in the *Times*.[62] In another case two unnamed publishers contacted the White House to complain that they, too, had been visited by the FBI.[63]

Despite this evidence, Eisenhower clearly had no intention to plumb leaks that might have existed in the executive branch; his reaction to the problem differed greatly from that of future president Nixon. To Eisenhower, direct action begged larger questions pertaining to the reporters and the way they conducted themselves. Eisenhower perceived a firm line between what should and should not be made public. Reporters who used unauthorized material often claimed that such intelligence was essential to the public, but as Eisenhower saw it, these "scoops" also gave reporters opportunities to headline their reportorial "expertise." Eisenhower did not believe such expertise existed. There were thousands of mouths in the government, and sensitive information was bound to find its way to journalists. Although most reporters used discretion and showed awareness of possible ill effects their stories could produce even after they had become yesterday's news, the few who did not were sufficient cause for alarm. "The news columns belong to the public," Eisenhower told John Hay Whitney, the new publisher of the *Herald Tribune*, in one of his final letters from the Oval Office. Pointing to an "abdication of responsibility" among several outlets that "have cheapened themselves," Eisenhower urged Whitney to keep his reporters confined to the task of presenting objective information. "Some papers, notably the *TIMES*, . . . have given their entire paper over to columnists. Almost every news item is published under a particular by-line and such persons are given, obviously, a high latitude in expressing their 'opinions.' This I deplore."[64]

Interestingly, Eisenhower never discussed these issues with individual reporters. In the end his practical solution to tensions in White House press relations seemed to be his fundamentals of coaxing, cooperation, and consensus building, although with the press these strategies had often failed to work. Eisenhower used the last date on his White House social calendar, January 16, 1961, to receive in a relaxed, informal affair about seventy regular members of the press corps. The atmosphere was almost as festive two days later, at Eisenhower's final news conference. When Robert Spivack of the often hostile *New York Post* asked whether the press had been fair, Eisenhower answered, "Well, when you come down to it, I don't see what a reporter could do much to a president, do you?"[65] A few laughed; others took his remark seriously. Most were not sure exactly what he meant.

Then the press had a delayed reaction to a piece of hidden-hand communication that they took as a solid clue. In his farewell television broadcast, the night before the final news conference, Eisenhower had offered prayers for "peace and prosperity" but warned of the

Cold War, its "indefinite duration," and the "unwarranted influence, whether sought or unsought, by the military-industrial complex." After propelling those words into the history books, Eisenhower continued with another passage that wound up in the craw of the journalistic community. Without a word of recognition for the press corps, Eisenhower lavishly honored and praised the development of electronic mass communication, expressing "gratitude to the radio and television networks for the opportunities they have given me over the years to bring reports and messages to our nation."[66]

A few days later, amid excitement over the beginning of the Kennedy era, the newspaper trade publication *Editor and Publisher* gave substantial space to what Eisenhower had said, its editors perplexed and sensing a "deliberate slight." "[W]hen thanks are being passed around we would think the President would have remembered that reporters were always by his side 'to bring his reports and messages to the nation,' even when cameras and microphones couldn't be there." An editorial in the same publication was more openly critical, concluding that Eisenhower "departed from our midst neither liked or disliked—but pretty much unknown."[67]

Although this stir was not lively, it was appropriate. Having gone out as a television president, Eisenhower was an "unknown" to close observers who had thought they really knew him, but an accepted member of the family to 180 million others.

11

A HERO'S IMAGE FULFILLED, AFTER 1960

After half a century of public service, a major contribution to the Allied victory in World War II, and eight years of peace
and prosperity as president, Eisenhower was entitled to an honored
position in the roll call of past national leaders. He did eventually receive this historical acclaim, but, in a sad postscript, not during his
lifetime. When he died in 1969, historians in a survey had rated him in
the same class as Millard Fillmore and Chester Arthur. Moreover, one
of the final living images of Eisenhower, almost totally out of character for the man who had urged harmony and dialogue and who had
had enormous respect for and fascination with the young, was as a
scourge of the "kooks" and "hippies" in the Vietnam protest movement. The Ike Age had not ended with a whimper. Yet it was corroded
greatly by the sixties' liberal resurgence and sudden tendency to recall
the 1950s as "the bland leading the bland." Eisenhower continued to
reflect on image making and public opinion in the 1960s, with revised
doubts about both.

Eisenhower's postpresidential years were ones of personal happiness; he was able to enjoy his family, friends, and hobbies while still
communicating with the American public—all on his terms. He wrote
articles in popular magazines and completed three books, including

his two-volume presidential memoir. His TV work, not as routine and pressured as during his presidency, was much more enjoyable. Besieged by requests for appearances, Eisenhower had little difficulty remaining a familiar visitor in living rooms across America. He found many of these media opportunities irresistible, even though his friends, usually concerned he was working too hard but also unsure whether certain appearances were appropriate for an elder statesman, sometimes warned against them.

Eisenhower undertook these media projects partially for income, activity, and a sense of nostalgia. Yet another major impetus, and a factor in some of his postpresidential dismay, was his hope of continuing as a voice of moderation extolling the simpler values of the American experience—a pursuit that had fractional appeal as the 1960s careened forward. When Harry Truman left the White House, he had remained a political wheelhorse and vocal conscience of the opposition. When Eisenhower left office, he did not provide the durable communications his moderate cause then needed. In characteristic fashion, his efforts were mostly nonpartisan "communications as usual," tailored to appeal to all the people, with no front against the liberal tide and no protection for what hit him from behind: a full-fledged conservative uprising in his own party. When he finally entered the fray with his emphatic support of the Vietnam War, it was on behalf of Lyndon Johnson, the Democratic president. The confusion assured Eisenhower that he would be perceived as a link between the 1950s and the very different decade that followed; he believed the turbulence of the 1960s legitimized his presidency by reflecting the soundness of his leadership. Yet it would require later historians to bring this connection to light.

One component of Eisenhower's doubts in the 1960s was the competition he internalized between himself and John Kennedy. It was not an obsession by any means; even at the peak of Kennedy's popularity, opinion polls showed the ex-president to be equally admired by the public. Moreover, Eisenhower was proud of his fifty-year record of public service. It was this record, though, that formed the backdrop of his many ill feelings. Eisenhower viewed the young Kennedy as a lot of smoke, with relatively little fire, who had nonetheless found a way to have himself painted in bigger-than-life terms. Eisenhower had forecast a Kennedy image phenomenon even before the 1960 election. What Eisenhower had feared might happen eventually did, in 1962, when Arthur Schlesinger, Sr., decided the time was right to have scholars rank the American presidents. When Eisenhower learned that he had finished number twenty-two, his feelings were hurt. "Jack Kennedy," he lamented, "is already up there with George Washington and Franklin Roosevelt."[1]

Few knew the extent to which Kennedy troubled Eisenhower; unlike Truman, who had similar ill feelings about Eisenhower, his successor a decade before, Eisenhower seldom spoke about JFK in public with the candid words used in private. Age and ideology separated Eisenhower and Kennedy. Interestingly, though, Eisenhower's critique of JFK largely bottomed out on the thing they had in common: public persuasion and the ability to wield an image. Perhaps this outcome was inevitable as one public relations titan transferred the power to another.

Eisenhower was scarcely out of the White House before he was back in front of a national TV audience. Just one month after settling on his farm near Gettysburg, Pennsylvania, he came to terms with CBS president William Paley on a three-part documentary series called "Eisenhower on the Presidency." Executive Producer Fred Friendly put himself in charge of the project and told Paley he was "bursting with enthusiasm over the Eisenhower portrait. . . . [O]ur approach will be to try to capture the living room type conversation that those of you, who know him well, say is so persuasive and easy."[2] Robert Montgomery came back to help with the production; when this series was completed in June 1961, Eisenhower was elated with the result.[3]

This production led to many others. Eisenhower invited NBC cameras to Gettysburg for a TV special timed to coincide with the centennial of the Civil War.[4] CBS spotlighted him again in its "Biography" series in 1962. Eisenhower also made numerous live appearances. He was occasionally seen on Sunday afternoon interview programs. One of his most innovative television appearances came in July 1963, when he was the feature attraction of the CBS "Town Meeting of the World." Through interactive technology and the Telstar II satellite, Eisenhower exchanged views with Sir Anthony Eden in London, Jean Monnet from Brussels, and Heinrich von Brentano in Bonn. The broadcast was widely seen in the U.S., although it lost its overseas audience when the French, unsure of its political content, disconnected the European downlink.[5]

One of the most cherished moments of Eisenhower's life was his return to Europe in August 1963 for the filming of the CBS special

"D-Day Plus Twenty Years." To host the program Eisenhower chose Walter Cronkite, who had recently been named anchor of the CBS Evening News. "I have at last found one news program," Eisenhower wrote, "that not only commands my respect, but demands my attention."[6] With Eisenhower behind the wheel of an Army jeep, Cronkite and viewers were escorted across the Normandy beaches and finally taken to a spot that overlooked the graves of fallen U.S. soldiers. Just as Jim Hagerty predicted when he first proposed this telecast in 1954, Eisenhower's return to Normandy drew large ratings and critical acclaim when it was broadcast on June 5, 1964.[7]

The heaviest concentration of Eisenhower's postpresidential media appearances came at the peak of Kennedy's White House popularity. It was a peaceful public coexistence, although Eisenhower was less enchanted with the new president than most Americans. There were things he liked about Kennedy, particularly JFK's respect for both his office and his elders, including Eisenhower. Kennedy had exhibited this respect in their consultations before and after the transition. Still, Eisenhower felt that Kennedy was too young, inexperienced, and impressionable to lead the nation through the perils of the Cold War. Time and again, Kennedy's decision making seemed to bear out that view, so much so that the ex-president believed it only a matter of time before events would catch up and mark, in Eisenhower's words, "a terrible outcry" and "virtual repudiation of the present administration."[8] By the time of the D-Day filming, however, this period of repudiation had not arrived. Kennedy's honeymoon persisted, with some of his approval ratings over 80 percent; meanwhile, Eisenhower quietly defined "Camelot" as an ounce of public relations worth a pound of good leadership.

Eisenhower had begun to lock onto this notion during the 1960 campaign. He had commented on Kennedy's magnetic television personality and realized that in combination with enticing liberal rhetoric, that personality would be a potent force. Yet Eisenhower could not accept Kennedy as the gallant, self-made protagonist the public perceived him to be; he suspected an apparatus at work that was somehow untouchable to the press and opinion leaders. Eisenhower related to close friends his fear "that if [the] Kennedys get in we will never get them out—that there will be a machine bigger than Tammany Hall ever was."[9] Just before leaving office, Eisenhower denigrated *Atlanta Constitution* editor Ralph McGill for his "naive belief that we have a new genius in our midst who is incapable of making any mistakes," implying that McGill had either been taken in or bought off in some way by the Kennedy family.[10] In a similar vein Eisenhower complained to close friend Ellis Slater that "some reporters and the Democrats in general are trying to do to him what Roosevelt and his gang did to Hoover," to "tear down everything that has been done" and "create the impression the administration has failed—all for the purposes of making themselves look better."[11]

Eisenhower made additional comments of this ilk after Kennedy entered the White House; to Hagerty, now the head of news at ABC, he directed comments regarding the adulatory treatment of Kennedy in the news media.[12] One revealing reaction—and notable, given Eisenhower's attitude toward the space program in the 1950s—occurred in February 1962, when John Glenn became the first American to orbit the earth and Kennedy received a matching share of the hero worship. Funding for that very mission had come out of Eisenhower's budget, not Kennedy's. According to Slater, the ex-president "felt it was unfortunate that at no time was any credit given to the organizers of the idea."[13]

Eisenhower would not have been nagged in the least by Kennedy's public esteem if he had felt it was deserved. But the New Frontier pinned the public to deficits in each Kennedy budget, while in Eisenhower's opinion the new president was also weakening the Western Alliance. Eisenhower was dumbfounded by Kennedy's handling of the April 1961 Bay of Pigs invasion. He had Kennedy personally reconstruct the entire episode for him and learned that someone had persuaded the young president to draw back air support for the intricate operation. With a satirical but pointed play on the title of Kennedy's Pulitzer Prize–winning book, Eisenhower summed up the Bay of Pigs as a "Profile in Timidity and Indecision."[14] The satire did not end with the Bay of Pigs. Former *New York Herald Tribune* reporter Earl Mazo, who grew close to the ex-president beginning in 1962, recalled in his 1971 oral history interview the pet names Eisenhower had given to some of the Kennedys. When speaking in private about President Kennedy, Eisenhower referred to "Little Boy Blue." Senator Edward Kennedy was the "Bonus Baby," while Attorney General Robert Kennedy was known as "that little something," with the word "something" exchanged for a profane expression; "God he couldn't stand the guy," said Mazo.[15]

Eisenhower appeared to have been closest to publicly dumping on

Kennedy in August 1961, when the Soviets, without a wink, sealed off East Germany with the Berlin Wall. Again, Eisenhower was flabbergasted, not just at Kennedy's inaction but the apparent exorcising of this affair from the public agenda. Although Eisenhower chose to temper his words outwardly, he went to the top management at CBS with questions as to why the news division there was not adequately treating the Berlin Wall as what Eisenhower felt it to be: a slap in Kennedy's face.[16] Nevertheless, in the first Gallup poll after the appearance of the Berlin Wall, three-fourths of the public approved of Kennedy's job performance.

Eisenhower was not completely satisfied with Kennedy's foreign policy masterstroke, the Cuban Missile Crisis in 1962. Some of Eisenhower's friends were put off that Kennedy had resolved the crisis by agreeing to protect in perpetuity a Communist regime ninety miles from the U.S. mainland. Although he approved of Kennedy's handling of the crisis, Eisenhower nonetheless placed several calls to former associate John McCone, now head of the CIA, to make sure Kennedy did not go too far with U.S. commitments and to assure himself the matter was being "carefully handled."[17]

Unsure as he was about his successor, the Kennedy years were among the most pleasing of Eisenhower's life. He balanced his public and private interests, mixing leisure and productivity. By the late summer of 1963, he had completed *Mandate for Change*, the first volume of his presidential memoir, and advance orders for the book were heavy. About that time, as Eisenhower had expected, the Kennedy shine finally started to recede. Kennedy was having a rough year with Congress, moving on civil rights without unanimous support, taunting the business community, and leaving unchecked Communist advances in Vietnam. After hitting 76 percent after the Cuban Missile Crisis, Kennedy's approval ratings by late 1963 were in the high fifties and on a downward slide. Thus Eisenhower had growing enthusiasm over the GOP's prospects in 1964, illustrated in his attempt to jockey his brother Milton into the race against the still popular but now more defeatable Kennedy.

But Kennedy was assassinated that November, with repercussions that put Eisenhower's image and aspirations in partial if not total eclipse for the remaining five years of his life. Eisenhower was genuinely grieved by Kennedy's death. By not having criticized Kennedy too harshly over the years, Eisenhower gained a final opportunity to play a calming, father-figure role as the incoming administration selected him, along with Johnson, the new president, to lead the official period of mourning.

Unfortunately for Eisenhower, though, this mourning period never ended. The public's reflexive support for the new administration, and Johnson's success in transforming the nation's shock into national unity, cast LBJ as a more formidable opponent in 1964 than Kennedy probably would ever have been. Slater, who had shared the preassassination optimism but was now, in his words, a "pessimist," wanted Eisenhower to get active and push Henry Cabot Lodge as a moderate GOP alternative to the rapidly rising Barry Goldwater.[18] Neither Lodge nor Pennsylvania governor William Scranton, another moderate possibility, were keen on challenging Johnson and the Kennedy afterglow. And Eisenhower, who rejected the conservative Goldwater, stuck to his past practice of refusing to choose between opposing Republican candidates, including Nelson Rockefeller, the only other contender. In this void the conservative revolt that Eisenhower had feared since his victory over Robert Taft in 1952 began to take shape. When it culminated in Goldwater's nomination, the moderate philosophy Eisenhower had espoused from the day he entered politics endured a humiliating thrashing.

What made Eisenhower look even worse was the role he selected for himself at the 1964 Republican convention, the scene of the final battle royale. Former president Truman had been a floor figure at his party's later conventions; he had even tried to broker the candidacy of Averell Harriman in 1956. In contrast, Eisenhower's showcase at his party's 1964 convention was the ABC-TV broadcast booth. This arrangement was Jim Hagerty's latest idea. Hagerty wanted his former boss to serve as ABC's political analyst, and Eisenhower accepted, despite concern from his closest friends, including Sig Larmon, that a television role would demean his stature as party leader. Interestingly, the same advice had prompted the former president to turn down a similar deal two years before to serve as an election commentator on CBS.[19] Slater granted that Eisenhower distinguished himself in the ABC telecasts but noted, "It's rather plain to see that twelve years and even eight have taken their toll. . . . It's so often the case, that a man who is a leader fades into dimness soon after he leaves the public scene."[20]

He may have looked good on TV, but the convention and the remainder of the Goldwater campaign, including the candidate's devastating loss to Johnson after Eisenhower's reluctant but very public endorsement, was a severe personal blow to the ex-president. "Never had Eisenhower appeared so bumbling or ineffective," observed Stephen Ambrose.[21]

Equally ineffective was Eisenhower's final crusade: his attempt to rally public support for a battlefield conclusion to the war in Vietnam. Eisenhower's hawkish stance was consistent with his military character but not with his past experience as president. He regretted war but believed that once engaged the nation must be committed to total victory and vindication of requisite sacrifices and heartbreak, although he had in fact ended the Korean War the way U.S. involvement in Vietnam would end after many more years of strife—not on the battlefield but at the peace table. Lyndon Johnson persisted in the war in part because Eisenhower advised him to do so. The fallacy of Eisenhower's conviction that Vietnam was more analogous to World War II than to Korea would not be clear until after he died. While Eisenhower lived, the Vietnam War all but dissolved his public image as a consensus-nurturing "man of all the people." Eisenhower let fly a personal salvo of anger and contempt that the public had never seen from him before. His first sweeping attack on the antiwar movement came in a TV broadcast in September 1966, in which Eisenhower used Vietnam to campaign for universal military training—a means, he said, of raising the "spiritual and moral level" of the nation's youth above that of the "kooks" of the "lunatic fringe," who he felt were undermining the nation's social fabric.[22] He expanded the assault in August 1967 in a *Reader's Digest* article aptly entitled "We Should Be Ashamed." That November, in a half-hour telecast, he made more stern comments about the "kooks" and "hippies" in response to questions from CBS correspondent Harry Reasoner.[23] In one of his final TV appearances, inspired by another critical *Reader's Digest* article, Eisenhower pled in April 1968 for wartime public support, again savaging antiwar factions, which he believed were embarrassing the nation and dishonoring those already lost in Vietnam by their appeals for "surrender."[24]

Now in his late seventies with rapidly failing health, Eisenhower had remarkable determination to continue his public dialogue. The chaos of the 1960s had given him motives to communicate with whatever audience cared to listen. As for Vietnam, he was not just backing the war but attempting to promote, one last time, the peace, prosperity, and progress ideals he had fashioned as president, principles

that had been found in the 1950s but were now, to his mind, lost. He
was repulsed by loud new opinion leaders, specifically those from the
cross section of Americans who had been of crib and bicycle age when
he was first elected president, who knew nothing but liberalism and
seemed to have no sense of the alternatives the past offered. Eisenhower appealed more and more to the part of the public that his vice
president, elected president by the end of the decade, would define
as the "silent majority." Eisenhower reached out to these less vocal
Americans with his final book, a memoir of prepresidential years,
entitled *At Ease: Stories I Tell to Friends.* This book stayed atop the best-
seller lists throughout 1967; yet as its title suggested, it was curiously
out of place within the crossfire of the 1960s, and Eisenhower knew it.

Eisenhower could not put his finger on exactly what had gone
wrong with public opinion in the 1960s. On at least two occasions,
though, he isolated as a contributing factor the hallowed image of the
martyred John Kennedy. Hagerty recalled one of these occasions—
a letter he received from Eisenhower in November 1966. Eisenhower
began by reminiscing about their exploits and achievements in the
White House. Eisenhower had gone back and calculated that they had
had an 83 percent success rate with the Democratic Congresses of the
1950s; he expressed great pride in this success. But then Eisenhower
began flailing against members of a new "personality cult" who "be-
little the achievements of the devoted men and women who served in
the executive branch from 1953 to 1961." According to Hagerty, Eisenhower was upset by liberal partisans and journalists, people he iden-
tified with Kennedy in their tendency to "equate oratorical strength
with editorial bombast" and "achievement with exaggerated use of
the vertical pronoun."[25]

Eisenhower started on the Kennedy phenomenon again in July
1967, when he was interviewed by Raymond Henle of the Herbert
Hoover Library. Not only did Eisenhower feel that the nation was still
stigmatized by a JFK "aura"; he believed the Kennedy family had capitalized on the assassination for maximum public relations by ensuring
the tragedy was not forgotten. "There is a very definitely financed
program," Eisenhower declared. "[E]very day you'll find one of the
Kennedys somewhere in the papers. It's Robert or Teddy or Jackie
and, if they can't get anybody else, well, they get young John or somebody." Talking about the Kennedys reminded Eisenhower of advice
given by General Fox Connor, his military mentor fifty years earlier
and an important personal influence. Connor had told him, "Take

your job seriously, never yourself." Eisenhower remarked, "These people [the Kennedys] are just the reverse: take yourself seriously and to hell with the job. . . ."[26]

When Richard Nixon was elected president, Eisenhower was gravely ill, and he was on his deathbed the following spring when Joe McGinniss's interpretation of the Nixon victory, *The Selling of the President*, became a national best-seller. Considering the number of times Eisenhower had used the word "selling" in his administration, he might have taken an interest in the McGinniss account. It was certain that Eisenhower, like McGinniss, saw a new Nixon in 1968; unlike the author, however, Eisenhower appreciated what he saw. Confined to a bed at Walter Reed Hospital, Eisenhower's only sustained glimpses of the 1968 Nixon were from television. "It seems to me," he wrote Nixon in mid-October, "your standing is going up everyday."[27] Two weeks before the election, Eisenhower sent Nixon another letter praising his campaign and enthusiastically predicting a "strong, clear mandate." He told Nixon, "You have stood steady and talked straight. . . ."[28]

Although Eisenhower was removed from the campaign, his influence hovered over the Nixon effort, in some ways more than it had in 1960. Eisenhower endorsed Nixon before his nomination was decided at the 1968 Republican convention. Nixon, for his part, remembered Eisenhower's 1956 lesson and brushed off repeated requests by opponent Hubert Humphrey to appear with him in a debate. Nixon also made full use of Eisenhower imagery, something he had shied away from eight years earlier. Eisenhower's grandson David, then engaged to Nixon's daughter Julie, headed a grassroots organization called "Youth for Nixon."[29] The young couple often appeared with Nixon in TV campaign appearances, which could not have pleased Eisenhower more.

Herbert Klein, Nixon's press secretary in the 1950s and 1960s, felt that the biggest difference between 1960 and 1968 was Nixon's willingness in the second campaign to accept the role of campaigner and leave strategy and image making to others, as Eisenhower had in 1952 and 1956. Klein's assessment was confirmed during the actual course of the campaign in some of Nixon's letters to Eisenhower. In one Nixon explained that he had not even seen some TV tributes that Eisenhower had recorded but had left them instead to his "experts in the promotion business." Nixon wrote, "[I do not] know how [they] will be used: simply because I am doing what I know you want me to do: concentrating every minute available on an all-out effort to win this election!"[30]

According to Klein, Nixon also "borrowed strategy on timing from the Kennedy effort in 1960[,] . . . added other communications techniques which were ahead of their time and provided a modern example for varied campaigns in the seventies."[31] Many of the people who orchestrated this "modern example" in 1968 were familiar faces from the Eisenhower era, Klein included. In addition, H. R. Haldeman, the ad executive loaned to Nixon by J. Walter Thompson in 1956, was Nixon's chief of staff. Harry Treleaven, who had worked at the same agency since 1950, was Nixon's advertising director. Maurice Stans, employed in the postmaster general's office in the 1950s under former RNC chairman Arthur Summerfield, was finance chairman. Personal adviser Robert Finch had helped run the California Citizens for Eisenhower group in 1956. Nixon's 1968 road manager, John Ehrlichman, had directed Washington state's Citizens in 1956. Even an aging Leonard Hall, offended by Nixon in 1960, had chipped in advice.

Nixon later revealed that his 1968 campaign emulated much of what Eisenhower had pioneered on TV in the 1950s. "President Eisenhower played a significant role in developing ways to use television which were different from the traditional speeches," Nixon noted in 1987. One technique that Nixon felt was crucial to his 1968 success was the televised "man in the arena" event, which had spun out of the people's news conference created by Young and Rubicam. This concept had premiered on October 12, 1956, and at Eisenhower's insistence was used again five nights later, at Cornell University, with Nixon in the ring. "I vividly recall a telephone call he made," Nixon explained. "He told me that this format was by far the most effective. He particularly liked it because it was before 'young people' as he put it." With football coach Bud Wilkinson serving on-camera as inquisitor, Nixon refined the "man in the arena" concept in his 1968 primary campaign and used it again in the fall, a "direct result," he said, "of the 1956 question and answer sessions" on TV.[32]

On March 28, 1969, Eisenhower's former vice president was in the White House, and a host of people that Eisenhower had recruited were again running parts of the government. Having been concerned with his legacy, Eisenhower may have taken some comfort in these circumstances when he died that day at age seventy-eight. Yet Nixon wound up boosting his former boss in ways that Eisenhower could never have foreseen short of using a soothsayer or a crystal ball. Nixon's 1972 campaign, which contained the Watergate episode, was a turning point in Eisenhower's posthumous image making, now entirely in the hands of historians. As Nixon's presidency headed toward collapse, groundwork fell into place for a "new" Eisenhower.

Eisenhower's high-profile, personal presidential campaigns, which had influenced Nixon's strategy in 1968, were even more of a model in Nixon's ill-fated reelection. Few pairs of presidential elections, in fact, have been more similar in behind-the-scenes calculations and outcomes than Eisenhower's campaign in 1956 and Nixon's in 1972. The 1956 GOP campaign had featured a "big vote premise," "maximum utilization" of TV, minimum utilization of the candidate, precision appeals to Democrats, demoralization of the opposition, a centralized chain of command, and an almost endless stream of campaign contributions. In 1972 these tactics were repeated but carried to illegal extremes; their revelation in court proceedings, a Senate investigation, and House impeachment hearings led to Nixon's unprecedented presidential resignation in 1974.

Gerald Ford attempted to restabilize the White House, only to see his support vanish after he pardoned Nixon, and then seemed ineffective in a period of unemployment and inflation in the double-digit range. Ford's successor, Jimmy Carter, likewise struggled in the Oval Office with the same economic dilemmas and then with a U.S. foreign policy apparently beyond his grasp. Carter's 21 percent approval rating in the middle of the Iran hostage crisis in 1980 was a milestone; in the fifty years that such polling had been conducted on a regular basis, no president had come so close to zero approval.

Perhaps beginning with Kennedy's approval slide in 1963, clearly advanced by Lyndon Johnson's frustrations with the war in the late 1960s, and jet-propelled by Watergate and its aftermath, a new scholarly appreciation arose for the complexities of the American presidency and for the handful of people who had managed the office particularly well. It was about this time in the late 1970s that Eisenhower's trove of personal papers, those he had used in his memoirs fifteen years before, were opened to historians for the first time. What scholars such as Ambrose, William Ewald, Fred Greenstein, Robert Griffith, and others discovered was like a gust of fresh air amid questions about the presidency that had persisted into the 1980s. Although they did not present Eisenhower's presidency as the picture of innocence, these scholars were impressed that he had led the nation honorably and with peace and prosperity for eight consecutive years. Ewald, writing in 1981, felt these years had been the "best in memory." [33]

Other historians may have agreed. In 1962 they had rated Eisenhower number twenty-two among the presidents. Twenty years later, the *Chicago Tribune* conducted another poll of historians. This time Eisenhower was ninth from the top—"up there" with Washington, Lincoln, Wilson, and the Roosevelts. [34]

CONCLUSION

The Ike age marked neither the beginning nor the end of consensus leadership in the United States. Nor did mass communication explain all of the changes in the political system during the mid–twentieth century.

In the view of historian Alonzo Hamby, Eisenhower's primary challenge was identical to that of all the presidents from Franklin Roosevelt on, continuing at least through Ronald Reagan. The right-angle turn was not in the advancing mass media. Instead, it was in the New Deal and the public's expectation for what Hamby called "collectivist" democratic liberalism. Prior to the New Deal, the nation's overriding concerns were individual matters such as property rights; there was "virtually no leeway for argument about ideological basics." After the New Deal, with the Herbert Hoover experience as a backdrop, presidents had to be less individualistic "leaders of the people" in the charismatic as well as liberal model of FDR. None of the post–New Deal presidents had been "made" by the media so much as they had seized opportunities to "exercise their leadership inside the limits of a broad, deeply felt American consensus." The best were those who "managed to combine media mastery with brokerage skills and to reconcile with seeming effortlessness whatever contradictions existed between the two." "For the first time in American history," Hamby observed, "the people as a whole could listen to, then see, political leaders on a day-to-day basis."[1] Eisenhower was influential among these presidents because he was the first to use television, the most advanced medium of the post–New Deal period.

Eisenhower has been incorrectly passed off as a minor communicator, though, perhaps in the same category as Harry Truman, Gerald Ford, and Jimmy Carter, when in fact he was a great one. There is no question that Eisenhower had few of the natural tools that would otherwise be needed to distinguish a leader in this way. He did not possess the inspiring voice of FDR, the photogenic qualities of Kennedy, nor the smoothness of Reagan. Still, during the time he was president, Eisenhower offered the only standard by which leaders were judged when they appeared on television. Adlai Stevenson, one of the truly great orators, was criticized again and again because he did not measure up to Eisenhower on the important new medium. Moreover, too much concentration on Eisenhower's physical features diverts attention from the essence of this president's communicative achievement, which was, as Hamby said, the use of public channels in concert with political skills that left few traces of contradiction. Eisenhower did not offer a lone communication blockbuster, such as a "Checkers" speech, for historical edification. More integral to his presidential legacy was that there were no major potholes or disasters. To communicate without drawing attention to one's communication efforts is the hallmark of any activity in that field; while Eisenhower's communications seemed on the surface to be flat, there was a colorful landscape of consultants, stage managers, researchers, and advertising experts behind the scenes who wanted this event to turn out precisely the way it did. Beginning in the 1950s, teams of media experts would be standard features in the highest levels of American leadership. Eisenhower marshaled them and helped define, in Hamby's terminology, the necessary appearance of "effortlessness."

This appearance of effortlessness is not the only explanation for the generally silent acceptance of Eisenhower's communication endeavors. The 1980s revisionist historians found numerous barriers in the Eisenhower field, including the worn perceptions of Eisenhower as a "grandfather president" promoted by people who were influenced more by the 1960s than the 1950s. Perhaps more formidable, though, was Eisenhower himself. So committed was Eisenhower to harmony and consensus that he concealed his personal determination toward achieving them, even though he often rocked the boat with historical consequences.

For example, a standard interpretation of his presidency is Eisenhower's own: his two-volume memoir, *Mandate for Change* (1963) and *Waging Peace* (1965), in which he essentially argued that a person could be president without fitting the definition of a "politician."

Because his own communication activities would have violated that thesis, Eisenhower kept discussion of them to a minimum, despite media "firsts" he could have spotlighted. Memos, diary entries, and records relating to his selling directives, news conference rehearsals, the "Tribune of the People" effort, plans for maximum utilization of TV, and frustrations with the news media were not part of his sourcework. Nor was his relationship with Robert Montgomery. Despite White House records that pinpoint regular contacts between the two men, Eisenhower mentioned Montgomery only once. Eisenhower's objective in the memoirs, as he stated, was to explain his policy and statecraft, but it seems that as well as a "hidden-hand leader," in Fred Greenstein's terms, Eisenhower was also a hidden-hand historian. Wanting to be above the fray, Eisenhower set his agenda apart from the subject of personal pursuit, helping to leave his reputation benign and his communication strategies unstudied.

Another interpretation, or lack of one, that continued through time was that of contemporary writers, reporters, and politicians. In the 1950s these figures scored Eisenhower on political issues but never perceived the forest of mass persuasion among the many individual technical trees. There was periodic conjecture during the Eisenhower era that the president had wide latitude with the mass media; such conjecture included the complaints of editor James Wechsler in 1955 and author Douglass Cater in 1959. This speculation never reached a critical mass, and there was no impetus for further examination. Again, Montgomery provides a good illustration. The White House hid neither the actor's existence on staff nor his physical attendance at most telecasts. It did not have to. Montgomery was able to work in almost total anonymity because he was not considered particularly newsworthy. In 1954 and 1955, his first full years on the job, there were three mentions of him in *U.S. News and World Report*; one story on him in *Life* and one in *Newsweek*; and no stories in *Time*. In the *New York Times* there were a total of ten mentions of him over two full years. As it turned out, the most elaborate treatments of the leading-man-turned-presidential-adviser were feature stories in *Good Housekeeping*, *Women's Home*, and *Coronet* magazines.[2] Press and public considered it quaint that a Hollywood celebrity was in the White House helping a popular president.

The 1950s tended to see presidential mass communication as content with surface aesthetics; most of Eisenhower's contemporaries were blind to his underlying political tactics. Realizing that this blindness helped Eisenhower's image as a nonpolitician, the White House did not elucidate. The one contemporary group that truly grasped Eisenhower's dominance in the media saw the whole topic disappear through its fingers due to its transparency, its lack of markings. This group was the Democratic party. Many Democrats analyzed Eisenhower's media operations with such accuracy that some of their statements could have been confused with White House files and GOP records. They were convinced that the "I Like Ike" imagery was an effect not managed by Eisenhower himself but rather manicured by others. Repeatedly, savvy Democrats portrayed Montgomery, Jim Hagerty, Leonard Hall, Lou Guylay, and the army of media specialists at BBDO as the true nemeses of the Democratic party in the 1950s. Stevenson's critiques were mild compared to the very specific analyses offered to the public by Paul Butler, George Ball, and other Democrats who had hands-on media experience. In the end the Democratic assessment of Eisenhower's media work sounded like sour grapes; even when Democratic party officials expressed it to their own congressional leaders during the Gore Committee hearings in 1956 and 1957, their account was taken about as seriously as Stevenson's chances of moving into the White House that decade.

Kennedy's television-assisted victory in 1960 further obscured Eisenhower's media past, besides depleting whatever interest there was in it. This timing was unfortunate, because not until the period just before the start of the 1960 campaign had political scientists at American universities begun to speculate on what Eisenhower had worked with mass communication.

These insights came from scientific national voting surveys conducted by the Survey Research Center at the University of Michigan in both the 1952 and 1956 campaigns. By the late 1950s the SRC had published a database from the 1956 election that enabled comparisons of voters' attitudes between the elections and, thus, glimpses of how the public perceived Eisenhower in his first four years as president. There were some noteworthy differences. In 1956, for example, 49 percent of respondents said they got most of their political news from television, compared to 24 percent who listed newspapers and 10 percent who said radio. In 1952, only 31 percent had chosen TV; radio had come second, with 28 percent, and newspapers third, with 22 percent.

The SRC data also suggested that Eisenhower capitalized on TV's popularity and its ability to conveniently implant positive visual images about himself and his administration. Not only did the total number of favorable references to Eisenhower increase between 1952 and 1956; more than 21 percent of the favorable references pertained to Eisenhower's kindness, warmth, and likability—twice the percentage of such responses in 1952. These were strikingly high proportions, because the surveys used an open-ended format in which the hundreds of respondents were free to say whatever they wanted. Eisenhower maintained his perceived height in terms of "integrity" and "good, capable, experienced leadership." Unlike in 1952, Eisenhower's reputation was no longer rooted in his military background. In 1952 Eisenhower had been a general; in 1956 he was the president, an obvious outcome but significant because the reinforcement of a presidential image had been a goal of his White House communications. Most of the unfavorable responses in 1956 pertained to Eisenhower's health and age, and there were few of these compared to the number of positive observations about his personality and leadership. When people saw Eisenhower on TV, he looked buoyant and healthy despite his hospitalizations. This image reflected another goal, targeted by the administration's media campaign after the heart attack.

The same data confirmed conclusions most Democrats and Republicans had already reached about Eisenhower's opponent in the two elections. The percentage of favorable references to Stevenson declined between 1952 and 1956. Even though eyewitnesses recalled Stevenson as a spellbinding public speaker, perhaps one of the best to run for president in the twentieth century, the greatest percentage of open-ended responses—twice as many in 1956 than 1952—referred to his poor speaking abilities. In addition, the SRC data may have provided some of the first scientific support regarding the effect of "negative" television campaign advertisements. A comparison of voters who had referred to Stevenson's divorce showed that although the divorce had occurred in 1949, it was mentioned more often in 1956 than in 1952. It may have been that more people knew about the divorce because Stevenson was more familiar in 1956; it may also have been the result of the "Mamie" TV spot, seen again and again on home screens in the fall of 1956.[3]

For a brief time in the late 1950s, before Kennedy burst into the picture in 1960, scholars were fascinated by this apparent Eisenhower image phenomenon. While his reputation as an average-person-turned-war-hero explained Eisenhower's 1952 feat in being elected president on his first try for public office, it seemed inconceivable to scholars that he could maintain his attraction on memories of VE Day. ~~Above all else, he had to have knowledge and political skill to be a~~ successful president. But Eisenhower also had to look like a chief executive, not an Army commander, before the eyes of the American public, which tested him on their ballots and in highly publicized opinion research. Eisenhower assumed the mantle of a president, statesman, and world leader, while keeping his attraction as a concerned, passionate symbol of average people.

Professors Donald Stokes, Warren Miller, and Angus Campbell observed in 1958 that "Mr. Eisenhower's appeal, already strongly personal in 1952, became overwhelmingly so in 1956."[4] Political scientist Ithiel de Sola Pool, in focusing on the 1952 campaign, maintained that Stevenson "did a remarkable job" of creating a favorable image on radio, while TV worked best for Eisenhower, a "rather abstract figure of a savior and conqueror, gracious to his men as a hero should be, but hardly a simple human being with foibles." According to Pool, "what TV did was to chip the graven stereotype" in ways that had nothing to do with the content of his messages, such as "walking, conversing, and interacting with people." Importantly, "Eisenhower made no fool of himself" and consciously fitted his image to "the great expectations that had been built up."[5]

Because Eisenhower's political style depended less on confrontation and more on consensus building, he was interested in salesmanship and had a willingness to use the mass media. As Hamby stated, the consensus era and the media were related, and Eisenhower's knowledge of their relationship was extensive. Yet it did not reach 100 percent. Eisenhower was not instinctively an innovator. Like most effective managers, Eisenhower knew what he liked and knew how to get it—by delegating the tasks of innovation and vision to people like Hagerty, Montgomery, and Hall. Yet the image makers were not policymakers; the two counsels were separate, and Eisenhower was usually the single common member. Some of Eisenhower's decisions missed image possibilities that could have helped him and uplifted the nation and the world. For example, Eisenhower decided in 1960 to continue the U-2 flights over the USSR, risking his meetings with Khrushchev, which caved in as a result. Historians later discovered a missed opportunity that constituted another glaring mistake: they found that had Eisenhower been so inclined, the U.S. could easily have orbited a satellite ahead of Sputnik and avoided much national distress.

But Eisenhower did not miss such opportunities often. He chose, with positive effects, to put his news conferences on the record during the McCarthy controversy in 1953 and 1954, and he himself almost always determined the timing of the live telecasts, such as those during the Suez, Lebanon, and Quemoy-Matsu crises. The trip to Paris after the 1957 stroke, and the TV broadcast that followed, also resulted from decisions by Eisenhower; and it was Eisenhower who finally approved, against much internal opposition, Khrushchev's visit in 1959.

Still, Eisenhower's delegation of consensus-building duties contributed to what even he believed was the major shortcoming in his presidency: his failure to fortify the Republican party.[6] In the 1950s the party's most severe problem was spotty organization at the local level, much the same problem it has had thus far in the 1990s. In 1954 and 1956, and to a lesser extent in 1958, the GOP tried to recruit new members through television appeals; they sidestepped precinct, district, and state committees, and later they found this method to have been a mistake. Television was similarly useless in the party's candidate recruiting problem. In 1956 twenty-two House contests had no Republican candidates; in 1958 many GOP contenders were virtually enlisted off the street and defeated by familiar Democrats.

More than one-third of the treasury of Eisenhower's Republican National Committee passed through the ad agency BBDO, tracing the party's centralized structure. The party's preoccupation with centralization was evident in its disregard for a grassroots vanguard it did have: the Citizens for Eisenhower organizations. Eisenhower tried to explain to the RNC the value of any show of political activism that went beyond ten minutes in a voting booth; because the Citizens groups drew volunteers by the hundreds of thousands, he urged RNC leaders to integrate these groups into the party's local machinery. He wanted local membership roles to be preserved, and he wanted the national and state committees to attempt to interest these volunteers in more sustaining relationships with the GOP—relationships based on moderate principles, not Eisenhower hoopla. Given the type of politics Eisenhower advanced, this was to be sure a tall order. Yet the TV age had clearly reduced but not completely eliminated the significance of party identification locally; there was still a need for strong local party committees that could raise money, anoint candidates, and initiate campaigns. The Republican party of the 1950s could have profited from proselytizing even a fraction of the Citizens members. But the professionals at national headquarters had little serious interest in the amateurs who ran Citizens and its nonpartisan volunteers. The party's top-down philosophy was strikingly apparent in 1956, when the RNC appeased the Citizens group and its partner, the giant Young and Rubicam agency, by making a "sacrifice" of half the national television activities.[7]

Thirty years later, the Republican party still had clout at the top but no reliable means of winning races in every district in the country. Eisenhower deserves credit for resurrecting from near death the central operation of the GOP. Yet even as he insisted on citizen participation, he proceeded on the assumption, widespread at the time, that the new medium of television had the power to perform a quick partisan fix. Few politicians were more rapidly led into this belief; when the 1956 results were in, Eisenhower was still inclined to believe that mass persuasion through outlets such as television was the most efficient means for success. A week after the 1956 election, he discussed his Modern Republicanism with CBS chairman and close friend William Paley and told him, "The selling to the American public of this conversion has not been so well done."[8]

By attempting this conversion, though, at the least Eisenhower helped scholars and strategists understand more about the political media. According to the SRC, the Republican party, for all its national media self-promotion, was perceived only slightly more positively in 1956 than in 1952, while Eisenhower's personal appeal intensified.[9] This data, along with the fact that Eisenhower outpolled GOP candidates in almost every district in 1956, brought into question the coattail theory, articulated only the decade before in E. E. Schattschneider's influential *Party Government*, which had actually contained a formula, based on pluralities in pre-1940s presidential races, for the prediction of an eventual party makeup in Congress.[10] The coattail theory had few adherents by the end of the Ike age. Not only did it collapse in the abstract in scholarly books and articles; the concrete effect was seen at the two party headquarters, which had up to that point been instrumental in filling and developing slates of local candidates; the organizations relied on their standard-bearers to draw party candidates together and, in no small measure, to define the two-party system for Americans prior to elections. The Eisenhower media experience suggested that while a political party was still needed for fund-raising, recruitment, and other tasks, its fate would rest on individual candidates who followed in Eisenhower's footsteps and sought "personal" victories.

Charles Press wrote in 1958 that "the important element that remains is the candidate's ability to campaign hard and win district votes by his own efforts"; this process required candidates at various levels to form their own organizations and rely neither on the strength of a party's national ticket nor on its headquarters.[11] Hall, who under Eisenhower had relied on a top-down concept of party management, had additional thoughts on this matter in 1960. "[W]e still have much to learn about how best to use [television] in a national campaign," Hall maintained in a *Life* article. "Important as television and new transportation methods are, they don't replace the local organization. There is no substitute for this vital element, and there is no substitute for doorbell-ringing and shoe leather." He also correctly predicted that the influence of the national party chair would diminish further as TV filtered down to local races. "[T]here is no longer any place for the traditional party boss," Hall observed. "He was killed by modern communications."[12]

If they had set realistic goals, the Republicans under Eisenhower could have made short but beneficial gains toward grooming badly needed new candidates, increasing their rolls, and offsetting their Depression era image. With the mass media, Eisenhower tried for a touchdown and wound up sacked at his own line, leaving the GOP with more troubles as it headed into the 1960s and beyond.

The Kennedy phenomenon in the 1960s chilled Eisenhower historiography, and the troubled 1970s gave it new energy; now, study of Eisenhower may have reached the doorstep of yet another new phase. Historians must decide how the past relates to living readers of the present amid constantly changing perspectives. One well-covered area in Eisenhower history, his military chess game with the USSR, seems less relevant, or relevant in different ways, following the breakup of the Soviet Union in 1991. The domestic economy and America's status in the world marketplace were also issues that had changed by the 1990s; indeed, after Ronald Reagan left office in 1989, having racked up the largest deficits in American history, it was hard to regard Eisenhower's balanced budgets in 1956, 1957, and 1960, prominent themes in his history, as much more than achievements from a bygone era. Yet barring some dramatic technological breakthrough that makes television obsolete, Eisenhower will remain instantly recognizable and meaningful to future readers through study of his public communication. More Eisenhower studies and comparisons may be required when serious historians visit the administration of Reagan, who followed his actor friend Robert Montgomery into the White House, was known as a "great communicator," and who, like Eisenhower, had eight consecutive and mostly unmarred years as president.

The 1980s confirmed what had happened in the 1950s—that some politicians could swing an image hammer and hit a popularity bell on a continual basis; and this recurrence indicates new needs in Eisenhower research. Although specific domestic decisions and foreign policy maneuvers will continue to mark Eisenhower's story, printed words in history books are not especially suited to relating the reality that the general public, beginning with Eisenhower's time, has continuously witnessed personalities and events with its own eyes and ears. Eisenhower was one of the first presidents to sense that every executive move reverberated through an integrated system of instantaneous, pervasive, audiovisual communications. He also realized the public now received these communications on close to an involuntary basis. The study of presidents who were, and will be, very effective in these areas will require extra energy, because communication ventures are often most apparent in their failure, most obscure in their success.

The traditional question in Eisenhower studies is whether he was a good or a bad president; Stephen Ambrose framed the question in terms of "right or wrong decisions." A different way of framing the question would be: did Eisenhower deserve the overwhelming public acclaim he generated? The answer is "yes." It is true that Eisenhower let the country down in many ways: McCarthyism and civil rights unrest were unchecked, the family farm was squeezed, and America's image abroad was weakened. It is also true that much of what the public saw was merely Eisenhower's exterior. Nevertheless, Eisenhower's communication efforts were clear, honest, and consistent. The "wrong" (Sputnik, U-2) intruded. Yet Eisenhower established a remarkable record for telling the people what he was going to do, doing it, and then telling them it was done. For eight years Eisenhower stood for peace, prosperity, and progress—and he delivered.

Eisenhower's detractors concede this point but still argue that justified public acclaim is not enough, that the 1950s were static years that kept the country where it was, with no link to a better future.

Arthur Schlesinger, Jr., suggested that the revisionist characterization of Eisenhower as a good manager but one who "rows toward his destination with muffled oars" failed to consider the former president's "abdication of the educational role."[13] Thus, another new question arises: did Eisenhower realize the potential of his communicative pulpit and attempt to do more than just reinforce public acclaim?

The answer to this question, too, is "yes." Eisenhower did see himself as an educator. He used his public communication abilities in balancing the federal budget, balancing foreign trade, restraining military spending, comprehending the emergence of the nonaligned nations, and reaching out to this Third World through such things as U.S. foreign aid. Eisenhower's lessons, in fact, were designed to avert many of the problems the nation faces as it nears the end of the century. Eisenhower has been a better educator from the grave than he was during his lifetime, a situation that creates questions for future historians who study Eisenhower's communication strategies. The electronic White House pulpit may, for example, still be only as good as the number of votes a president can wield in Congress; Eisenhower never had as many as he wanted.

Or the pulpit may be only as good as the general public. Historians who depict the 1950s as bland usually blame Eisenhower for not piquing and shaking the masses. In his characteristic role as a "beacon of moderation," though, Eisenhower had tried to stir thinking. Yet the feedback told him that most people did not care about budget balancing and the like; they preferred visions with a lot more pizzazz and immediate gratification, such as expanded entitlement programs and Kennedy's call for a moon program.[14] Such shallow desires were among the reasons Eisenhower never had deep respect for public opinion and condemned Kennedy for appealing to sentiment and emotion. Of course, Eisenhower himself did not entirely reject the gratification approach; he gave the public interstate highways and an end to the war in Korea, stalemated though it was. "Gratification" and "consensus" may be similar terms in post–New Deal leadership. Yet Eisenhower's experiences may suggest that the public is ultimately more crucial to any political education process than some would expect. Social scientists have, in fact, speculated that in a society that relies on communication, the predisposed attentiveness and receptiveness of the public is a force in itself—one that may create more questions for historians as they study the presidents.

Although White House communications in the 1950s were clear, honest, and sometimes purposeful, they were not without darker over-tones. Eisenhower was driven by a public relations mentality and was not averse to privileging image over substance. He assembled the best group of press tacticians, TV consultants, media buyers, creative specialists, and public opinion researchers that money could buy—and Eisenhower could afford them. In many instances Eisenhower saved money by using his influence and personal magnetism to enlist these people. Other politicians did not have these advantages. He delegated duties to media people and, to a small degree, became their pawn. To a larger degree, he strove to keep his public relations an internal matter, between himself, his staff, and the media industry giants who were among his best friends. When the Democrats made an issue of his preemptive use of the media, he did not respond. When he wrote his memoirs, with presidential papers that contained confirming evidence, he ignored the subject.

Nevertheless, despite their partial unseemliness, Eisenhower's presidential communications formed a positive reflection of his presidency. The many recent histories of this period have at least characterized President Eisenhower for what he was: a politician. Eisenhower spent the final twenty-five years of his life criticizing politics. Yet Eisenhower's greatest single achievement as president may have been in honoring the political process. Only a politician can be considered a great president; Eisenhower became a great president, despite his self-conscious rejection of the "politician" label, because his communication skills helped him meet political challenges. Although his media tactics remain open to question, a hundred words of scorn can be countered by the single, realistic observation that he used public channels the way any good and honest politician would, and in doing so, he stood head and shoulders above his challengers. As de Sola Pool said in 1958, he "made no fool of himself."

By focusing mostly on policy, statecraft, and hidden-hand leadership strategies, revisionist scholars in the 1980s revamped Eisenhower's historical image. Eisenhower has come to be viewed not as a retiring political has-been but as an up-to-date, intelligent, and assertive chief executive. The televised Eisenhower affirms and enhances this view. Not only did Eisenhower take advantage of the mass media at their landmark period of rapid expansion; he also acted before anybody was really ready to take note. His faith in mass communication was thus an area in which Eisenhower did not just hold the line but was ahead of his time. It is not too late for historians to recognize this accomplishment, though Eisenhower himself will no longer benefit from the recognition. Nor is it too late to draw from what his administration produced: a multitude of seminal insights about how politics fits into a media age that now has no foreseeable end.

NOTES

Abbreviations

AESP   Adlai E. Stevenson Papers
AWD   Ann Whitman Diary Series
CDJP   C. D. Jackson Papers
CDJR   C. D. Jackson Records
COHP   Columbia University Oral History Project
DDED   DDE Diary Series
DNCR   Democratic National Committee Records
EAS   Eisenhower Administration Series
ECS   Eisenhower Campaign Series
EGF   Eisenhower General File
ELAV   Eisenhower Library audiovisual collection
ELOH   Eisenhower Library Oral History
EOF   Eisenhower Official File
EPCS   Eisenhower Press Conference Series
EPPC   Eisenhower Postpresidential Convenience File
EPPSN   Eisenhower Postpresidential Special Names Series
ESDS   Eisenhower Stag Dinner Series
ESS   Eisenhower Speech Series
GBP   George Ball Papers
GHR   Gabriel Hauge Records
HBP   Harry Butcher Papers
HLOH   Hoover Library Oral History
JFKPP   John F. Kennedy Prepresidential Papers
JHP   James C. Hagerty Papers
KLAV   Kennedy Library audiovisual collection
KLOH   Kennedy Library Oral History
MEP   Milton Eisenhower Papers
RFKP   Robert F. Kennedy Papers
RHP   Robert Humphreys Papers
RNCR   Republican National Committee Records
TSR   Thomas E. Stephens Records
WRP   William E. Robinson Papers
YRR   Young and Rubicam Records

Introduction

1. See diaries, Sept. 24, Sept. 25, Sept. 26, 1955, JHP; diary, Sept. 29, 1955, AWD; Eisenhower, *Mandate for Change*, pp. 535–44; and Nixon, *Six Crises*, pp. 131–67.

2. Hagerty, COHP, p. 300.

3. Transcripts of the Hagerty-White news briefings appear in Dr. White Press Conference file, Box 57, JHP, and Illness Press Conference file, Box 4, JHP.

4. See news conference transcript, Sept. 26, 1955, Box 4, EPCS.

5. Hall, "Len Hall Hails the Revolution," p. 130.

6. Diaries, Oct. and Nov. 1955, AWD.

7. News release, Sept. 27, 1955, Box 4, EPCS.

8. *New York Times*, Oct. 6, 1955.

9. "President Shows Health," *New York Times*, Nov. 29, 1955.

10. Eisenhower, *Eisenhower Diaries*, p. 304.

11. Reaction among reporters to the heart attack appears in Donovan, p. 45; Folliard, p. 43; Morgan, p. 10; and Scherer, p. 31, all in COHP.

12. Robert Riggs, "Democrats Accuse Eisenhower of Hagertizing," *Louisville Courier-Journal*, Sept. 2, 1956.

13. Greenstein, *Hidden-Hand Presidency*, pp. 92–99.

14. Ambrose, *Eisenhower: The President*, p. 53.

15. Ferrell, Introduction to Hagerty, *Hagerty*, p. xiii.

16. Griffith, "Corporate Commonwealth," pp. 89–96.

17. Ambrose, *Eisenhower: 1890–1952*, p. 176.

Chapter One

1. Ambrose, *Eisenhower: 1890–1952*, p. 66.

2. Milton Eisenhower, *President Is Calling*, pp. 53–69.

3. Ambrose and Immerman, *Milton Eisenhower*, pp. 42–52.

4. Winkler, *Politics of Propaganda*, pp. 29–37. Also see "War Information—Domestic Phase," undated, Box 1, MEP.

5. Press conference transcript, July 14, 1942, Box 1, HBP.

6. Diary, July 14, 1942, Box 9, and press conference transcript, July 14, 1942, Box 1, both in HBP.

7. Diary, June 6, 1944, Box 11, HBP.

8. Diary, Dec. 6, 1944, Box 11, HBP.

9. "Bridge at Remagen," 1945, ELAV.

10. Diary, Dec. 10, 1942, DDED.

11. Hamby, *Liberalism*, p. 100.

12. Diary, Mar. 8, 1947, DDED.

13. Eisenhower, *Mandate for Change*, p. 5; diary, Nov. 28, 1959, DDED.

14. Ambrose, *Eisenhower: 1890–1952*, pp. 454–56; Miller, *Ike the Soldier*, pp. 379–81.

15. Eisenhower, *Mandate for Change*, pp. 10–11.

16. Levy interview with author.

17. Lang and Lang, *Politics and Television*, pp. 84–91; also see David, Moos, and Goldman, *Presidential Nominating Politics*, pp. 67–100.

18. Hollitz, "Eisenhower and the Admen," pp. 25–39; Wood, "First Political Spot Ad Campaign," pp. 265–83.

19. Barkin, "Eisenhower's Television Planning Board," pp. 319–31, and "Eisenhower's Secret Strategy," pp. 18–28.

20. Wills, "Nixon Agonistes," pp. 93–107.

21. Folliard, COHP, p. 28.

22. Eisenhower, *Mandate for Change*, pp. 133–35, 193–94.

23. James Hagerty to Sherman Adams, Dec. 1952, Box 10, JHP.

24. Diary, Feb. 7, 1953, DDED.

25. Diary, Apr. 1, 1953, DDED.

26. Diary, July 24, 1953, DDED.

27. Diary, Apr. 1, 1953, DDED.

28. Ambrose, *Eisenhower: The President*, p. 53.

29. Arthur Krock, "Eisenhower Criticized," Apr. 5, 1953, and "Eisenhower Expected to Step Up Pace Soon," Apr. 26, 1953, both in *New York Times*.

30. James Reston, "President Tries Middle Way," *New York Times*, May 5, 1953.

31. James Reston, "Eisenhower-Taft Split," *New York Times*, May 31, 1953.

32. Ambrose, *Eisenhower: The President*, p. 81.

33. Maxwell Rabb to Adams, Jan. 8, 1953, Box 415, EOF.

34. Gabriel Hauge to Adams, May 14, June 3, 1953, Box 415, EOF.

35. Henry Cabot Lodge to Eisenhower, Oct. 30, 1953, Box 415, EOF.

36. Daily log, Dec. 2, 1953, CDJP.

37. Memorandum to cabinet, Nov. 5, 1953, DDED.

38. Memorandum to staff, Nov. 23, 1953, DDED.

39. Stanley Rumbough to Adams, Nov. 5, 1953, Box 415, EOF.

40. Lodge to Wilton Persons, Nov. 12, 1953, Box 415, EOF.

41. Charles Willis to Adams, Nov. 17, 1953, Box 415, EOF.

42. Parmet, *Eisenhower and the American Crusades*, pp. 57–60.

43. "Robert Montgomery," in Vinson, *Actors and Actresses*, pp. 448–49.

44. "Lady in the Lake," review, Jan. 24, 1947, and Bosley Crowther, "Subjective Film," Feb. 9, 1947, both in *New York Times*.

45. "Actors Elect Reagan," *New York Times*, Nov. 18, 1947.

46. "Behind the Scenes: Robert Montgomery," *New York Times*, Mar. 1, 1956.

47. Montgomery, *Open Letter*, p. 59.

48. Murray Snyder to Lewis Deschler, Dec. 30, 1953, Box 415, EOF.

49. Broadcast transcript, Dec. 24, 1953, Box 5, ESS.

Chapter Two

1. List of President Eisenhower's speeches, Box 34, JHP.

2. Edwards interview with author.

3. Hagerty, COHP, p. 427.

4. See Box 34, JHP; films and kinescopes of several 1954 telecasts appear in ELAV.

5. Eisenhower to Robert Montgomery, Aug. 25, 1954, DDED.

6. Diary, July 31, 1953, DDED.

7. Eisenhower to Montgomery, Jan. 26, 1956, Box 26, EAS.

8. Levy interview with author.

9. Eisenhower to Edgar Eisenhower, Nov. 22, 1955, DDED.

10. Eisenhower to William Paley, Jan. 15, 1964, Box 15, EPPSN.

11. Khrushchev, *Khrushchev Remembers*, p. 407.

12. See Greenstein, *Hidden-Hand Presidency*, pp. 15–54; Arthur Krock, "Impressions of the President and the Man," *New York Times Magazine*, June 23, 1957, pp. 5, 34–39.

13. Montgomery, *Open Letter*, pp. 62–64.

14. Eisenhower, *Mandate for Change*, p. 299.

15. Eisenhower to Montgomery, Mar. 16, 1954, DDED.

16. Ambrose, *Eisenhower: The President*, pp. 166–67.

17. "Robert Montgomery Presents: President as a Pro," *Life*, Apr. 19, 1954, pp. 28–29.

18. Diary, Apr. 6, 1954, JHP.

19. See Wheaton, COHP, pp. 120–23; Scherer, COHP, pp. 23–26.

20. Scherer, COHP, pp. 23–25; Montgomery, *Open Letter*, pp. 61–64.

21. Scherer, COHP, p. 24.

22. Ibid., p. 25.

23. Montgomery, *Open Letter*, p. 62.

24. Diary, Jan. 4, 1954, JHP.

25. "Behind the Scenes: Robert Montgomery," *New York Times*, Mar. 1, 1956.

26. Levy interview with author.

27. Diary, Feb. 7, 1953, DDED.

28. Griffith, "Corporate Commonwealth," pp. 93–94, 104.

29. Diaries, Apr. 27, 1950 and Sept. 25, 1951, DDED.

30. Gabriel Hauge to Eisenhower, Mar. 1954, Box 1, GHR.

31. Hagerty, COHP, pp. 486, 493.

32. See Leonard Hall to Eisenhower, Nov. 10, 1953, Box 30, EAS.

33. Larmon, COHP, p. 29.

34. Kelley, *Professional Public Relations*, p. 189.

35. See Public Opinion Index file, Box 7, YRR.

36. Kelley, *Professional Public Relations*, p. 172.

37. Newton interview with author; Hauge to Eisenhower, Oct. 25, 1954, Box 1, GHR.

38. Eisenhower to J. C. Cornelius, Feb. 2, 1954, DDED.

39. Eisenhower to Roy Howard, Feb. 2, Feb. 9, 1954, DDED.

40. Public Opinion Index file, Box 7, YRR.

41. Memorandum to staff, Nov. 23, 1953, DDED.

42. Eisenhower to William Robinson, Feb. 12, 1954, DDED.

43. Meeting summary, Eisenhower and Ezra Taft Benson, Oct. 29, 1955, DDED.

44. Cook, *Declassified Eisenhower*, pp. 178–81.

45. See Eisenhower to C. D. Jackson, May 17, 1954, DDED.

46. Discussion of Eisenhower's board of strategy appears in his Nov. 23, 1953 memorandum. Also see Hauge to Eisenhower, Nov. 11, 1953, Box 1, GHR; Eisenhower to Frank Stanton, Mar. 30, 1954, DDED; and Paley to Eisenhower, Mar. 19, 1960, DDED.

47. Eisenhower to Sigurd Larmon, Jan. 15, 1954, DDED; Larmon, COHP, pp. 50–55.

48. Larmon, COHP, pp. 49–50. Also see Chalmers Roberts, "The Day We Didn't Go to War," *The Reporter*, Sept. 14, 1954, pp. 31–35.

49. Eisenhower to Larmon, Jan. 15, 1954, DDED.

50. Eisenhower to Adams, Apr. 1, 1954, DDED.

51. Hagerty, COHP, p. 56.

52. Diaries, Mar. 2, Mar. 25, 1954, JHP.

53. Eisenhower to Henry Cabot Lodge, Sept. 8, 1954, DDED.

54. Eisenhower to Robinson, Aug. 4, 1954, DDED.

55. Diary, June 18, 1954, JHP.

56. Eisenhower, *Mandate for Change*, p. 440.

57. Lodge to Eisenhower, July 30, 1954, DDED.

58. Eisenhower to Everett Hazlett, Dec. 8, 1954, DDED.

Chapter Three

1. Pollard, "Eisenhower: The First Two Years," pp. 285–300.

2. Donovan interview with author.

3. "The President and the Press," Oct. 26, 1953, pp. 61–64, and "Correspondents' View," Nov. 30, 1953, p. 80, both in *Time*.

4. Eisenhower to John Hay Whitney, Nov. 24, 1960, DDED.

5. Eisenhower, HLOH, p. 105.

6. Eisenhower to Milton Eisenhower, Jan. 15, 1968, Box 1, MEP.

7. Griffith, *Politics of Fear*, p. 140. Additional accounts of the McCarthy-era press appear in Bayley, *Joe McCarthy and the Press*, and Aronson, *Press and the Cold War*.

8. Eisenhower to Everett Hazlett, July 21, 1953, DDED.

9. Memorandum to cabinet, Nov. 5, 1953, DDED.

10. Snyder, COHP, p. 38.

11. News conference transcript, Nov. 11, 1953, Box 69, JHP; James Reston, "Patriotism Backed," *New York Times*, Nov. 12, 1953; Robert Donovan, *New York Herald Tribune*, Nov. 12, 1953.

12. "The President and the Press," *Time*, Oct. 26, 1953, pp. 61–64.

13. Eisenhower, *Mandate for Change*, pp. 108, 232–33.

14. Daily log, Dec. 2, 1953, Box 56, CDJP.

15. "Atomic Power for Peace," USIA, Dec. 8, 1953, ELAV.

16. "Radio Press Conference," editorial, and Arthur Krock, "In the Nation," both in *New York Times*, Dec. 18, 1953.

17. Pollard, "Eisenhower: The First Two Years," p. 288.

18. Diary, Jan. 18, 1954, DDED.

19. Eisenhower, *Mandate for Change*, p. 290.

20. Ibid.

21. Diaries, Feb. 2, Feb. 8, 1954, JHP.

22. James Reston, "Other Cheek Is Struck," *New York Times*, Mar. 3, 1954.

23. Diary, Mar. 4, 1954, JHP.

24. Hagerty, COHP, p. 77.

25. Diary, Mar. 15, 1954, JHP.

26. Donovan, COHP, p. 9.

27. Hagerty, COHP, p. 441.

28. Donovan interview with author. Also see Smith, COHP, p. 26; Morgan, COHP, p. 9; and Scherer, COHP, p. 16.

29. Hagerty, COHP, pp. 183, 222.

30. Ibid., p. 179.

31. Diaries, June 3, June 7, 1954, JHP.

32. Eisenhower had used his influence with the networks to keep McCarthy off the air; some historians feel that this skirmish over equal time helped precipitate the Army-McCarthy hearings. See Greenstein, *Hidden-Hand Presidency*, pp. 194–95, and Crandell, "Eisenhower the Strategist," pp. 487–502.

33. Diary, Feb. 3, 1955, JHP.

34. Diary, June 7, 1954, JHP.

35. Hagerty, COHP, pp. 78–79.

36. Film, "Cabinet Meeting," Oct. 25, 1954, ELAV.

37. See Wayne Oliver, "How Those Press Conferences Are Set Up for TV," Associated Press report, Mar. 12, 1955, Box 103, JHP.

38. Hagerty, COHP, pp. 78–79.

39. Eisenhower to Milton Eisenhower, Aug. 28, 1956, DDED.

40. Diary, Jan. 18, 1955, JHP.

41. Scherer, COHP, pp. 3–6.

42. Excerpts were seen on the evening news programs; CBS carried the full news conference at 7:30 P.M., ABC at 9:30 P.M., and NBC at 11:30 P.M.; the telecast was also seen on the Dumont network. A kinescope of the news conference can be found in ELAV.

43. "President's News Conference Filmed for TV," and Jack Gould, "President's Press Conference an Example to Millions of Democracy at Work," both in *New York Times*, Jan. 20, 1955.

44. "Camera, Mr. President," editorial, Jan. 21, 1955, and Arthur Krock, "President Takes Risks in TV News Questions," Jan. 23, 1955, both in *New York Times*.

45. James Wechsler, "Any Resemblance between This Show and Real Life Is Infrequent," Jan. 23, 1955, and "The White House Show (Passed by the Censor)," Feb. 3, 1955, both in *New York Post*.

46. Oliver, "Those Press Conferences."

47. Hagerty, COHP, p. 81.

48. Donovan, COHP, p. 17.

49. Arthur Krock, "In the Nation," *New York Times*, Jan. 21, 1955.

50. Diary, Jan. 20, 1955, JHP. Although the Democrats did not formally appeal for equal time in the 1950s, the Republicans succeeded with such a challenge in 1964. The FCC's ruling in 1964 affirmed what Hagerty believed was true nine years before: the news conferences were not bona fide news events because the White House, not the press corps, controlled the format. See Columbia Broadcasting System, Inc., 3 R.R.2d 623 (1964), and Republican National Committee, 3 R.R.2d 647 (1964).

51. James Hagerty to Gabriel Hauge, June 8, 1955, Box 398, EOF.

52. See L. Richard Guylay to Hagerty, May 24, 1955, Box 397, EOF.

Chapter Four

1. Diary, Nov. 28, 1959, DDED; Eisenhower, *Mandate for Change*, pp. 17–20.

2. Eisenhower, COHP, pp. 85–86.

3. SRC figures appear in Austin, *Political Facts*, pp. 387–88.

4. Eisenhower, *Mandate for Change*, p. 431.

5. ~~Ibid.~~

6. Adkins, COHP, p. 24.

7. "Hard Campaigner Always," *New York Times*, July 13, 1956.

8. Hall, ELOH, p. 51.

9. "Hard Campaigner," *New York Times*.

10. Phillips, "Party Chairmen."

11. "Enrollment of New Republicans," Aug. 31, 1955, Box 3, ECS.

12. Republican National Committee organizational chart, Apr. 14, 1956, Box 230, RNCR. Also see Adkins, COHP, p. 55.

13. Guylay, COHP, p. 64.

14. Newton interview with author.

15. Guylay, COHP, p. 9.

16. James Reston, "The Busy Republicans," *New York Times*, Sept. 15, 1955.

17. See Henry Cabot Lodge to Eisenhower, July 30, 1954, DDED.

18. Plans Board files, Box 22, TSR.

19. Hall, ELOH, pp. 85–86.

20. Meeting summary, Eisenhower and Merriman Smith, Nov. 23, 1954, DDED.

21. Edward Bacher to Leonard Hall, Nov. 24, 1955, Box 101, RNCR.

22. Bacher to Hall, Apr. 13, 1954, and Hall memorandum to RNC staff, Apr. 23, 1954, both in Box 101, RNCR.

23. McCann-Erickson, Inc., figures from Bogart, *Age of Television*, p. 185.

24. "CBS Class A Prime Time Costs," undated, Box 383, DNCR.

25. Newton interview with author.

26. Ibid.

27. Ibid.

28. See Stag Dinner guest list files, Box 1, ESDS.

29. Senate report on 1956 campaign spending in *Congressional Record*, 85th Cong., 1st sess., 1957, 103, pt. 2:1727–34, and *Congressional Record*, 85th Cong., 1st sess., 1957, 103, pt. 4:4773–95 and 5588–5606.

30. Cabinet meeting notes, Sept. 28, 1956, DDED.

31. Alexander, *Money in Politics*, p. 281.

32. *Congressional Record*, 85th Cong., 1st sess., 1957, 103, pt. 4:4773–95 and 5588–5606.

33. Charles Willis to Sherman Adams, Oct. 23, 1953, Box 99, RNCR.

34. Hall memorandum to RNC staff, July 16, 1954, Box 101, RNCR; 1955 Campaign School file, Box 2, RHP.

35. Republican National Committee organizational chart, Apr. 14, 1956, Box 230, RNCR.

36. Eisenhower, *Mandate for Change*, pp. 440–42.

37. Diary, Dec. 20, 1954, JHP.

38. C. D. Jackson to Henry Luce, Dec. 21, 1954, CDJP.

39. Eisenhower to Gabriel Hauge, May 25, 1955, Box 6, AWD.

40. Diary, Feb. 14, 1955, JHP.

41. Diary, Feb. 17, 1955, JHP.

42. "What Ike Will Do in the Campaign," *U.S. News and World Report*, Mar. 2, 1956, pp. 19–21.

43. RNC guide for 1955 Campaign School, Sept. 7, 1955, Box 2, RHP.

44. Hall, "Len Hall Hails the Revolution," pp. 126–27.

45. RNC 1956 campaign plan, undated, Box 11, RHP.

46. L. Richard Guylay to Hall, Aug. 9, 1955, Box 103, RNCR.

47. RNC guide for 1955 Campaign School, Sept. 7, 1955, Box 2, RHP.

48. Guylay, COHP, p. 85.

49. Newton interview with author.

50. "Plan for Citizen Action," July 30, 1952, Box 1, ECS.

51. Eisenhower to Cliff Roberts, Oct. 30, 1954, DDED; Eisenhower to James Murphy, Nov. 2, 1954, Box 2, ECS.

52. See Sigurd Larmon to David Levy, Mar. 7, 1956, Box 5, YRR.

53. Willis to Hall, Feb. 15, 1955, Box 103, RNCR.

54. Zaghi, ELOH, p. 9.

55. "Top Ranking Radio-TV Agencies 1952–1955," *Broadcasting*, Dec. 3, 1956, pp. 30–31; "Revlon Shifts to BBDO," *Broadcasting*, Jan. 16, 1956, p. 31.

56. Hollitz, "Eisenhower and the Admen."

57. Newton interview with author.

58. Harding interview with author.

59. Monitoring file, Box 6; National Citizens for Eisenhower-Nixon Summary Report, Box 6; and "Status Report on Network Television," Sept. 21, 1956, Box 7, all in YRR.

60. Guylay, COHP, p. 78.

61. Newton interview with author.

62. Harding interview with author.

63. Eisenhower, *Mandate for Change*, p. 429.

64. "TV Film Has Duet by Eisenhowers," *New York Times*, June 24, 1956.

65. A summary of 1956 campaign spending appears in *Congressional Record*, 85th Cong., 1st sess., 1957, 103, pt. 4:4773–95 and 5588–5606.

66. Levy interview with author.

67. Newton interview with author.

68. Ibid.

69. RNC guide for 1955 Campaign School, Sept. 7, 1955, Box 2, RHP.

70. Diary, Sept. 10, 1955, AWD.

Chapter Five

1. Eisenhower, *Waging Peace*, p. 5.
2. Film, Eisenhower address, Feb. 29, 1956, ELAV.
3. Adams, COHP, p. 219.
4. Ambrose, *Eisenhower: The President*, pp. 271, 291–92.
5. Diary, Apr. 21, 1953, in Slater, *Ike I Knew*.
6. Ambrose, *Eisenhower: The President*, p. 289.
7. For this reason, Paul Dudley White, the attending physician, told reporters on Oct. 9, 1955, that he was not sure whether Eisenhower would be able to run for office; White echoed a similar sentiment on Dec. 17. News briefing transcripts, Box 57, JHP.
8. Meeting summary, Eisenhower and RNC staff, July 25, 1956, Box 3, ECS.
9. Eisenhower to Walter Hoving, Oct. 11, 1956, Box 415, EOF.
10. Ewald, *Eisenhower the President*, p. 158.
11. Hall, "Len Hall Hails the Revolution," p. 130.
12. Diaries, Dec. 12, Dec. 13, Dec. 14, 1955, JHP.
13. Guylay, COHP, pp. 55, 78–89.
14. Diary, Nov. 28, 1955, AWD.
15. Hall, "Len Hall Hails the Revolution," pp. 126–27.
16. Folger, COHP, p. 19; Hall, "Len Hall Hails the Revolution," p. 136.
17. Leonard Hall to Eisenhower, Jan. 23, 1956, Box 17, EAS; Eisenhower to Hall, Jan. 23, 1956, Box 709, EOF.
18. Meeting summary, Eisenhower and Nixon, Feb. 7, 1956, DDED.
19. Diaries, Feb. 8, Feb. 9, 1956, AWD.
20. News briefing transcript, Feb. 14, 1956, Box 57, JHP.
21. Diaries, Feb. 27, Feb. 29, 1956, AWD.
22. Films, news conference and Eisenhower TV address, Feb. 29, 1956, both in ELAV.
23. Scherer, COHP, pp. 13–14.
24. See C. A. Siepman, "TV and the Campaign," *Nation*, Mar. 17, 1956, pp. 218–20; "President Plans TV Drive," *New York Times*, May 14, 1956; "Hagerty Sees GOP Electronic Drive," *Christian Science Monitor*, May 16, 1956; and "Ike's Health, TV and the Campaign," *Newsweek*, May 16, 1956, pp. 31–32.
25. "President Plans TV Drive," *New York Times*.

Chapter Six

1. Guggenheim interview with author.
2. Schlesinger interview with author.

3. Scammon, *America Votes*, passim.

4. Leo Egan, "Butler of Indiana Heads Democrats," *New York Times*, Dec. 5, 1954.

5. Phillips, "Party Chairmen," pp. 10–11.

6. Paul Ziffren to Harold Leventhal, Mar. 24, 1954, Equal Time file, Box 419, DNCR.

7. "Uses of Broadcast Facilities by Candidates for Public Office," Federal Communications Commission, Document 54–1155, 1954, appearing in Box 385, DNCR.

8. Paul Butler to Harold Fellows, Mar. 21, 1956, Box 418, DNCR.

9. Fellows to Butler, Mar. 23, 1956, Box 418, DNCR.

10. Harding interview with author.

11. Joseph Heffernan to Butler, July 29, 1955, Box 383, DNCR.

12. Diamond and Bates, *The Spot*, pp. 46–51.

13. Emerson Foote to Butler, Mar. 14, 1955, Box 413, DNCR.

14. See "Democrats Find Few Takers for '56 Campaign Account," *Advertising Age*, Aug. 22, 1955, p. 1; "Donkey Business," *Broadcasting*, Oct. 24, 1955; and Thomas M. Jones, "Who Will Handle Advertising of '56 Presidential Campaigns?," *Printer's Ink*, Nov. 11, 1955, pp. 23–25, 108–9.

15. Ad Agency file, Box 375, DNCR.

16. Butler to Herbert Bayard Swope, Aug. 6, 1955, Box 413, DNCR.

17. Kummel interview with author.

18. Newton interview with author.

19. Abraham Feinberg to Butler, Aug. 8, 1955, Box 413, DNCR.

20. Advertising billing report, *Broadcasting*, Dec. 3, 1956.

21. Feinberg to Butler, Aug. 8, 1955, Box 413, DNCR.

22. Eugene Kummel to Butler, Oct. 31, 1955, Box 376, DNCR.

23. Butler to Heffernan, Feb. 6, 1956, Box 413, DNCR.

24. Meeting summaries, Norman, Craig and Kummel and DNC, Feb. 10, Feb. 20, 1956, Box 419, DNCR.

25. Ibid.

26. Clayton Fritchey to Butler, July 1, 1955, Box 414, DNCR.

27. Butler to Sam Ervin, May 31, 1955, Box 393, DNCR.

28. Heffernan to Butler, July 29, 1955, Box 383, DNCR.

29. Jack Christie to *Broadcasting*, Apr. 18, 1957, Box 375, DNCR.

30. Don Durgin to Butler, Jan. 9, 1956, Box 383, DNCR.

31. DNC news release, Apr. 20, 1956, Box 385, DNCR.

32. Newton interview with author.

33. Butler to Democratic state and county committee chairs, June 14, 1955, Box 387, DNCR.

34. Ibid.

35. Radio-Television Program Audience file, Box 388, DNCR.

36. Meeting summaries, Norman, Craig and Kummel and DNC, Mar. 8, Aug. 31, 1956, Box 419, DNCR.

37. *Congressional Record*, 85th Cong., 1st sess., 1957, 103, pt. 4:4773–95 and 5588–5606. Also see Alexander, *Money in Politics*, p. 96.

38. Butler to John C. Kelly, Aug. 6, 1955, Box 413, DNCR.

39. Martin, *Stevenson and the World*, p. 255.

40. Speech transcript, Feb. 4, 1956, Box 77, AESP.

41. Speech transcript, Mar. 28, 1956, Box 82, AESP.

42. See Leo Egan, "Harriman Tactics," May 20, 1956, and "Harriman Forces," June 24, 1956, both in *New York Times*.

43. Richard J. H. Johnston, "Kefauver Scores Minnesota Upset," *New York Times*, Mar. 21, 1956. Also see Thomson and Shattuck, *1956 Campaign*, p. 62.

44. Jack Gould, "TV: Political Politeness," *New York Times*, May 22, 1956.

45. Lawrence W. Davies, "Stevenson Scores Victory," *New York Times*, June 6, 1956.

46. Delegate poll, June 8, 1956, from Davis, *Presidential Primaries*, p. 83.

47. CBS news release, May 23, 1955, Box 376, DNCR; Heffernan to Butler, July 29, 1955, Box 383, DNCR.

48. Butler to Lyndon Johnson, Nov. 10, 1955, Box 418, DNCR.

49. Dunn, *Financing Presidential Campaigns*, p. 99.

50. Butler to Leonard Hall, Feb. 7, 1956, and Butler to Frank Stanton, Feb. 8, 1956, both in Box 419, DNCR.

51. Martin, *Stevenson and the World*, pp. 354–55.

52. Butler to networks, Feb. 29, 1956; Robert Sarnoff to Butler, Mar. 1, 1956; Sig Mickelson to Butler, Mar. 1, 1956; John Poor to Butler, Mar. 5, 1956; Robert Kintner to Butler, Mar. 6, 1956, all in Box 419, DNCR.

53. Butler to Christie, Mar. 12, 1956, Box 378, DNCR.

54. Reggie Schuebel to Butler, Mar. 28, 1956, Box 378, DNCR.

55. Richard J. H. Johnston, "Butler Criticizes Illness Report," *New York Times*, June 13, 1956.

56. Morgan, COHP, p. 10.

Chapter Seven

1. Lang and Lang, *Politics and Television*, pp. 78–149.

2. Davis, *National Party Conventions*, pp. 189–90, 207–10; Parris, *Convention Problem*, pp. 142, 150.

3. Richard Hofstadter in introduction to "NBC Student Guide for National Conventions," brochure, National Broadcasting Company, New York, June 1956, Box 383, DNCR.

4. FCC figures from *Radio Annual and Television Yearbook, 1957*, p. 73.

5. See "The 120 Million Audience," *Time*, Aug. 13, 1956, pp. 36–37, and "Preview Convention '56: TV and Radio," *Newsweek*, Aug. 13, 1956, pp. 32–34. Figures on television coverage of the 1952 conventions can be found in "Television Convention," *Newsweek*, July 14, 1952, p. 85, and "One Big Stage," *Time*, July 25, 1952, pp. 38–41.

6. *Congressional Record*, 83d Cong., 2d sess., 1954, 100, pt. 5:6505. In May 1956, Bricker sponsored a bill to move several VHF stations to UHF; see *Congressional Record*, 84th Cong., 2d sess., 1956, 102, pt. 6:8210–11.

7. CBS news release, June 23, and NBC news release, June 14, 1956, Box 383, DNCR.

8. *Congressional Record*, 84th Cong., 2d sess., 1956, 102, pt. 6:8325–26.

9. "House Committee on Monopoly Hunt," *Broadcasting*, July 16, 1956. The NBC-Westinghouse deal was revoked by the Justice Department in 1958.

10. "First Report: CBS, NBC TV Sales," *Broadcasting*, Nov. 12, 1956, pp. 32–42.

11. Pulse, Inc., audience figures appearing in *Broadcasting*, July 23, 1956, p. 36.

12. CBS news release, May 14, 1956, Box 383, DNCR.

13. NBC news release, May 18, 1956, Box 383, DNCR.

14. NBC news release, Apr. 27, 1956, Box 418, DNCR.

15. NBC news release, Aug. 7, 1956, Box 383, DNCR.

16. Sig Mickelson, "The Electronic Revolution in Politics," CBS news release, July 3, 1956, Box 383, DNCR.

17. Jack Christie to Paul Butler, Jan. 6, 1956, Box 388, DNCR.

18. Diaries, Feb. 14, Feb. 17, 1955, JHP. Also see materials pertaining to the convention site selection in Box 226, RNCR.

19. Cotter and Hennessey, *Politics without Power*, pp. 114–15.

20. George McElrath to Butler, Oct. 25, 1955, Box 383, DNCR.

21. See Pre-Convention Planning file, Box 10, RHP.

22. Hugh Morrow, "Watch Your Step at the Conventions," *Saturday Evening Post*, July 5, 1952, pp. 28–29, 75–76. Also see Larry Wolters, "Video Coverage of the Conventions," *New York Times*, June 15, 1952.

23. "TV Fashion Advice," *New York Times*, Aug. 4, 1956. Also see Leonard Hall file, Box 17, EAS, and Convention file, Box 2, ECS.

24. Mickelson to Butler, June 18, 1956, Box 418, DNCR; Hall to Republican National Committee members and state chairs, July 18, 1956, Box 75, RNCR.

25. Thomson and Shattuck, *1956 Campaign*, pp. 119–20, 179–80.

26. Russell Baker, "Democrats to Go Television Blue," *New York Times*, Aug. 13, 1956.

27. W. H. Lawrence, "Democratic Keynote Talk Assails Nixon," *New York Times*, Aug. 14, 1956.

28. Meeting summary, Norman, Craig and Kummel and DNC, May 9, 1956, Box 419, DNCR.

29. "Pursuit of Happiness," DNC film, Aug. 14, 1956, KLAV.

30. "C.B.S. Head Backs TV Film Deletion," *New York Times*, Aug. 15, 1956; "Platform Editor," *Time*, Aug. 27, 1956, p. 54.

31. W. H. Lawrence, "Near a Majority," *New York Times*, Aug. 16, 1956.

32. William S. White, "Civil Rights Compromise Voted," *New York Times*, Aug. 16, 1956.

33. Martin, *Stevenson and the World*, pp. 350–52.

34. Edwards interview with author.

35. W. H. Lawrence, "Kefauver Nominated," *New York Times*, Aug. 18, 1956.

36. "The Coverage Was There But Was the Audience?," *Business Week*, Sept. 1, 1956, p. 27.

37. NBC coverage, Aug. 17, 1956.

38. "The Biggest Studio," *Time*, Aug. 27, 1956, p. 43.

39. John Crosby and Lucia Carter, "Two Critics Comment on TV's Coverage of the Conventions," *Chicago Sun-Times*, Aug. 15, 1956.

40. Jack Gould, "Routine Show," *New York Times*, Aug. 19, 1956.

41. Edwards interview with author.

42. Hall, "Len Hall Hails the Revolution," p. 134. Also see Democratic National Convention file, Box 718, EOF.

43. Eisenhower to Everett Hazlett, Aug. 20, 1956, DDED.

44. Eisenhower to Hall, Aug. 18, 1956, DDED.

45. CBS kinescopes of each of the five sessions of the Republican convention can be found in ELAV.

46. See Box 3, ECS. Some of the other events are recalled in Folger, COHP, p. 17.

47. W. H. Lawrence, "Eisenhower Flies to Convention," *New York Times*, Aug. 22, 1956.

48. Hall, ELOH, pp. 51–55.

49. Nixon-Stassen file, Box 717, EOF.

50. NBC coverage, Aug. 22, 1956.

51. W. H. Lawrence, "Eisenhower and Nixon Renominated," *New York Times*, Aug. 23, 1956.

52. W. H. Lawrence, "Eisenhower's Acceptance," *New York Times*, Aug. 24, 1956.

53. Williams, "Choosing Candidates," p. 268.

54. Discussion of proposed reforms in the conventions appears in Wildavsky, "National Conventions," and Shafer, *Evolution and Reform*.

55. "Were You Watching?," *Newsweek*, Sept. 10, 1956, p. 54.

56. Marya Mannes, "TV: Too Much of a Good Thing?," *The Reporter*, Sept. 6, 1956, pp. 21–22.

57. Viewership of the 1952 conventions is discussed in Thomson, *Television and Presidential Politics*, pp. 44–45.

58. A. C. Nielsen Company news release, Sept. 19, 1956, Box 383, DNCR.

59. "Were You Watching?," *Newsweek*.

60. See Robert Kennedy, KLOH, p. 660. The importance Kennedy backers placed on JFK's TV appeal appear in circulars written by Kennedy aide Theodore Sorensen and distributed to delegates at the 1956 convention. These appear in Box 810, JFKPP.

61. Jack Gould, "TV: Witty Commentator," *New York Times*, Aug. 17, 1956.

62. Eisenhower to Robert Montgomery, Sept. 4, 1956, Box 710, EOF.

63. Hall, "Len Hall Hails the Revolution," p. 127.

64. Guylay, COHP, pp. 9, 83.

65. May and Fraser, *Campaign '72*, p. 174.

66. Edwards interview with author.

67. Press Party file, Box 6, GBP.

Chapter Eight

1. See Stokes, Campbell, and Miller, "Electoral Decision," and Press, "Voting Statistics." Results of this voting research are discussed in the Conclusion.

2. See Alexander, *Money in Politics*, for 1952 expenditures; 1956 expenditures appear in the Gore Committee Report, *Congressional Record*, 85th Cong., 1st sess., 1957, 103, pt. 2:1727–34 and pt. 4:4773–95 and 5588–5606.

3. "Status Report on Network Television," Box 7, YRR.

4. RNC guide for 1958 Campaign School, Oct. 1958, Box 2, RHP; BBDO, "Public Opinion Survey on Political Issues," Dec. 1954, Box 3, ECS.

5. RNC 1956 campaign plan, undated, Box 11, RHP.

6. Sigurd Larmon to David Levy, Mar. 7, 1956, Box 5, YRR.

7. Levy interview with author.

8. Speech transcript, Apr. 17, 1956, Box 15, ESS; Levy to Thomas Lapham, Box 5, YRR; "Copy Memorandum, Citizens for Eisenhower," May 8, 1956, Box 6, YRR.

9. Lists of President Eisenhower's Speeches, Box 34, JHP.

10. Levy to Young and Rubicam staff, July 1956, Box 6, YRR.

11. Hollitz, "Eisenhower and the Admen."

12. Levy interview with author.

13. "Citizens for Eisenhower-Nixon TV Operations," Versions 1 and 2, Sept. 13, 1956, Box 6, YRR. Also see Levy to Young and Rubicam staff, Aug. 28, 1956, in same box.

14. William Morris Agency to Preston Wood, telex, Sept. 12, 1956, Box 9, YRR.

15. Levy interview with author; Dorothy Houghton to Larmon, Sept. 27, 1956, Box 5, YRR.

16. Ben Duffy to Sherman Adams, Sept. 21, 1956, Box 714, EOF.

17. C. P. Russell, "Two Parties Pledge Proper Spending," *New York Times*, Sept. 11, 1956.

18. Newton interview with author.

19. George Ball to William Blair, June 14, 1956, Box 3, GBP.

20. "Adlai's 1956 Team," *U.S. News and World Report*, Sept. 28, 1956, pp. 86–87.

21. William Blair, "Stevenson Is Expected to Name Fritchey," *New York Times*, Aug. 21, 1956.

22. Ball interview with author.

23. Ball, *Past Has Another Pattern*, pp. 143–44.

24. Ball to Stevenson, May 1956, Box 3, GBP.

25. Kummel interview with author.

26. Norman, Craig and Kummel campaign plan, Aug. 10, 1956, Box 384, DNCR; meeting summary, Norman, Craig and Kummel and DNC, Aug. 28, 1956, Box 4, GBP.

27. Ball interview with author.

28. Norman, Craig and Kummel memorandum on television time purchases, undated, Box 384, DNCR.

29. Bill Wilson to Eugene Kummel, Walter Craig, and Newton Minow, Sept. 18, 1956, Box 6, GBP.

30. Kinescope, Stevenson telecast, Sept. 13, 1956, KLAV.

31. Blair interview with author.

32. Wilson interview with author.

33. Meeting summary, Norman, Craig and Kummel and Jim Finnegan, Sept. 15, 1956, and Wilson to Advance Men, Sept. 18, 1956, both in Box 6, GBP.

34. Stevenson to Gerald Johnson, Sept. 19, 1956, Box 433, AESP.

35. James Reston, "Washington—'Via Ovicapitum Dura Est,' Stevenson," *New York Times*, Sept. 16, 1956.

36. Young and Rubicam monitoring reports, Sept. 24, Sept. 29, 1956, Box 6, YRR.

37. Blair interview with author.

38. Fritchey interview with author.

39. Windes, "Stevenson's Speech Staff," p. 42.

40. Schlesinger interview with author.

41. Wilson interview with author.

42. Helitzer interview with author.

43. Ball to Finnegan, Sept. 21, 1956, Box 5, GBP.

44. "TV Election Plug Dropped by CBS," *New York Times*, Oct. 27, 1956; DNC news release, Oct. 18, 1956, Box 385, DNCR; Stevenson itinerary, Oct. 19, 1956, Box 4, GBP.

45. Miller interview with author; meeting notes, Reggie Schuebel and Ball, Oct. 5, 1956, GBP.

46. Hagerty, COHP, p. 129.

47. Eisenhower to Everett Hazlett, Nov. 2, 1956, DDED.

48. News conference transcript, Oct. 11, 1956, Box 5, EPCS.

49. Drafts, H-bomb contingency speech, dated Oct. 15–16, 1956, Box 17, ESS.

50. Kinescope, Stevenson telecast, Oct. 15, 1956, KLAV.

51. Newton interview with author.

52. Drew Pearson, "Adlai Displeases Election Advisors," *Washington Post*, Oct. 10, 1956.

53. Jack Gould, "Campaign on TV," *New York Times*, Oct. 28, 1956.

54. Sevareid had been enlisted to narrate some of Stevenson's spots; see DNC Television Scripts file, Aug. 31, 1956, Box 4, GBP.

55. Ball interview with author.

56. See Stevenson, *New America*.

57. Walter O'Meara to Ball, Oct. 2, 1956, Box 3, GBP.

58. Wilson interview with author.

59. "M" to Ball, Oct. 10, 1956, Box 5, GBP.

60. Film, Young and Rubicam "College" spot, Oct. 1956, ELAV.

61. Film, Young and Rubicam "Mamie" spot, Oct. 1956, ELAV.

62. Film, Young and Rubicam "Taxi Driver" spot, Oct. 1956, ELAV.

63. "Citizens for Eisenhower-Nixon TV Operations," Version 1, Sept. 13, 1956, Box 6, YRR.

64. Film, "Decision for Tomorrow," Oct. 17, 1956, ELAV.

65. Levy interview with author.

66. Kinescope, "The People Ask the President," Oct. 12, 1956, ELAV.

67. Peter Lisagor, *Chicago Daily News*, Oct. 13, 1956; Russell Baker, "Eisenhower Finds U.S. Well Served," *New York Times*, Oct. 13, 1956; Eisenhower to Larmon, Oct. 13, 1956, Box 6, YRR.

68. Kinescope, Eisenhower "coffee klatsch," Oct. 24, 1956, KLAV.

69. Jack Gould, "Show Business Influence on Politics," *New York Times*, Oct. 15, 1956.

70. Kinescope, "Ike Day," Oct. 13, 1956, ELAV.

71. Speech transcript, Oct. 15, 1956, Box 3, GBP.

72. Claude Traverse to John Sharon, Oct. 24, 1956, Box 5, GBP.

73. Eisenhower, *Waging Peace*, pp. 74, 88.

74. Hagerty, COHP, pp. 222–23; film, Eisenhower address, Oct. 31, 1956, ELAV.

75. Martin, *Stevenson and the World*, p. 386.

76. Val Adams, "Free Time Ruling Is Given by FCC," *New York Times*, Nov. 6, 1956.

77. Speech transcript, *New York Times*, Nov. 2, 1956.

78. Harrison Salisbury, "Stevenson Says U.S. Policy Fails," *New York Times*, Nov. 2, 1956.

79. Minow interview with author.

80. Blair interview with author.

81. "Beyond a Cease Fire," editorial, *Washington Post*, Nov. 3, 1956.

82. "The First Tuesday," *New York Times*, Nov. 4, 1956.

83. Eisenhower to Alfred Gruenther, Nov. 3, 1956, DDED.

84. Speech transcript, Nov. 5, 1956, Box 101, AESP.

85. Campaign report, Paul Hoffman, Oct. 29, 1956, Box 714, EOF.

86. Kinescope, "Four More Years," Nov. 5, 1956, ELAV.

87. Levy interview with author.

88. Schlesinger, *Robert Kennedy*, p. 136; also see Robert Kennedy, KLOH, pp. 660–61.

89. Nixon, *RN*, pp. 180–81.

Chapter Nine

1. See diary, Nov. 4, 1956, in Slater, *Ike I Knew*.

2. Alcorn, COHP, pp. 89–92.

3. Ewald, *Eisenhower the President*, pp. 284–85.

4. Diaries, May 27, Sept. 10, Nov. 28, 1959, DDED.

5. Ambrose, *Eisenhower: The President*, pp. 376–93.

6. The selling of the Eisenhower Doctrine culminated in an Oval Office address on May 21, 1957. See film, "The Need for Security in Waging the Peace," ELAV.

7. Congress ultimately approved $2.7 million for foreign aid in 1957.

8. Ewald, *Eisenhower the President*, p. 232.

9. See Eisenhower to Emmet Hughes, Apr. 29, 1957, DDED.

10. Larson, *A Republican*, pp. 185–86.

11. Lyndon Johnson to Eisenhower, June 6, 1957, Box 573, EOF.

12. Meeting summary, Dec. 3, 1957, DDED.

13. Eisenhower to John Foster Dulles, June 3, 1957, DDED.

14. Henry Loomis to Arthur Larson, July 9, 1957, DDED.

15. L. Arthur Minnich to Maurice Stans, July 16, July 29, 1958, DDED.

16. Eisenhower to Everett Hazlett, July 22, 1957, DDED.

17. Eisenhower to Murray Snyder, Feb. 21, 1957, DDED.

18. Film, Eisenhower address on "Situation in Little Rock," Sept. 24, 1957, ELAV.

19. Film, "Science in National Security," Nov. 7, 1957, ELAV.

20. Larson, *The President*, pp. 155–56.

21. Film, "Our Future Security," Nov. 13, 1957, ELAV.

22. Ann Whitman to Hazlett, Dec. 1, 1957, DDED.

23. Montgomery, *Open Letter*, p. 65.

24. Film, "Report of the NATO Conference," Dec. 23, 1957, ELAV.

25. Eisenhower to Hazlett, Feb. 26, 1958, DDED; Montgomery, *Open Letter*, pp. 64–69.

26. "Goodbys to Standbys," *Newsweek*, July 16, 1957, pp. 80–81.

27. Department of Navy endorsements file, Jan. 1957, Box 263, EGF.

28. FCC endorsements file, June 1957, Box 384, EGF.

29. News release, Advisory Commission on the Arts, Apr. 11, 1959, Box 430, EGF.

30. Eisenhower to Robert Montgomery, May 22, July 3, 1958, Jan. 3, 1961, DDED.

31. See Pollard, "Truman," pp. 273–86.

32. Wheaton, COHP, p. 48.

33. James Hagerty to Beth Short, Apr. 4, 1958, Box 8, JHP.

34. Mike Moroney to Hagerty, Mar. 21, 1958, Box 8, JHP.

35. Interview transcript, "The Today Show," NBC, July 14, 1959, Douglass Cater file, Box 5, JHP.

36. See Ambrose, *Eisenhower: The President*, pp. 312–13, 427–35.

37. Diary, Jan. 16, 1958, AWD.

38. Meeting summary, Eisenhower and legislative leaders, Feb. 4, 1958, DDED.

39. Diary, Oct. 28, 1959, in Kistiakowsky, *Scientist at the White House*.

40. Eisenhower, *Waging Peace*, p. 256. Also see Satellite file, Box 9, JHP.

41. Meeting summary, Eisenhower and James Killian, Feb. 6, 1958, DDED.

42. Killian to Hagerty, Mar. 31, 1958, Box 9, JHP.

43. TV Guide file, Box 10, JHP.

44. Diary, Dec. 17, 1958, AWD.

45. Film, Eisenhower on "Landing of U.S. Marines in Beirut," July 15, 1958, and "Report Regarding the Formosa Straits," Sept. 11, 1958, both in ELAV.

46. Diary, Aug. 3, 1958, in Slater, *Ike I Knew*.

47. Eisenhower to Hagerty, Dec. 29, 1958, Box 5, JHP.

48. Hagerty to Eisenhower, Dec. 8, Dec. 9, Dec. 25, 1958, Box 9, JHP.

49. Ambrose, *Eisenhower: The President*, pp. 517–19.

50. Meeting summary, Eisenhower and Dulles, Feb. 3, 1959, DDED.

51. Diaries, July 28, Aug. 1, 1958, AWD.

52. Eisenhower, *Waging Peace*, p. 412.

53. Press Office budget, Dec. 12, 1952, Box 10, JHP.

54. Hagerty to Roger and Bruce Hagerty, Jan. 6, 1961, Box 8, JHP.

55. Drew Pearson, "Washington Merry Go Round," *Washington Post*, Apr. 27, 1957.

56. Hagerty, COHP, p. 326.

57. Diaries, July 13, Aug. 1, 1959, AWD.

58. Telephone summary, Eisenhower and Christian Herter, July 8, 1959, DDED.

59. Diary, Aug. 1, 1959, AWD.

60. See Hagerty, COHP, pp. 148–53, 370–79. Also see Dave Reque, "Ike's Trip Cues Video Progress," *Washington Daily News*, Aug. 30, 1959.

61. Hagerty, COHP, p. 183.

62. Eisenhower, *Waging Peace*, p. 415. Also see European Trip file, Aug.–Sept. 1959, Box 19, JHP.

63. Kinescopes of many CBS "Eyewitness to History" broadcasts appear in ELAV.

64. *New York Times*, Dec. 19, 1959.

65. Positive foreign reaction to the trips is summarized in USIA-London to USIA-Washington, Sept. 16, 1959, Box 20, and John Calhoun to Andrew Goodpaster, Dec. 22, 1959, Box 22, both in JHP.

66. William Hopkins to White House, Aug. 10, 1959, Box 11, AWD.

67. "Eyewitness to History," CBS, Sept. 15, 1959, ELAV.

68. Meeting summary, Eisenhower and Goodpaster, Sept. 28, 1959; Eisenhower to C. D. Jackson, Sept. 23, 1959, DDED.

69. See Coverage file, Sept. 1959, Box 21, JHP.

70. Hagerty, COHP, p. 143.

71. Hagerty to Eisenhower, Oct. 27, 1959, Box 9, JHP.

72. Eisenhower to Hagerty, Dec. 29, 1959, Box 5, JHP.

73. Hagerty to Thomas Dewey, Jan. 7, 1960, Box 8, JHP.

Chapter Ten

1. James Hagerty to Eisenhower, Mar. 21, 1960, Box 11, AWD.

2. James Reston, "Flights Stopped," *New York Times*, May 9, 1960.

3. Hagerty, COHP, pp. 148–50.

4. See Japan file, Box 32, JHP.

5. Khrushchev, *Khrushchev Remembers*, p. 477.

6. Film, "Summit Conference Report," May 25, 1960, ELAV.

7. Ambrose, *Eisenhower: The President*, p. 577.

8. Eisenhower, *Waging Peace*, p. 602.

9. Diary, Nov. 9, 1960, AWD.

10. Diary, Nov. 9, 1960, in Slater, *Ike I Knew*.

11. Diary, Mar. 13, 1957, DDED.

12. Diary, Dec. 6, 1958, DDED.

13. Diary, June 29, 1954, AWD.

14. Ewald, *Eisenhower the President*, p. 178.

15. Nixon, *RN*, pp. 167–68.

16. Eisenhower, *Mandate for Change*, pp. 68–69.

17. "Nixon Tells How to Win TV Friends," *New York Times*, Sept. 15, 1955.

18. Eisenhower to Leonard Hall, Oct. 13, 1956, Box 17, EAS.

19. Nixon letter to author, Apr. 17, 1987.

20. Nixon, *Six Crises*, pp. 253–54.

21. Ibid., p. 303.

22. Diary, Mar. 13, 1957, DDED.

23. Diary, Dec. 6, 1958, DDED.

24. Diary, Jan. 13, 1960, DDED.

25. Film, "Dinner with Ike," Jan. 27, 1960, ELAV.

26. Newton interview with author. Also see diary, July 5, 1960, DDED. Folger became Nixon's 1960 finance chair.

27. Telephone summary, Eisenhower and Alton Jones, Aug. 8, 1960, DDED.

28. Newton interview with author.

29. Diary, Aug. 10, 1960, AWD.

30. Diary, Aug. 1960, in Slater, *Ike I Knew*.

31. Diary, Aug. 12, 1960, AWD.

32. Klein, *Perfectly Clear*, p. 102; Newton interview with author.

33. Nixon, *Six Crises*, p. 323.

34. Eisenhower, *Waging Peace*, pp. 598–99.

35. Telephone summary, Eisenhower and Nixon, Sept. 25, 1960, DDED.

36. Hagerty, COHP, pp. 123–24.

37. Telephone summary, Eisenhower and Nixon, Oct. 1, 1960, DDED.

38. Telephone summary, Eisenhower and Nixon, Oct. 14, 1960, AWD.

39. News conference transcript, Aug. 24, 1960, EPCS.

40. Eisenhower, HLOH, pp. 88–89.

41. Ewald, *Eisenhower the President*, p. 302.

42. Film, "Ike in Philly," Oct. 28, 1960, ELAV.

43. Eisenhower to William Robinson, Sept. 21, 1966, Box 17, EPPSN.

44. Ewald, *Eisenhower the President*, p. 312.

45. Newton interview with author; Ewald, *Eisenhower the President*, p. 308.

46. Meeting summary, Eisenhower and Ann Whitman, Nov. 9, 1960, DDED.

47. Meeting summary, Eisenhower and Whitman, Nov. 28, 1960, DDED.

48. Eisenhower to Nixon, Apr. 25, 1961, Box 14, EPPSN.

49. Eisenhower, *Waging Peace*, p. 602.

50. See Hamby, *Liberalism*, pp. 183–230.

51. Theodore Sorenson, "The Democratic Nominee for Vice President in 1956," Aug. 1956, and Sorenson memo, "Kennedy and the Vice Presidency," undated, both in Box 810, JFKPP.

52. Newton interview with author.

53. Several episodes of the "Big Picture" and most of the "Crusade in Europe" television series appear on film in ELAV.

54. Diary, Nov. 9, 1960, in Slater, *Ike I Knew*.

55. John Kennedy, "Force That Has Changed the Political Scene," *TV Guide*, Nov. 14, 1959, pp. 5–7.

56. Wilson interview with author.

57. News briefing transcript, Apr. 7, 1959, Box 53, JHP.

58. Diary, July 22, 1959, AWD.

59. Diaries, Feb. 10, Feb. 11, 1960, in Kistiakowsky, *Scientist at the White House*.

60. Eisenhower, *Waging Peace*, p. 614.

61. Hagerty to Eisenhower, Feb. 23, 1959, Box 9, JHP.

62. Diary, Aug. 22, 1960, in Kistiakowsky, *Scientist at the White House*.

63. Diary, May 7, 1958, AWD.

64. Eisenhower to John Hay Whitney, Nov. 24, 1960, DDED.

65. News conference transcript, Jan. 18, 1961, Box 76, JHP.

66. Film, "Farewell Address," Jan. 17, 1961, ELAV.

67. *Editor and Publisher*, Jan. 21, 1961, pp. 6, 15.

Chapter Eleven

1. Quote is William Ewald's paraphrasing of Eisenhower's reaction. See Ewald, ELOH, p. 46.

2. Fred Friendly to William Paley, Feb. 27, 1961, Box 15, EPPSN.

3. Eisenhower to Paley, June 6, 1961, Box 15, EPPSN. Also see diary, June 5, 1961, in Slater, *Ike I Knew*.

4. Film, "Eisenhower on Lincoln," NBC, 1962, ELAV.

5. Film, "Town Meeting of the World," CBS, July 10, 1963, ELAV.

6. Eisenhower to Paley, Dec. 18, 1962, Box 15, EPPSN.

7. Film, "D-Day Plus Twenty Years," CBS, June 5, 1964, ELAV. Also see diary, Mar. 15, 1954, JHP.

8. Diary, June 5, 1961, DDED.

9. Diary, Aug. 1960, in Slater, *Ike I Knew*.

10. Eisenhower to "Bob," Jan. 3, 1961, DDED.

11. Diary, Jan. 7, 1961, in Slater, *Ike I Knew*.

12. Hagerty, COHP, pp. 101–2.

13. Diary, Feb. 22, [1962], in Slater, *Ike I Knew*.

14. Diary, June 5, 1961, DDED.

15. Mazo, COHP, p. 12.

16. Eisenhower to Paley, Aug. 28, 1961, Box 15, EPPSN.

17. Diaries, Oct. 29, Nov. 2, Nov. 5, 1962, DDED.

18. Diary, Jan. 21, 1964, in Slater, *Ike I Knew*.

19. Eisenhower to Paley, Oct. 2, 1962, Box 15, EPPSN.

20. Diary, July 16, 1964, in Slater, *Ike I Knew*.

21. Ambrose, *Eisenhower: The President*, p. 653.

22. Film, "DDE on Universal Military Training," WHP-TV, Sept. 1966, ELAV.

23. Eisenhower, "We Should Be Ashamed," *Reader's Digest*, Aug. 1967, pp. 67–71; audio recording, "Eisenhower and Bradley on Vietnam," CBS, Nov. 28, 1967, ELAV.

24. Film, "A Call for Reason," Apr. 1968, ELAV; Eisenhower, "Let's Close Ranks on the Home Front," *Reader's Digest*, Apr. 1968, pp. 49–53. Also see Eisenhower to Hazel Hess, Aug. 18, 1967, Box 1, EPPC.

25. Eisenhower to James Hagerty, Oct. 18, 1966, in Hagerty, COHP, pp. 101–2.

26. Eisenhower, HLOH, p. 32.

27. Eisenhower to Nixon, Oct. 16, 1968, Box 14, EPPSN.

28. Eisenhower to Nixon, Oct. 24, 1968, Box 14, EPPSN.

29. Francis Levine, "David Eisenhower Takes Job," *Washington Star*, June 25, 1968.

30. Nixon to Eisenhower, Oct. 27, 1968, Box 14, EPPSN.

31. Klein, *Perfectly Clear*, p. 16.

32. Nixon letter to author, Apr. 17, 1987.

33. Ewald, *Eisenhower the President*, p. 324.

34. The poll is discussed in Schlesinger, "Ike Age Revisited," p. 2. Also see "The People Still Like Ike," *Chicago Tribune*, Mar. 29, 1980; "How They Rank," *Dallas Times Herald*, Mar. 25, 1984; and Steve Neal, "Ike's Stature Rises as Time Goes By," *Chicago Tribune*, Nov. 30, 1985.

Conclusion

1. Hamby, *Liberalism*, pp. 4–8.

2. See *U.S. News and World Report*, Sept. 3, 1954, Jan. 7, Nov. 25, 1955;

Newsweek, Apr. 19, 1954; *New York Times*, Jan. 7, Jan. 29, Feb. 11, Mar. 16, Mar. 28, Apr. 25, Aug. 24, 1954, July 1, Aug. 7, Sept. 8, 1955; *Good House-keeping*, Nov. 1955; *Women's Home*, Dec. 1955; and *Coronet*, Sept. 1954.

3. SRC data appears in Stokes, Campbell, and Miller, "Electoral Decision," pp. 373–79; Key, *Public Opinion and Democracy*, pp. 346–47; and Nimmo and Savage, *Candidates*, p. 145.

4. Stokes, Campbell, and Miller, "Electoral Decision," p. 377.

5. Pool, "TV," pp. 254–61.

6. Eisenhower, *Waging Peace*, p. 652.

7. Guylay, COHP, p. 78.

8. Eisenhower to William Paley, Nov. 14, 1956, DDED.

9. Stokes, Campbell, and Miller, "Electoral Decision," pp. 373–75.

10. Schattschneider, *Party Government*, pp. 75–76.

11. Press, "Voting Statistics," p. 1050.

12. Hall, "Len Hall Hails the Revolution," pp. 126–27.

13. Schlesinger, "Ike Age Revisited," p. 6.

14. See Eisenhower, *Waging Peace*, pp. 655–66.

BIBLIOGRAPHY

Manuscript Sources

Abilene, Kansas
  Dwight D. Eisenhower Library
    Audiovisual collection (ELAV)
    Harry Butcher Papers (HBP)
    Milton Eisenhower Papers (MEP)
    James C. Hagerty Papers (JHP)
    Gabriel Hauge Records (GHR)
    Robert Humphreys Papers (RHP)
    C. D. Jackson Papers (CDJP)
    C. D. Jackson Records (CDJR)
    Post-Presidential Papers
      Convenience File (EPPC)
      Special Names Series (EPPSN)
    Republican National Committee Records (RNCR)
    William E. Robinson Papers (WRP)
    Thomas E. Stephens Records (TSR)
    White House Central Files
      The General File (EGF)
      The Official File (EOF)
    Ann Whitman File
      Administration Series (EAS)
      Campaign Series (ECS)
      DDE Diary Series (DDED)
      Press Conference Series (EPCS)
      Speech Series (ESS)
      Stag Dinner Series (ESDS)
      Ann Whitman Diary Series (AWD)
    Young and Rubicam Records (YRR)
Boston, Massachusetts
  John F. Kennedy Library
    Audiovisual collection (KLAV)
    Democratic National Committee Records (DNCR)
    John F. Kennedy Pre-Presidential Papers (JFKPP)
    Robert F. Kennedy Papers (RFKP)
Princeton, New Jersey
  Seeley G. Mudd Manuscript Library

George W. Ball Papers (GBP)

Adlai E. Stevenson Papers (AESP)

Interviews

BY AUTHOR

George Ball; Athens, Ohio; Apr. 21, 1988
William McCormick Blair; Washington, D.C.; May 18, 1988
Robert Donovan; Washington, D.C.; Mar. 7, 1988
Douglas Edwards; Sarasota, Fla.; Aug. 29, 1988
Clayton Fritchey; Washington, D.C.; Feb. 27, 1987
Charles Guggenheim; Washington, D.C.; Feb. 24, 1987
Joan Hafey; New York, N.Y.; Jan. 21, 1988
Harry Harding; New York, N.Y.; Jan. 21, 1988
Mel Helitzer; Athens, Ohio; Aug. 11, 1988
Eugene Kummel; New York, N.Y.; Mar. 21, 1989
David Levy; Beverly Hills, Calif.; Jan. 26, 1988
Robert Ellis Miller; Los Angeles, Calif.; Aug. 19, 1988
Newton Minow; Chicago, Ill.; Jan. 5, 1989
Carroll Newton; Sarasota, Fla.; Sept. 2–3, 1988
Arthur Schlesinger, Jr.; New York, N.Y.; Mar. 21, 1989
William Parmenter Wilson; New York, N.Y.; July 8, 1988

BY COLUMBIA UNIVERSITY ORAL HISTORY PROJECT (COHP)

Elie Abel
Sherman Adams
Bertha Adkins
Meade Alcorn
Robert Donovan
Roscoe Drummond
Dwight Eisenhower
Milton Eisenhower
Robert Finch
Clifford Folger
Edward Folliard
L. Richard Guylay
James Hagerty
Sigurd Larmon
William Lawrence
Earl Mazo
Edward P. Morgan
Howard Pyle
Harrison Salisbury
Ray Scherer
Howard K. Smith
Murray Snyder
Abbott Washburn
Anne Wheaton

BY DWIGHT D. EISENHOWER LIBRARY (ELOH)

Milton Eisenhower
William Ewald
Leonard Hall
Frederick Zaghi

BY HERBERT HOOVER LIBRARY (HLOH)

Dwight Eisenhower

BY JOHN F. KENNEDY LIBRARY (KLOH)
Robert Kennedy

Books and Articles

Adams, Sherman. *Firsthand Report*. New York: Harper, 1961.
Alexander, Charles C. *Holding the Line: The Eisenhower Era, 1952–1961*.
    Bloomington: Indiana University Press, 1975.
Alexander, Herbert. *Money in Politics*. Washington, D.C.: Public Affairs,
    1972.
Allen, Craig. "Eisenhower's Congressional Defeat of 1956." *Presidential
    Studies Quarterly* 22 (1992): 57–71.
———. "Our First 'Television' Candidate: Eisenhower Over Stevenson
    in 1956." *Journalism Quarterly* 65 (1988): 352–59.
———. "Robert Montgomery Presents: Hollywood Debut in the Eisen-
    hower White House." *Journal of Broadcasting and Electronic Media* 35
    (1991): 431–48.
Alsop, Joseph, and Stewart Alsop. *The Reporter's Trade*. New York:
    Reynal, 1958.
Ambrose, Stephen E. *Eisenhower: 1890–1952*. New York: Simon and
    Schuster, 1983.
———. *Eisenhower: The President*. New York: Simon and Schuster, 1984.
———. *Nixon: The Education of a Politician*. New York: Grosset and
    Dunlap, 1987.
Ambrose, Stephen E., and Richard Immerman. *Milton S. Eisenhower:
    Educational Statesman*. Baltimore: Johns Hopkins University Press,
    1983.
Aronson, James. *The Press and the Cold War*. Indianapolis: Bobbs-Merrill,
    1970.
Austin, Erik. *Political Facts of the United States since 1789*. New York:
    Columbia University Press, 1986.
Ball, George W. *The Past Has Another Pattern*. New York: W. W. Nor-
    ton, 1982.
Barkin, Steven. "Eisenhower's Secret Strategy." *Journal of Advertising
    History* 9 (1987): 18–28.
———. "Eisenhower's Television Planning Board." *Journal of Broadcast-
    ing and Electronic Media* 27 (1983): 319–31.
Bayley, Edwin. *Joe McCarthy and the Press*. New York: Pantheon, 1981.
Beck, Kent M. "What Was Liberalism in the 1950s?" *Political Science
    Quarterly* 102 (1987): 233–58.
Blumler, Jay G., and Denis McQuail. *Television in Politics: Its Uses and
    Influence*. Chicago: University of Chicago Press, 1969.

Boddy, William. *Fifties Television: The Industry and Its Critics*. Urbana: University of Illinois Press, 1990.

Bogart, Leo. *The Age of Television*. New York: Frederick Ungar, 1972.

Brands, H. W. "The Age of Vulnerability: Eisenhower and the National Insecurity State." *American Historical Review* 94 (1989): 963–89.

Burdick, Eugene, and Arthur J. Brodbeck, eds. *American Voting Behavior*. Glencoe, Ill.: Free Press, 1959.

Butcher, Harry C. *My Three Years with Eisenhower*. New York: Simon and Schuster, 1946.

Campbell, Angus, Philip E. Converse, Warren E. Miller, and Donald E. Stokes. *The American Voter*. New York: John Wiley and Sons, 1960.

Cater, Douglass. *The Fourth Branch of Government*. Boston: Houghton Mifflin, 1959.

Cochran, Bert. *Adlai Stevenson: Patrician among the Politicians*. New York: Funk and Wagnalls, 1969.

Congressional Quarterly. *Guide to U.S. Elections*. Washington, D.C.: Congressional Quarterly, 1975.

Cook, Blanche Wiesen. *The Declassified Eisenhower*. Garden City, N.Y.: Doubleday, 1981.

Cotter, Cornelius P., and Bernard C. Hennessey. *Politics without Power*. New York: Atherton, 1964.

Craig, Herbert R. "Distinctive Features of Radio-Television in the 1952 Presidential Campaign." Master's thesis, University of Iowa, 1954.

Crandell, William F. "Eisenhower the Strategist: The Battle of the Bulge and the Censure of Joseph McCarthy." *Presidential Studies Quarterly* 17 (1987): 487–502.

David, Paul, Malcolm Moos, and John Goldman. *Presidential Nominating Politics in 1952*. Baltimore: Johns Hopkins University Press, 1954.

Davis, James W. *National Party Conventions in an Age of Party Reform*. Westport, Conn.: Greenwood Press, 1983.

———. *Presidential Primaries: Road to the White House*. New York: Thomas Y. Crowell, 1967.

Diamond, Edward, and Stephen Bates. *The Spot*. Cambridge, Mass.: MIT Press, 1984.

Donovan, Robert. *Eisenhower: The Inside Story*. New York: Harper, 1956.

Dunn, Delmer. *Financing Presidential Campaigns*. Washington, D.C.: Brookings Institution, 1972.

Eisenhower, Dwight D. *At Ease: Stories I Tell to Friends*. Garden City, N.Y.: Doubleday, 1967.

———. *Crusade in Europe*. Garden City, N.Y.: Doubleday, 1948.

———. *The Eisenhower Diaries*. Edited by Robert Ferrell. New York: W. W. Norton, 1981.

———. *Ike's Letters to a Friend*. Edited by Robert Griffith. Lawrence: University Press of Kansas, 1984.

———. "Let's Close Ranks on the Home Front." *Reader's Digest*, April 1968, pp. 49–53.

———. *Mandate for Change, 1953–1956*. Garden City, N.Y.: Doubleday, 1963.

———. *Waging Peace, 1956–1961*. Garden City, N.Y.: Doubleday, 1965.

———. "We Should Be Ashamed." *Reader's Digest*, August 1967, pp. 67–71.

Eisenhower, Milton S. *The President Is Calling*. Garden City, N.Y.: Doubleday, 1974.

Ewald, William Bragg. *Eisenhower the President: Crucial Days, 1951–1960*. Englewood Cliffs, N.J.: Prentice-Hall, 1981.

Hagerty, James C. *The Diary of James C. Hagerty*. Edited by Robert Ferrell. Bloomington: Indiana University Press, 1983.

Gallup, Inc. *Gallup Poll Public Opinion, 1935–1971*. New York: Random House, 1972.

Greenstein, Fred I. *The Hidden-Hand Presidency: Eisenhower as Leader*. New York: Basic Books, 1982.

Griffith, Robert. "Dwight D. Eisenhower and the Corporate Commonwealth." *American Historical Review* 87 (1982): 87–122.

———. *The Politics of Fear: Joseph McCarthy and the Senate*. 2d ed. Amherst: University of Massachusetts Press, 1987.

Hall, Leonard. "Len Hall Hails the Revolution Wrought by TV." *Life*, 25 April 1960, pp. 126–34.

Hamby, Alonzo L. *Liberalism and Its Challengers*. New York: Oxford University Press, 1985.

Hanna, Edward, Henry Hicks, and Ted Koppel, eds. *The Wit and Wisdom of Adlai Stevenson*. New York: Hawthorn Books, 1965.

Hersey, John. "Survival: Lieutenant John F. Kennedy." *Reader's Digest*, August 1944, pp. 75–80.

Hoffman, Paul. "How Eisenhower Saved the Republican Party." *Colliers*, 26 October 1956, pp. 44–47.

Hollitz, John E. "Eisenhower and the Admen: The Television 'Spot' Campaign of 1952." *Wisconsin Magazine of History* 66 (1982): 25–39.

Hughes, Emmet J. *The Ordeal of Power: A Political Memoir of the Eisenhower Years*. New York: Atheneum, 1963.

Jamieson, Kathleen Hall. *Packaging the Presidency*. New York: Oxford University Press, 1984.

Kelley, Stanley, Jr. *Professional Public Relations and Political Power*. Baltimore, Md.: Johns Hopkins University Press, 1956.

Kennedy, John F. "A Force That Has Changed the Political Scene." *TV Guide*, 14 November 1959, pp. 4–7.

Key, V. O., Jr. *Public Opinion and Democracy*. New York: Alfred A. Knopf, 1961.

Khrushchev, Nikita. *Khrushchev Remembers*. Boston: Little, Brown, 1974.

Kistiakowsky, George B. *A Scientist at the White House*. Cambridge, Mass.: Harvard University Press, 1976.

Klein, Herbert G. *Making It Perfectly Clear*. Garden City, N.Y.: Doubleday, 1980.

Knepprath, Hubert Eugene. "The Elements of Persuasion in the Nationally Broadcast Speeches of Eisenhower and Stevenson during the 1956 Presidential Campaign." Ph.D. diss., University of Wisconsin, 1962.

Lang, Kurt, and Gladys Lang. "The Mass Media and Voting." In *American Voting Behavior*, edited by Eugene Burdick and Arthur J. Brodbeck, pp. 217–35. Glencoe, Ill.: Free Press, 1959.

———. *Politics and Television*. Chicago: Quadrangle, 1968.

———. "The Unique Perspective of Television and Its Effects." *American Sociological Review* 17 (1953): 3–12.

Larson, Arthur. *Eisenhower: The President Nobody Knew*. New York: Charles Scribner's Sons, 1968.

———. *A Republican Looks at His Party*. New York: Harper and Row, 1956.

Lazarsfeld, Paul F., Bernard R. Berelson, and Hazel Gaudett. *The People's Choice*. 2d ed. New York: Columbia University Press, 1948.

Lazarsfeld, Paul F., Bernard R. Berelson, and William McPhee. *Voting*. Chicago: University of Chicago Press, 1954.

McGinniss, Joe. *The Selling of the President, 1968*. New York: Trident, 1969.

MacGregor, Mary C. "Television's Impact on the 1952 Presidential Election." Master's thesis, Ohio University, 1986.

McKeever, Porter. *Adlai Stevenson: His Life and Legacy*. New York: William Morrow, 1989.

Marcus, Robert D., and David Burner, eds. *America since 1945*. New York: St. Martin's, 1985.

Margolis, Joel Paul. "The Conservative Coalition in the United States Senate." Ph.D. diss., University of Wisconsin, 1973.

Martin, John Bartlow. *Adlai Stevenson of Illinois*. Garden City, N.Y.: Doubleday, 1976.

———. *Adlai Stevenson and the World*. Garden City, N.Y.: Doubleday, 1977.

May, Ernest, and Janet Fraser, eds. *Campaign '72: The Managers Speak*. Cambridge, Mass.: Harvard University Press, 1973.

Mickelson, Sig. *The Electronic Mirror: Politics in an Age of Television*. New York: Dodd and Mead, 1972.

———. *From Whistle Stop to Soundbite*. New York: Praeger, 1989.

Miller, Merle. *Ike the Soldier*. New York: G. P. Putnam's Sons, 1987.

Montgomery, Robert. *Open Letter from a Television Viewer*. New York: James H. Heineman, 1968.

Moon, Gordon Ames II. "James Campbell Hagerty's Eight Years in the White House." Master's thesis, University of Wisconsin, 1962.

Ney, Edward N. "TV and Political Campaigns." Young and Rubicam Issues, no. 9 (pamphlet). New York: Young and Rubicam, 1975.

Nimmo, Daniel D. *Popular Images of Politics*. Englewood Cliffs, N.J.: Prentice-Hall, 1976.

Nimmo, Daniel D., and Robert Savage. *Candidates and Their Images*. Pacific Palisades, Calif.: Goodyear, 1976.

Nixon, Richard M. *RN: The Memoirs of Richard Nixon*. New York: Grosset and Dunlap, 1978.

———. *Six Crises*. Garden City, N.Y.: Doubleday, 1962.

Oxford Research Associates. *Influence of Television on the Election of 1952*. Oxford, Ohio: Miami University Press, 1954.

Packard, Vance. *The Hidden Persuaders*. New York: David McKay, 1957.

Parmet, Herbert. *Eisenhower and the American Crusades*. New York: Macmillan, 1972.

Parris, Judith. *The Convention Problem*. Washington, D.C.: Brookings Institution, 1972.

Patterson, James T. *Mr. Republican: A Biography of Robert A. Taft*. Boston: Houghton Mifflin, 1972.

Phillips, Cabell. "Party Chairmen: Study in Feuds and Funds." *New York Times Magazine*, 1 July 1956, pp. 10–11, 28.

Pollard, James E. "Eisenhower and the Press: The Final Phase." *Journalism Quarterly* 38 (1961): 181–86.

———. "Eisenhower and the Press: The First Two Years." *Journalism Quarterly* 32 (1955): 285–300.

———. "Eisenhower and the Press: The Partial News Vacuum." *Journalism Quarterly* 33 (1956): 3–8.

———. *The Presidents and the Press*. Washington, D.C.: Public Affairs Press, 1964.

———. "Truman and the Press: The Final Phase." *Journalism Quarterly* 30 (1953): 273–86.

Pool, Ithiel de Sola. "TV: A New Dimension in Politics." In *American Voting Behavior*, edited by Eugene Burdick and Arthur J. Brodbeck, pp. 236–61. Glencoe, Ill.: Free Press, 1959.

Press, Charles. "Voting Statistics and Presidential Coattails." *American Political Science Review* 52 (1958): 1041–50.

Radio Annual and Television Yearbook, 1957. New York: Radio Daily, 1957.

Reinsch, J. Leonard. *Getting Elected: From Radio and Roosevelt to Television and Reagan*. New York: Hippocrene, 1988.

Roper, Elmo. *You and Your Leaders.* New York: William Morrow, 1957.

Runyon, John H., Jennefer Verdini, and Sally S. Runyon. *Source Book of American Presidential Campaigns and Elections, 1948–1968.* New York: Frederick Ungar, 1971.

Rutland, Robert A. "President Eisenhower and His Press Secretary." *Journalism Quarterly* 34 (1957): 452–56.

Scammon, Richard M., ed. *America Votes: A Handbook of Contemporary American Election Statistics.* New York: Macmillan, 1958.

Schattschneider, E. E. *Party Government.* New York: Farrar and Rinehart, 1942.

Schlesinger, Arthur, Jr. "The Ike Age Revisited." *Reviews in American History* 11 (1983): 1–11.

———. *The Imperial Presidency.* Boston: Houghton Mifflin, 1973.

———. *Robert Kennedy and His Times.* Boston: Houghton Mifflin, 1978.

Schwartz, Tony. *The Responsive Chord.* Garden City, N.Y.: Doubleday, 1973.

Shafer, Byron E. *Evolution and Reform: The National Party Convention in American Politics.* New York: Russell Sage Foundation, 1988.

Slater, Ellis D. *The Ike I Knew.* N.p.: Ellis D. Slater Trust, 1980.

Sorauf, Frank J., and Paul Allen Beck. *Party Politics in America.* Glenview, Ill.: Scott, Foresman, 1988.

Steinberg, Cobbett. *TV Facts.* New York: Facts on File Publications, 1985.

Steiner, Paul, ed. *The Stevenson Wit and Wisdom.* New York: Pyramid, 1965.

Stevenson, Adlai E. *The New America.* New York: Harper, 1957.

———. *The Papers of Adlai Stevenson.* Edited by Walter Johnson. Boston: Little, Brown, 1976.

Stokes, Donald, Angus Campbell, and Warren Miller. "Components of Electoral Decision." *American Political Science Review* 52 (1958): 367–87.

Tananbaum, Duane. *The Bricker Amendment Controversy.* Ithaca, N.Y.: Cornell University Press, 1988.

Thayer, George. *Who Shakes the Money Tree?* New York: Simon and Schuster, 1973.

Thomson, Charles. *Television and Presidential Politics.* Washington, D.C.: Brookings Institution, 1956.

Thomson, Charles, and Frances M. Shattuck. *The 1956 Presidential Campaign.* Washington, D.C.: Brookings Institution, 1960.

Vinson, James, ed. *Actors and Actresses.* Chicago: St. James, 1984.

Watson, Mary Ann. *Expanding Vista: Television in the Kennedy Years.* New York: Oxford University Press, 1990.

White, Theodore H. *The Making of the President, 1960.* New York: Atheneum, 1961.

Wildavsky, Aaron. "On the Superiority of National Conventions." *Review of Politics* 25 (1962): 307–19.

Williams, David. "Choosing Presidential Candidates." *Political Quarterly* 23 (1952): 268–79.

Wills, Garry. "Nixon Agonistes: The Checkers Speech." In *America since 1945*, edited by Robert D. Marcus and David Burner, pp. 93–107. New York: St. Martin's, 1985.

Windes, Russel, Jr. "Adlai E. Stevenson's Speech Staff in the 1956 Campaign." *Quarterly Journal of Speech* 46 (1960): 32–43.

Winkler, Allan M. *The Politics of Propaganda*. New Haven, Conn.: Yale University Press, 1978.

Wood, Stephen C. "Television's First Political Spot Ad Campaign: Eisenhower Answers America." *Presidential Studies Quarterly* 20 (1990): 265–83.

INDEX

ABC, 97, 103, 140, 185; and White House, 57–58, 62, 108, 223 (n. 42); political ads on, 75–76, 89; 1953 merger, 113; conventions on, 115–20; Hagerty at, 166, 194, 196–97

Abilene telecast (1952), 24–25, 79, 136, 157, 184

Adams, Sherman, 1, 3, 21, 22–23, 26, 30, 73, 87, 164, 166

Adenauer, Konrad, 169

Adkins, Bertha, 67, 68, 117

AFL-CIO, 104, 164

Air Force One, 168

Alcorn, Meade, 150, 177

Allen, George, 155

Alsop, Joseph, 187

American Association of Advertising Agencies (AAAA), 36–37, 42, 100

Anderson, Robert, 74, 175

Associated Press, 61

Atlanta Constitution, 193–94

Baker, Russell, 143

Ball, George, 140, 141, 144; criticizes GOP image making, 134, 143–44, 206; media work of, 134–35, 146

Barton, Bruce, 16, 79–80

Baruch, Bernard, 99

Bassett, James, 69

Batten, Barton, Durstine and Osborn (BBDO), 8, 16, 42, 69, 99, 100, 130; "Eisenhower Answers America," 17, 130–31; public opinion research of, 37–39, 129, 132, 139; enlistment by RNC, 38, 79–81, 150, 177; financial resources of, 71, 75–76, 89, 103, 132–33, 209; TV time buying, 75–76, 80–81, 101–3; Young and Rubicam rivalry, 78–81; political ads of, 82–83, 132, 138, 140–48; "These Peaceful, Prosperous Years," 83; criticism of, 104–5, 143–44, 206; "You and Your Government," 140–41; "coffee klatsch," 143; 1956 TV birthday party ("Ike Day"), 143; and 1960 campaign, 177–80; and Kennedys, 184

Benson, Ezra Taft, 35, 40

Berlin, 152, 164, 165, 194–95

Black, Douglas, 36

Blair, William McCormick, 133, 136, 137, 147

Bricker, John, 19, 28, 45, 50, 55, 113–14, 229 (n. 6)

Brightman, Sam, 102

Brinkley, David, 120, 125, 161; debut at 1956 convention, 115, 125

Brownell, Herbert, 74

Brown v. Board of Education, 39, 152

Bulganin, Nikolai, 4

Burr, John, 78

Butcher, Harry: at CBS, 13; World War II media relations, 13–14, 48; as model for Hagerty, 14, 44; offends Eisenhower, 15, 44

Butler, Paul, 96–97, 116–19, 132, 206; equal time requests, 97–98, 107–9; ad agency search, 98–101; and Stevenson, 102, 104, 119, 133–34; fund-raising, 103–4, 132; attacks Hall and Hagerty, 109

Cagney, James, 131, 159
Carter, Jimmy, 201, 204
Carter, Lucia, 120
Castro, Fidel, 164, 187
Cater, Douglass, 160, 205
CBS, 16, 24, 31, 42, 71, 187, 192–93, 195, 197, 210; news division, 13, 52, 114–15, 125, 167–68; and White House, 57–58, 61–62, 223 (n. 42); political ads on, 75–76, 89, 101–2, 108, 143; debates on, 107–8; political anxieties of, 113–14; conventions on, 115–20, 125
Celler, Emanuel, 114
Chancellor, John, 123
Chicago Daily News, 143
Chicago Sun Times, 120
Chicago Tribune, 202
China, 41, 60–61, 163–64, 209
Christie, Jack, 102
Churchill, Winston, 31–32
Citizens for Eisenhower, 42, 43, 177; in 1952 campaign, 16–17, 20–21, 77–78, 141; in 1956 campaign, 77–81, 129–32, 141–43, 210; and RNC, 77–82, 209–10; and Eisenhower, 78–82. *See also* Young and Rubicam
Clay, Lucius, 78
Clement, Frank, 118
Cleveland Press, 134
Connor, Fox, 198
Cooper, John Sherman, 84
Craig, Walter, 100–101
Creel Committee, 12
Cronkite, Walter, 115, 117, 140, 168, 193
Crosby, John, 120
Cuba, 164, 187, 194–95
Curtis, Carl, 133

De Gaulle, Charles, 169

Democratic National Committee (DNC): media difficulties of, 4–5, 62, 89, 93, 97–104, 107–9, 137; and Eisenhower, 93, 98, 100, 107–9, 206; 1953 optimism, 96; and Norman, Craig and Kummel, 100–103, 118, 134; and Stevenson, 102, 104, 107–8, 119, 133–35; finances, 103–4, 138; conventions, 115–20, 124–25. *See also* Norman, Craig and Kummel
Dewey, Thomas, 43, 55, 66–67, 80, 105, 170
Dirksen, Everett, 44, 84
Donovan, Robert, 51, 56, 62, 186
Doyle Dane Bernbach, 99
Duff, James, 84, 149
Duffy, Ben, 16, 42, 69, 80, 132, 143, 178, 184
Dulles, John Foster, 3, 154–55, 165–66, 187; image problem of, 40; failed telecast of, 157–58
Dumont network, 62, 113, 223 (n. 42)
Dunne, Irene, 131, 143
Durgin, Donald, 103
Durstine, Roy, 80

Eden, Anthony, 192
Editor and Publisher, 189
Edwards, Douglas, 114, 115, 120
Edwards, India, 117
Ehrlichman, John, 200
Eisenhower, David, 4, 199
Eisenhower, Dwight D.: heart attack, 1–5, 74, 86–93; moderate philosophy, 6–7, 15, 18–20, 64–65, 203–4, 213; communication goals, 6–9, 12–13, 17–18, 20, 22–23, 40–42; as TV viewer, 7–8, 31, 120–21; and John Kennedy, 7–8, 183–86, 191–95, 198–99; as politician, 9, 70, 204–6, 208, 214;

in World War II, 10–15; media tycoons, 15–16, 36–37, 51, 78, 98; TV coaching of, 16, 24–25, 31–35, 130–31, 186, 205–6; as communicator, 16, 31–34, 91, 139–40, 141, 143, 203–8; 1952 campaign, 16–17, 20–21, 24–25, 77–78, 82, 130–31, 206–8; and Citizens for Eisenhower, 16–17, 77–82, 177, 179, 209–10; and Nixon, 17, 91–92, 122, 173–83, 199–201; and Congress, 18–23, 28–29, 43–45, 73, 77, 83–84, 123, 147–49, 153–56, 183–84, 198; disdain of press, 19, 48–55, 186–89; 1954 campaign, 28–29, 45, 58, 65, 88; and public opinion research, 37–40, 152, 159–60; foreign public relations, 41, 153–56, 167–70, 171–73; and Hagerty, 43–45, 166–67, 194; and GOP, 64–67, 77, 83–84, 148–50, 177, 209–11; fund-raising efforts, 72, 177–79, 182–83; 1956 campaign, 73–74, 83–85, 86–93, 120–23, 127–29, 131–32, 138–49, 150, 206–8; debates on, 108, 174, 180–81, 199; and Stevenson, 120, 138–39; and space program, 156–57, 161–63, 194; and 1958 campaign, 163–64, 177; and 1960 campaign, 173–74, 177–83; rated by historians, 190, 191–92, 201–2, 212–13, 239 (n. 34); and youth, 190, 197–98, 200; and media in postpresidential years, 192–98; memoirs, 195, 198, 204–5; and 1964 campaign, 196–97; and 1968 campaign, 199–201
Eisenhower, Mamie, 31, 83, 87–88, 108–9, 131–32, 141–42, 143, 207

Eisenhower, Milton, 138, 175; influences Dwight, 11–13; and OWI, 12; 1964 election, 195
Ewald, William, 152, 154, 182, 201–2

Federal Communications Commission (FCC), 114, 159; TV freeze, 7, 105; equal time, 58, 62, 70, 97–98, 107–9, 145–46, 180, 223 (n. 50)
Finch, Robert, 200
Finnegan, James, 133, 136, 146
Folger, J. Clifford, 72, 177–78, 230 (n. 46)
Folliard, Edward, 17, 186
Foote, Emerson, 99
Ford, Gerald, 128, 201, 204
Freeman, Orville, 105
Friendly, Fred, 192
Fritchey, Clayton, 102, 133–34, 137

Gabrielson, Guy, 66–67, 68
Gallup, George, 37–38, 39, 147–48, 171; and Larmon, 38
Gallup Poll, 22, 38–39, 132, 144, 147–48, 149, 152, 159–60, 164, 171, 173, 175, 193, 195
Gettysburg, Pa., 5, 87, 89–90, 192
Godfrey, Arthur, 31
Goldwater, Barry, 73, 196–97
Gore Committee, 72, 132–33, 206, 231 (n. 2)
Gould, Jack, 61, 106, 120, 125, 143
Gruenther, Albert, 147
Guggenheim, Charles, 95
Guylay, L. Richard, 178, 206; slogans and imagery of, 69; and TV networks, 75–76, 89–90, 102; and BBDO–Young and Rubicam intermediary, 80–81; and Eisenhower, 89–90; image of "stability," 125–26

duties at White House, 28–36, 56, 59, 142, 145, 156–59, 186; coaching of Eisenhower, 31–35, 130; not analyzed by press, 33, 205; criticism of, 104, 109, 141, 206; denied senior post, 156, 158–59; and 1960 debate, 174, 180

Morgan, Edward P., 109

Moroney, Mike, 160

Morse, Wayne, 77

Morton, Thruston, 84

Mundt, Karl, 44

Murrow, Edward R., 13, 114, 115, 140

Mutual network, 108

National Aeronautics and Space Administration (NASA), 163, 213

National Security Council, 3, 154, 187

NBC: Montgomery at, 26, 34–35, 158; news division, 34, 52, 92, 114–15, 125, 161, 167–68, 192; and White House, 57–58, 61–62, 223 (n. 42); political ads on, 75–76, 89, 98–99, 101–2, 108, 135, 142; debates on, 107, 181; conventions on, 112, 115–20, 122–23, 125; political anxieties of, 113–14, 229 (n. 9)

Nehru, Jawaharlal, 169

New Orleans Item, 134

News conferences, 3, 4, 6, 8, 13, 18, 22–23, 92, 139, 160, 188; on television, 47–48, 55–63, 122, 156, 159; on journalistic "record," 52–55; on radio, 54–55; rehearsals for, 60, 142, 162; first live broadcast, 122; Young and Rubicam's, 142–43, 176, 200

Newsweek, 68, 113, 124, 205

Newton, Carroll, 69, 71, 81, 84; time buying for GOP, 75–76, 102–3; "piggybacks," 76; congressional testimony, 132–33; and Nixon, 178–81. *See also* Batten, Barton, Durstine and Osborn (BBDO)

New York Daily News, 88

New York Herald Tribune, 50, 51, 101, 120; ties to administration, 36, 40, 42, 56, 62, 78, 188, 194; leaks to, 187

New York Post, 61, 188

New York Times, 4, 26, 36, 50, 51, 54, 55, 62, 69, 93, 106, 109, 120, 125, 143, 205; unfriendly to Eisenhower, 19–20, 56, 61, 172; unfriendly to Stevenson, 136, 140, 146, 147; leaks to, 187; attacked by Eisenhower, 188

Nixon, Richard M., 2–3, 58, 69, 119, 121–23, 128, 199–201; "Checkers" telecast, 17, 32, 90–91, 137, 176, 204; and Eisenhower, 74, 173–83, 187–88, 198, 199–201; TV knowledge of, 91–92, 126, 175–77; attacked by Stevenson, 136, 147; 1960 debates, 174, 180–81; "man in the arena" events, 176–77, 200; and BBDO, 178–80; conflict with Hall, 178–81; 1956 and 1972 campaigns compared, 201

Norman, Craig and Kummel: enlisted by DNC, 98–103, 118–19; and "The $64,000 Question," 100; and DNC money troubles, 103, 132, 138; political ads of, 107, 134–37; "The Man from Libertyville," 107, 136–37; under Stevenson, 133–36; Harrisburg telecast, 135–36

Normandy, 11, 14, 56, 192–93

107, 130, 134–39, 145–47, 181; "piggyback" ads, 76, 102; long form (half-hour) political ads, 82–83, 102, 134–41, 143–48; closed-circuit fund-raisers, 83, 90–91, 138, 177; debates on, 106, 107–8, 174, 180–81, 199. *See also* Batten, Barton, Durstine, and Osborn (BBDO); Norman, Craig and Kummel; Young and Rubicam

Telstar satellite, 192

Thornton, Daniel, 77, 149

Time, 22, 48, 50, 120, 170, 181, 205

Traverse, Claude, 144

Treleaven, Harry, 200

Truman, Harry S., 38, 43, 83, 138, 142, 191, 196; and Eisenhower's 1948 prospects, 15; news conferences of, 19, 52; criticizes Eisenhower, 21–22, 50–51, 192; media use of, 40, 160, 166, 204; and Stevenson, 96–97, 105, 119

TV Plans Board, 17, 69

U-2 incident, 161, 170–73, 208, 212

United Nations, 53, 144–45, 173

United Press, 70

U.S. Army Pictorial Service, 14, 185

U.S. Information Agency (USIA), 41, 153–55

U.S. News and World Report, 205

Vanocur, Sander, 181

Vietnam, 32, 49, 190, 191, 197–98

Voice of America, 20, 41, 155

Von Bretano, Heinrich, 192

Waring, Fred, 31

Warner, James, 187

Washington Post, 17, 50, 147

Washington Star, 50

Waterman, Alan, 163

Wayne, John, 31

Wechsler, James, 61, 205

Weeks, Sinclair, 35

Weintraub, William, 100

Welch, Joseph, 45

Welles, Orson, 138, 144

Wheaton, Anne, 68, 160

White, Harry Dexter, 21–22, 43, 50–53

White, Paul Dudley, 2–3, 91–92, 226

White House Correspondents Association, 62

White House TV studio, 8, 28, 33 (n. 7)

Whitman, Ann, 162, 182

Whitney, John Hay, 72, 188

Willis, Charles, 23, 29, 73

Wilson, Charles, 35, 38

Wilson, William, 135–36, 141, 186

Wilson, Woodow, 29, 52

Wirtz, Willard, 133

Young and Rubicam, 8, 16, 99, 136–37; Larmon and, 38, 42, 100, 178; enlistment by Citizens for Eisenhower, 78–79, 129, 210; BBDO rivalry, 78–81; 1956 election eve telecast, 81, 148; political ads of, 129–32, 141–44; "star committee," 131; "Mamie" spot, 131–32, 141–42, 207; 1956 political travelogue, 142; "taxi driver" spot, 142; "people's news conference," 142–43, 176–77, 200

Ziffren, Paul, 97

PERMISSIONS

Portions of this book appeared originally in somewhat different form in the following articles:

"Our First 'Television' Candidate: Eisenhower over Stevenson in 1956," *Journalism Quarterly* 65, no. 2 (1988): 352–59.

"News Conferences on TV: Ike Age Politics Revisited," *Journalism Quarterly*, forthcoming.

"Eisenhower's Congressional Defeat of 1956," *Presidential Studies Quarterly* 22 (1992): 57–71. Used by permission of the Center for the Study of the Presidency, publisher of *Presidential Studies Quarterly*.